GARFIELD

Road Pizza

BY JIM DAVIS

Ballantine Books • New York

Published in the United States by Ballantine Books, an imprint of Random House, a division of Penguin Random House LLC, New York.

BALLANTINE and the HOUSE colophon are registered trademarks of Penguin Random House LLC.

NICKELODEON is a Trademark of Viacom International, Inc.

All of the comics in this work have been previously published.

ISBN 978-0-593-15648-3
Ebook ISBN 978-0-593-15649-0

Printed in China on acid-free paper

randomhousebooks.com

9 8 7 6 5 4 3 2 1

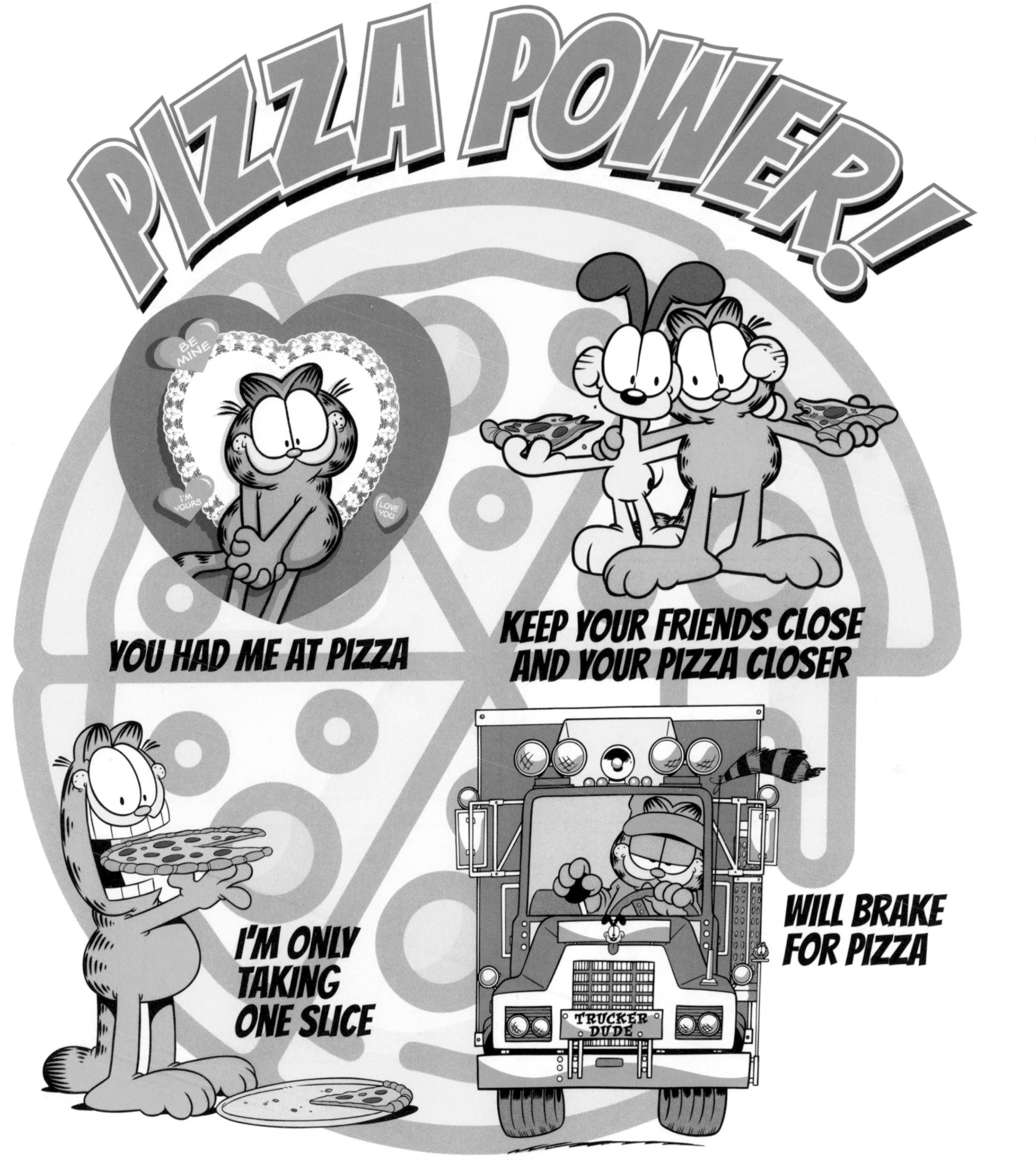
PIZZA POWER!!
BE MINE
I'M YOURS
LOVE YOU
YOU HAD ME AT PIZZA
KEEP YOUR FRIENDS CLOSE AND YOUR PIZZA CLOSER
I'M ONLY TAKING ONE SLICE
TRUCKER DUDE
WILL BRAKE FOR PIZZA

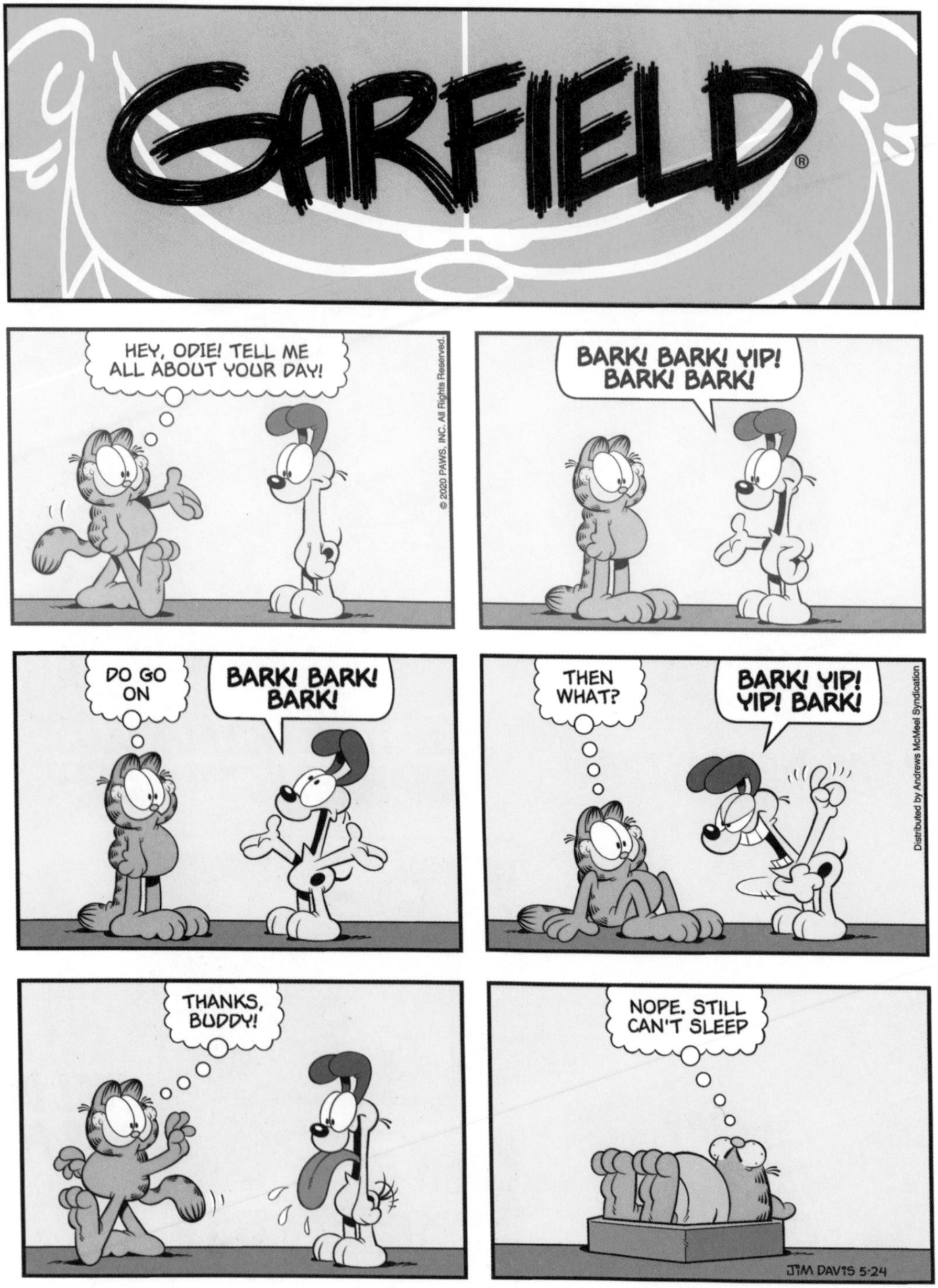
GARFIELD®
HEY, ODIE! TELL ME ALL ABOUT YOUR DAY!
© 2020 PAWS, INC. All Rights Reserved.
BARK! BARK! YIP! BARK! BARK!
DO GO ON
BARK! BARK! BARK!
THEN WHAT?
BARK! YIP! YIP! BARK!
Distributed by Andrews McMeel Syndication
THANKS, BUDDY!
NOPE. STILL CAN'T SLEEP
JIM DAVIS 5-24

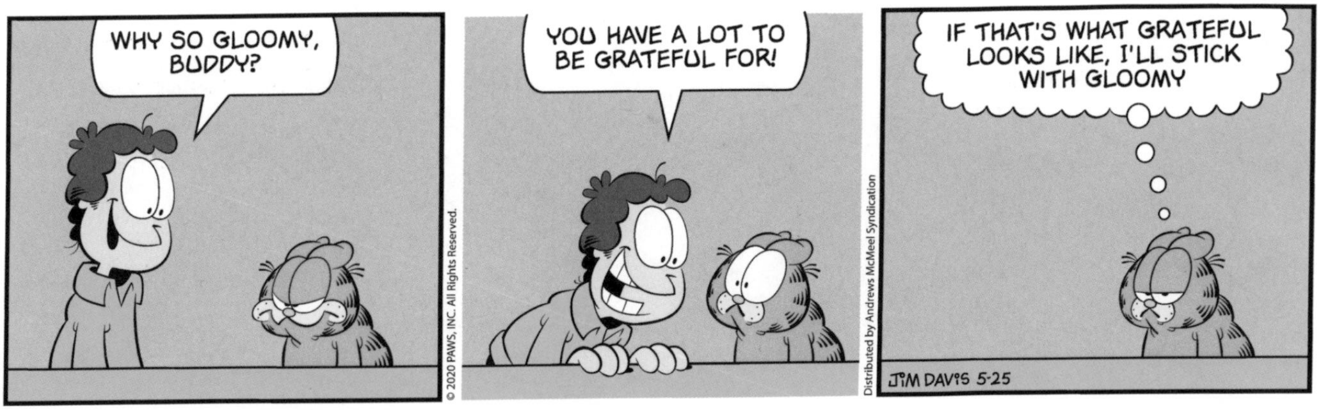
WHY SO GLOOMY, BUDDY?
YOU HAVE A LOT TO BE GRATEFUL FOR!
IF THAT'S WHAT GRATEFUL LOOKS LIKE, I'LL STICK WITH GLOOMY
© 2020 PAWS, INC. All Rights Reserved.
Distributed by Andrews McMeel Syndication
JIM DAVIS 5-25

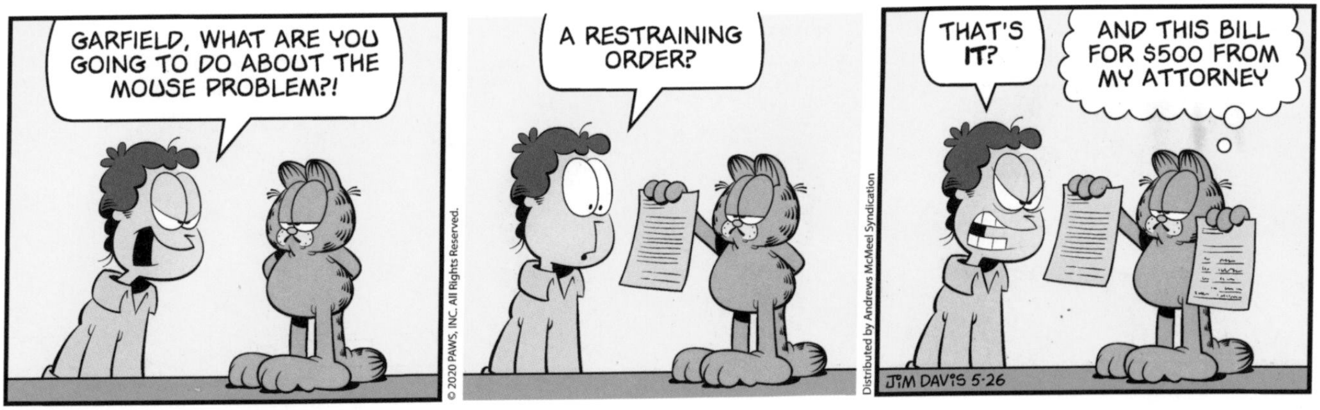
GARFIELD, WHAT ARE YOU GOING TO DO ABOUT THE MOUSE PROBLEM?!
A RESTRAINING ORDER?
THAT'S IT?
AND THIS BILL FOR $500 FROM MY ATTORNEY
© 2020 PAWS, INC. All Rights Reserved.
Distributed by Andrews McMeel Syndication
JIM DAVIS 5-26

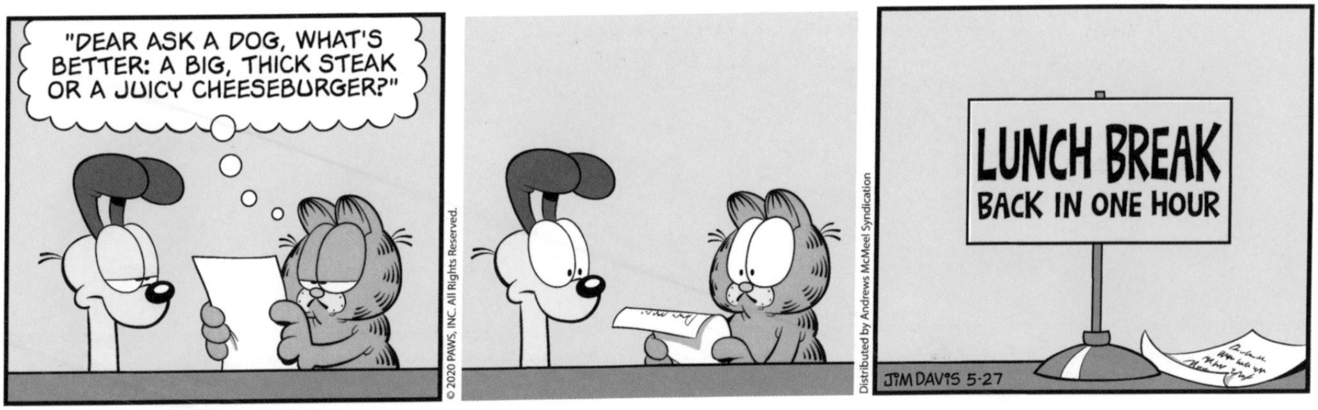
"DEAR ASK A DOG, WHAT'S BETTER: A BIG, THICK STEAK OR A JUICY CHEESEBURGER?"
LUNCH BREAK
BACK IN ONE HOUR
© 2020 PAWS, INC. All Rights Reserved.
Distributed by Andrews McMeel Syndication
JIM DAVIS 5-27

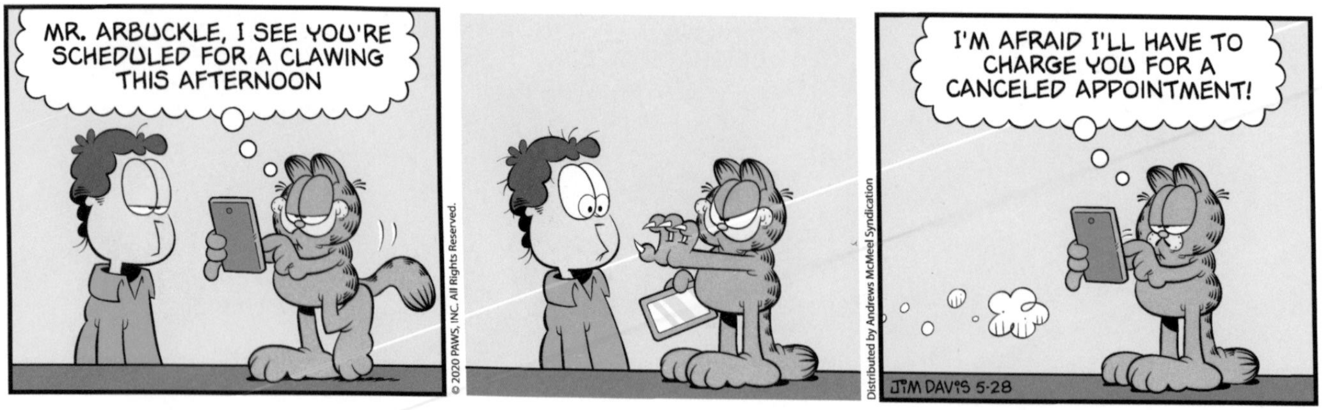
MR. ARBUCKLE, I SEE YOU'RE SCHEDULED FOR A CLAWING THIS AFTERNOON
© 2020 PAWS, INC. All Rights Reserved.
Distributed by Andrews McMeel Syndication
I'M AFRAID I'LL HAVE TO CHARGE YOU FOR A CANCELED APPOINTMENT!
JIM DAVIS 5-28

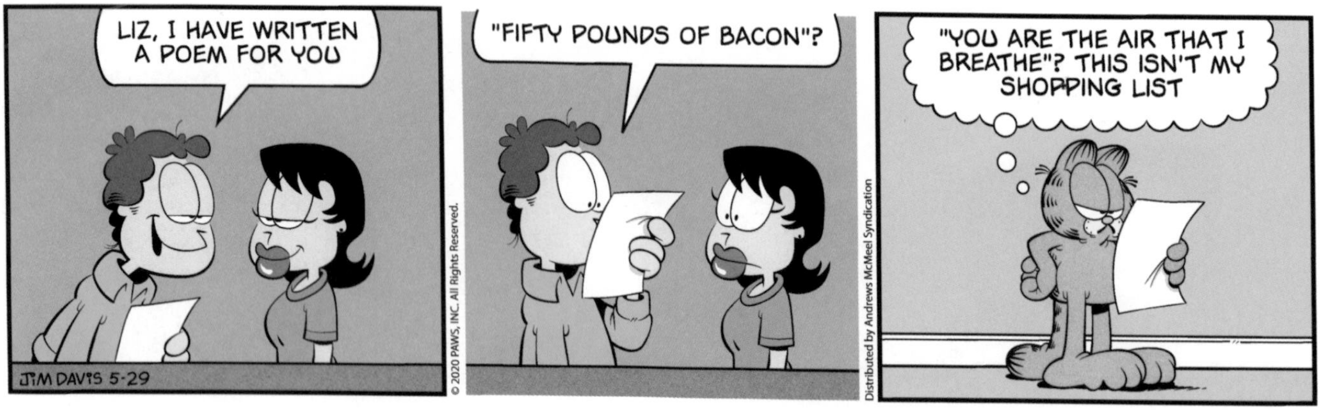
LIZ, I HAVE WRITTEN A POEM FOR YOU
JIM DAVIS 5-29
© 2020 PAWS, INC. All Rights Reserved.
"FIFTY POUNDS OF BACON"?
Distributed by Andrews McMeel Syndication
"YOU ARE THE AIR THAT I BREATHE"? THIS ISN'T MY SHOPPING LIST

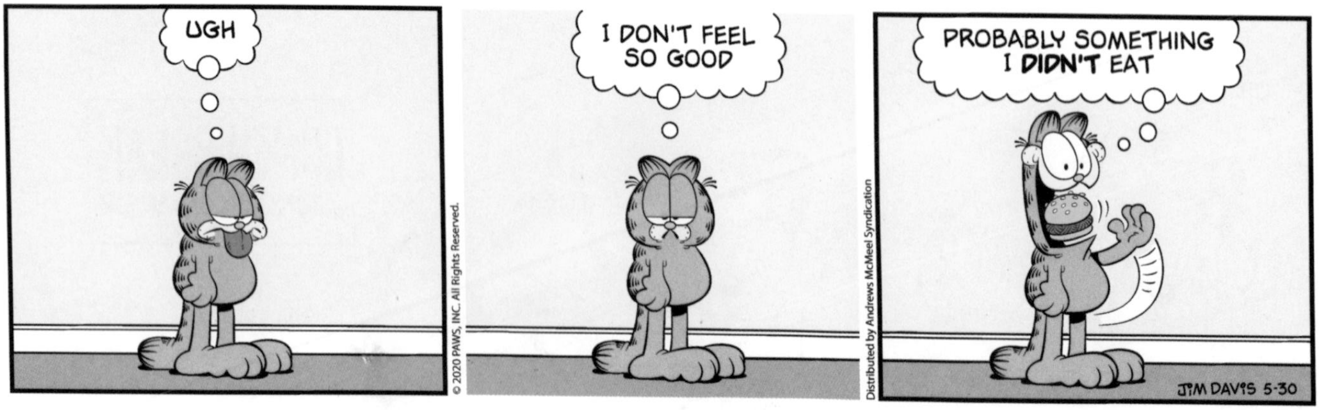
UGH
© 2020 PAWS, INC. All Rights Reserved.
I DON'T FEEL SO GOOD
Distributed by Andrews McMeel Syndication
PROBABLY SOMETHING I **DIDN'T** EAT
JIM DAVIS 5-30

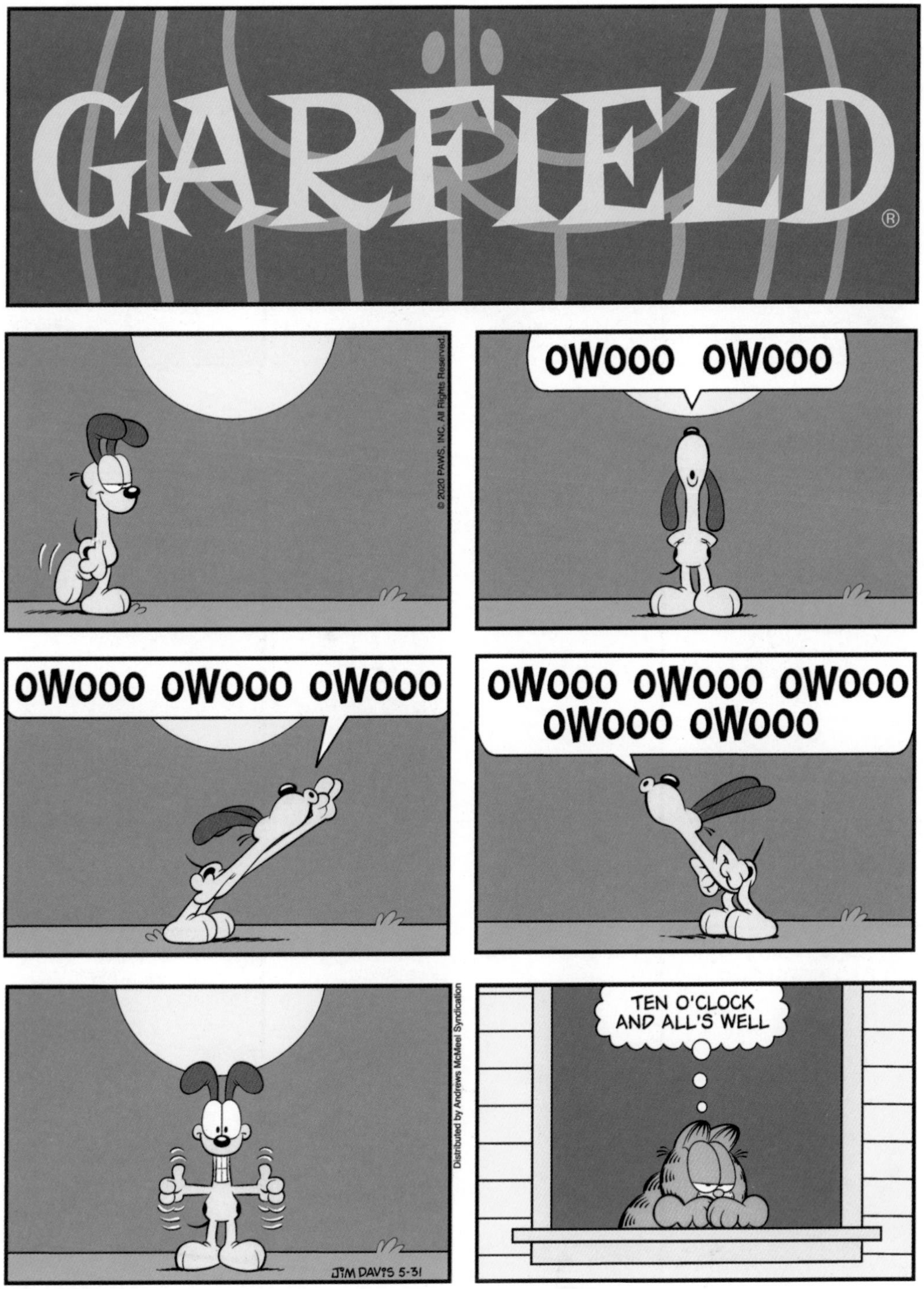
GARFIELD®
© 2020 PAWS, INC. All Rights Reserved.
OWOOO OWOOO
OWOOO OWOOO OWOOO
OWOOO OWOOO OWOOO
OWOOO OWOOO
Distributed by Andrews McMeel Syndication
JIM DAVIS 5-31
TEN O'CLOCK
AND ALL'S WELL

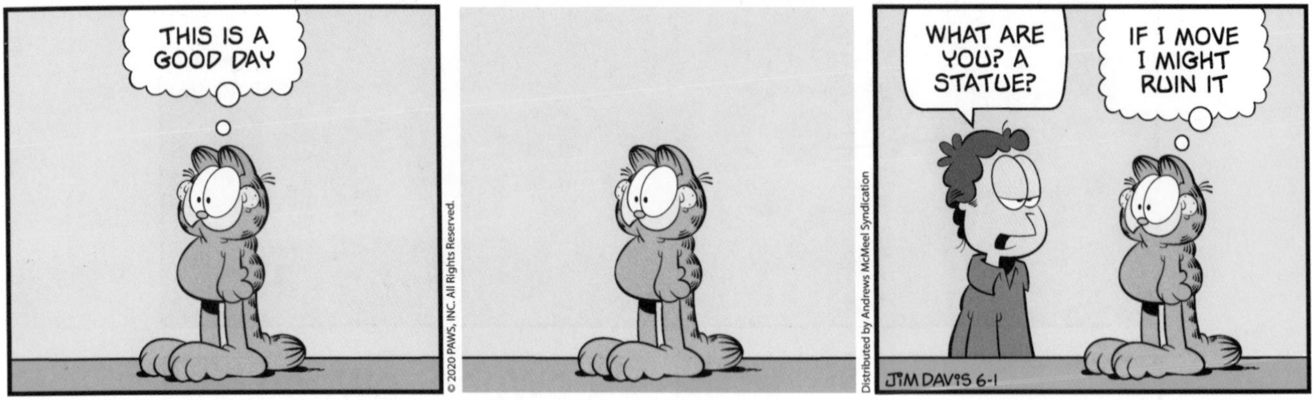
THIS IS A GOOD DAY
WHAT ARE YOU? A STATUE?
IF I MOVE I MIGHT RUIN IT
JIM DAVIS 6-1

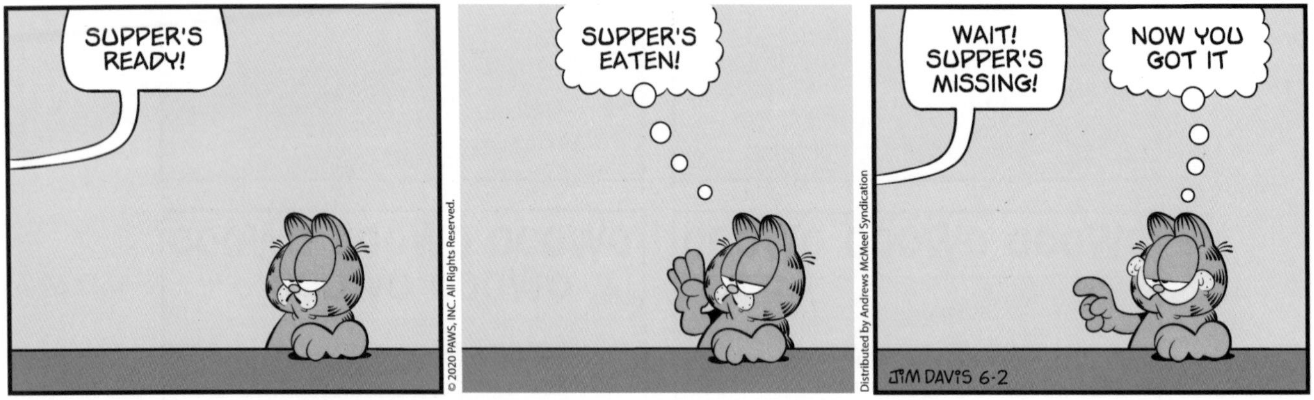
SUPPER'S READY!
SUPPER'S EATEN!
WAIT! SUPPER'S MISSING!
NOW YOU GOT IT
JIM DAVIS 6-2

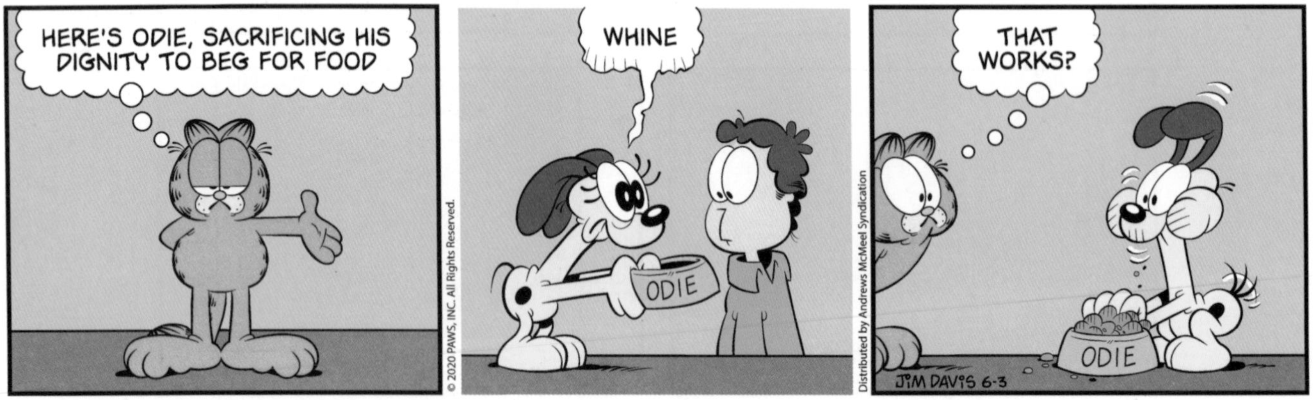
HERE'S ODIE, SACRIFICING HIS DIGNITY TO BEG FOR FOOD
WHINE
ODIE
THAT WORKS?
ODIE
JIM DAVIS 6-3

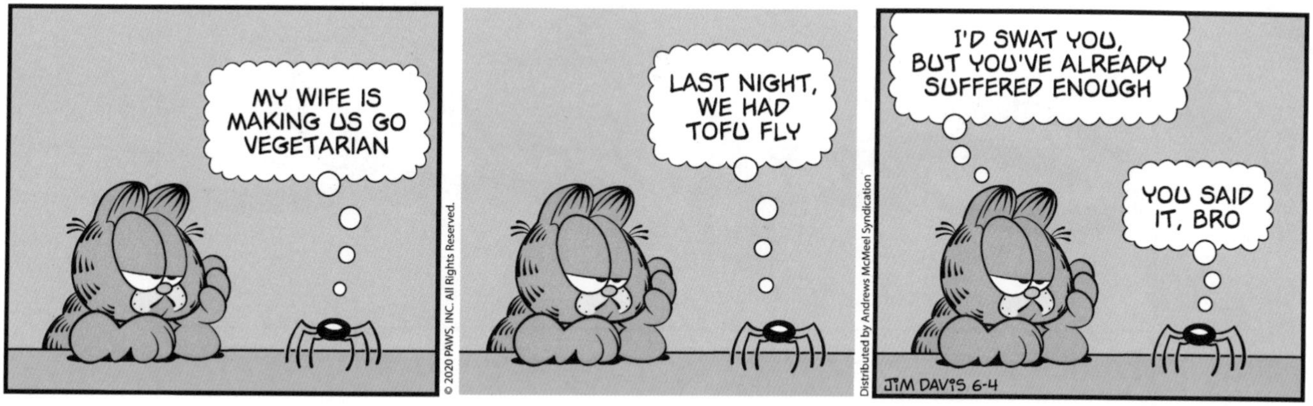
MY WIFE IS MAKING US GO VEGETARIAN
LAST NIGHT, WE HAD TOFU FLY
I'D SWAT YOU, BUT YOU'VE ALREADY SUFFERED ENOUGH
YOU SAID IT, BRO
JIM DAVIS 6-4
© 2020 PAWS, INC. All Rights Reserved.
Distributed by Andrews McMeel Syndication

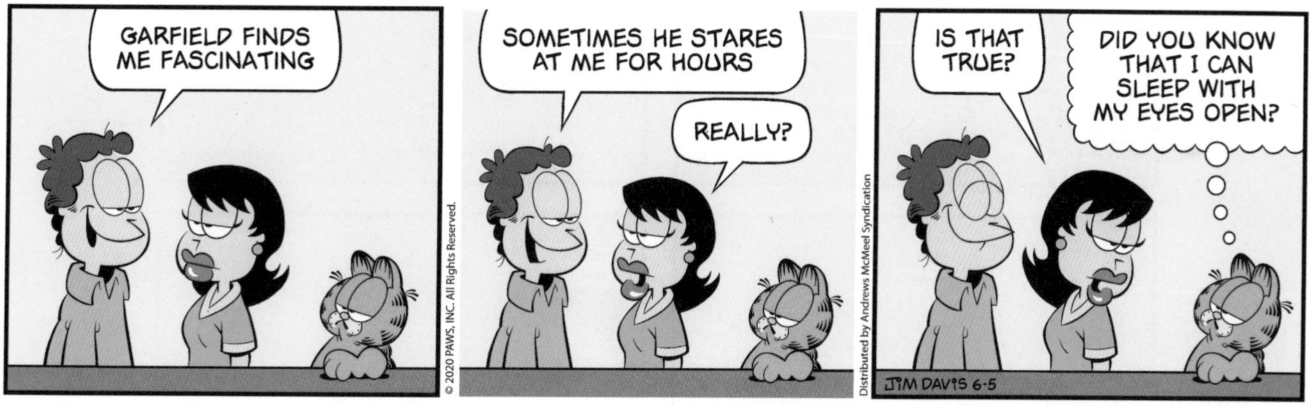
GARFIELD FINDS ME FASCINATING
SOMETIMES HE STARES AT ME FOR HOURS
REALLY?
IS THAT TRUE?
DID YOU KNOW THAT I CAN SLEEP WITH MY EYES OPEN?
JIM DAVIS 6-5
© 2020 PAWS, INC. All Rights Reserved.
Distributed by Andrews McMeel Syndication

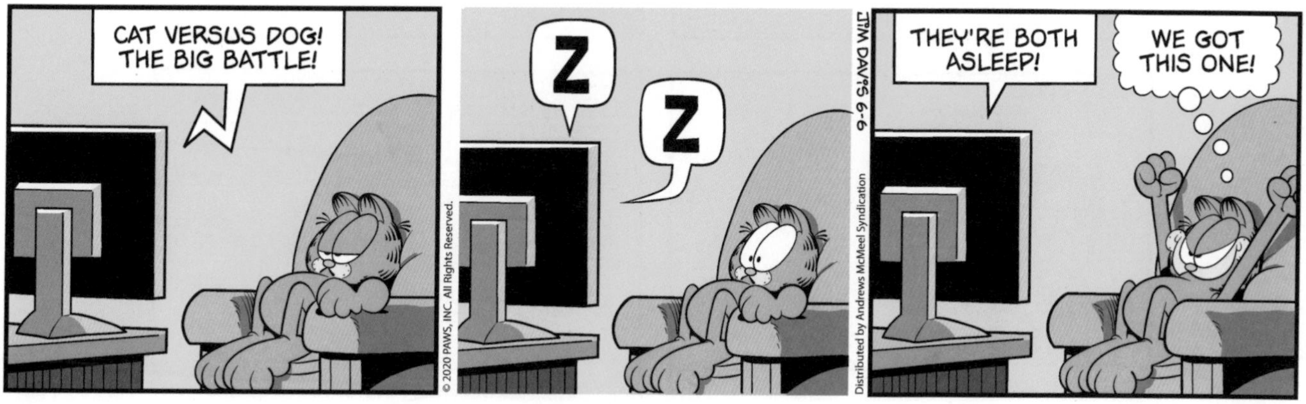
CAT VERSUS DOG! THE BIG BATTLE!
Z
Z
THEY'RE BOTH ASLEEP!
WE GOT THIS ONE!
JIM DAVIS 6-6
© 2020 PAWS, INC. All Rights Reserved.
Distributed by Andrews McMeel Syndication

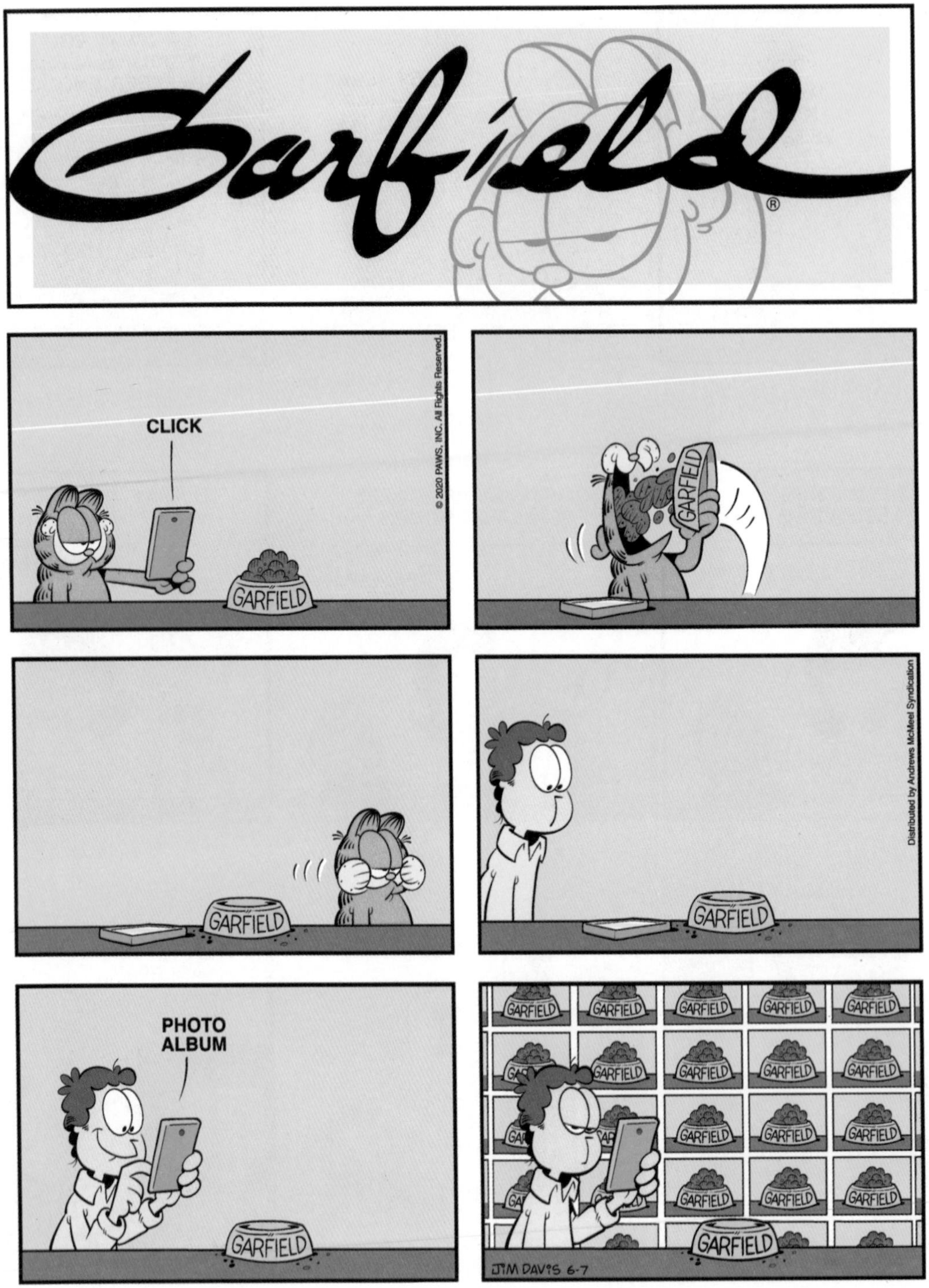

Garfield®
© 2020 PAWS, INC. All Rights Reserved.
CLICK
GARFIELD
GARFIELD
GARFIELD
Distributed by Andrews McMeel Syndication
GARFIELD
PHOTO ALBUM
GARFIELD
GARFIELD
JIM DAVIS 6-7

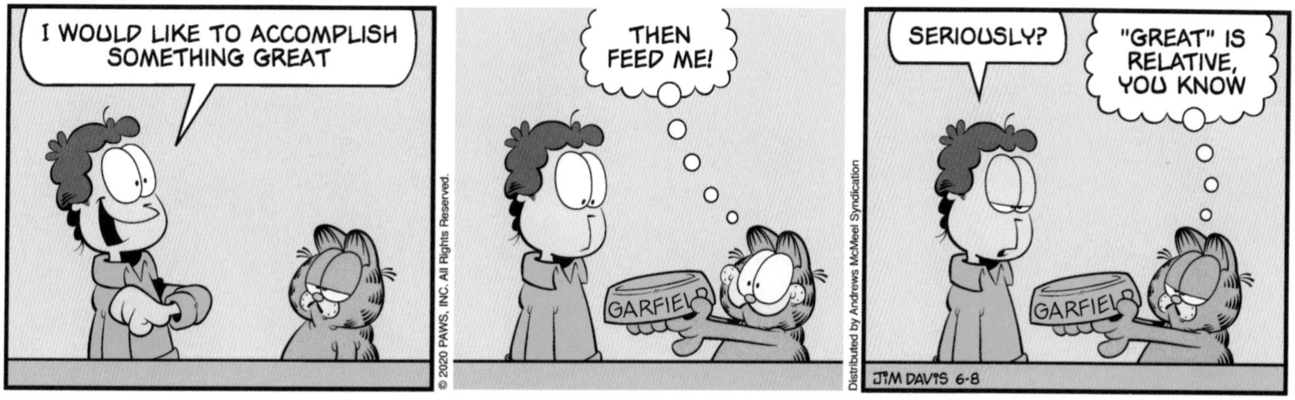
I WOULD LIKE TO ACCOMPLISH SOMETHING GREAT
THEN FEED ME!
GARFIELD
SERIOUSLY?
"GREAT" IS RELATIVE, YOU KNOW
GARFIELD
JIM DAVIS 6-8
© 2020 PAWS, INC. All Rights Reserved.
Distributed by Andrews McMeel Syndication

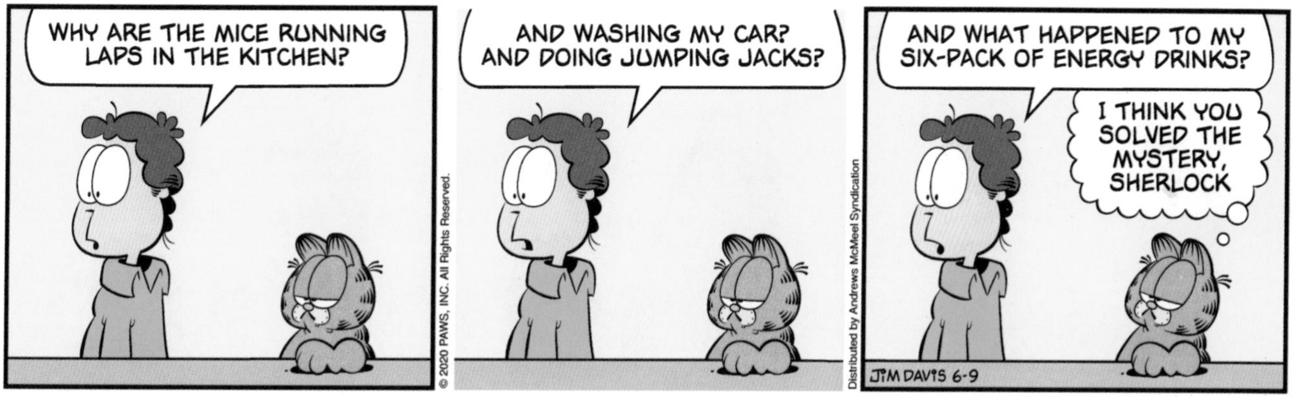
WHY ARE THE MICE RUNNING LAPS IN THE KITCHEN?
AND WASHING MY CAR? AND DOING JUMPING JACKS?
AND WHAT HAPPENED TO MY SIX-PACK OF ENERGY DRINKS?
I THINK YOU SOLVED THE MYSTERY, SHERLOCK
JIM DAVIS 6-9
© 2020 PAWS, INC. All Rights Reserved.
Distributed by Andrews McMeel Syndication

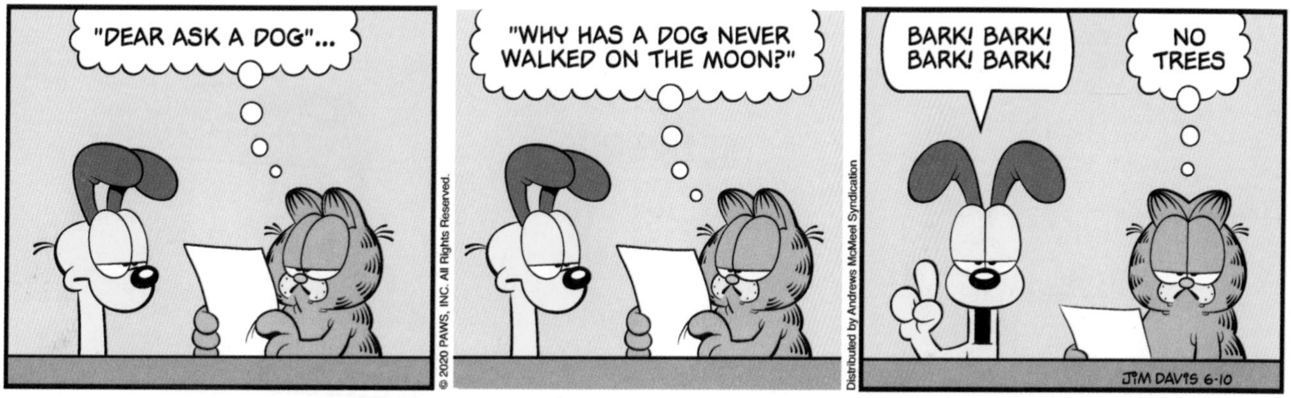
"DEAR ASK A DOG"...
"WHY HAS A DOG NEVER WALKED ON THE MOON?"
BARK! BARK! BARK! BARK!
NO TREES
JIM DAVIS 6-10
© 2020 PAWS, INC. All Rights Reserved.
Distributed by Andrews McMeel Syndication

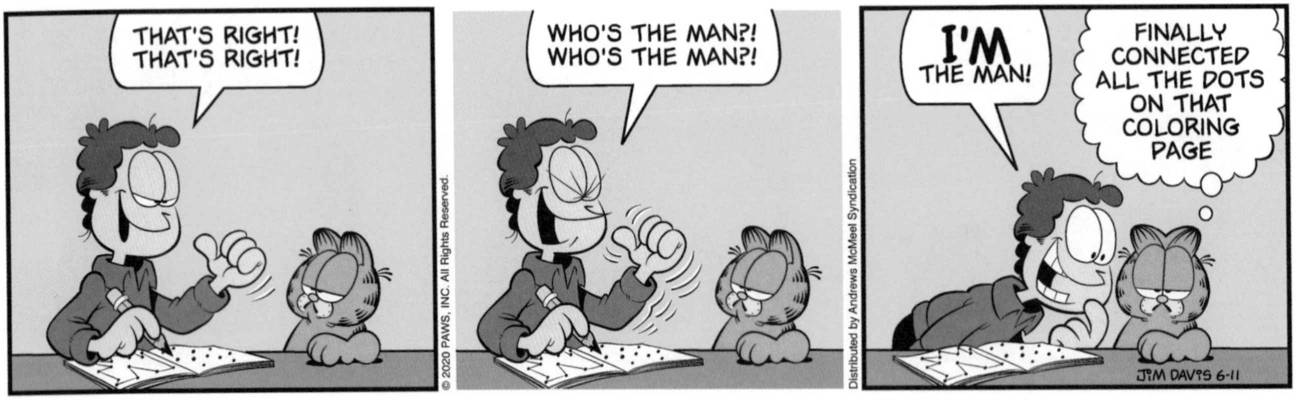
THAT'S RIGHT! THAT'S RIGHT!
WHO'S THE MAN?! WHO'S THE MAN?!
I'M THE MAN!
FINALLY CONNECTED ALL THE DOTS ON THAT COLORING PAGE
JIM DAVIS 6-11
© 2020 PAWS, INC. All Rights Reserved.
Distributed by Andrews McMeel Syndication

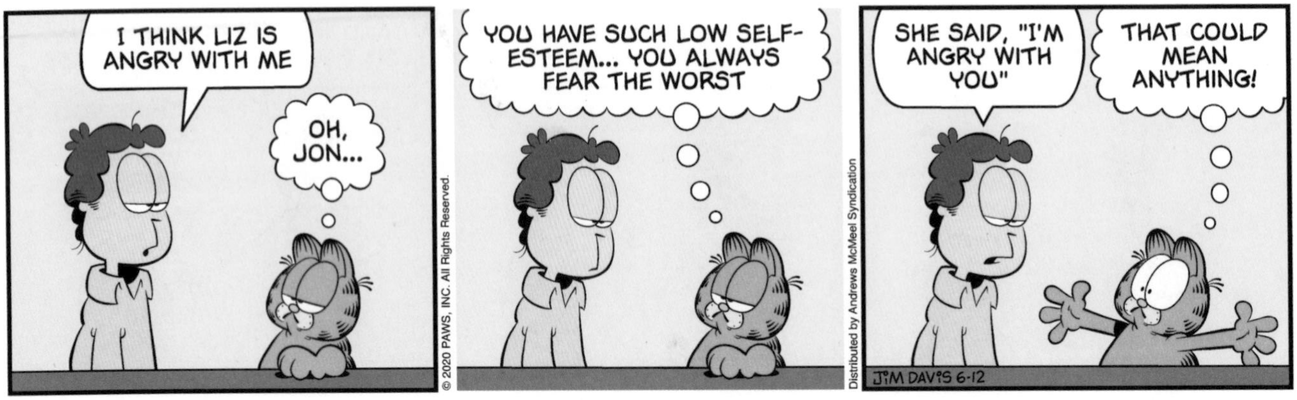
I THINK LIZ IS ANGRY WITH ME
OH, JON...
YOU HAVE SUCH LOW SELF-ESTEEM... YOU ALWAYS FEAR THE WORST
SHE SAID, "I'M ANGRY WITH YOU"
THAT COULD MEAN ANYTHING!
JIM DAVIS 6-12
© 2020 PAWS, INC. All Rights Reserved.
Distributed by Andrews McMeel Syndication

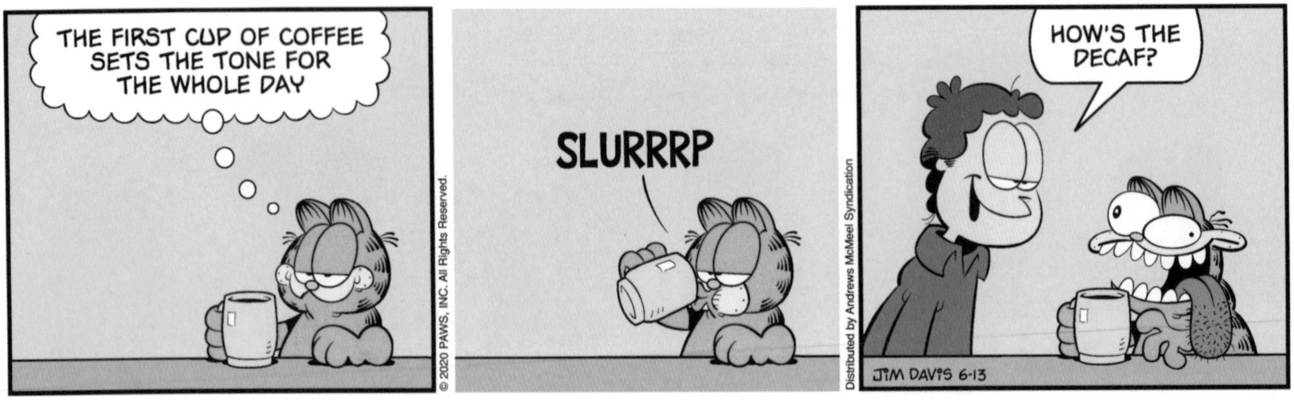
THE FIRST CUP OF COFFEE SETS THE TONE FOR THE WHOLE DAY
SLURRRP
HOW'S THE DECAF?
JIM DAVIS 6-13
© 2020 PAWS, INC. All Rights Reserved.
Distributed by Andrews McMeel Syndication

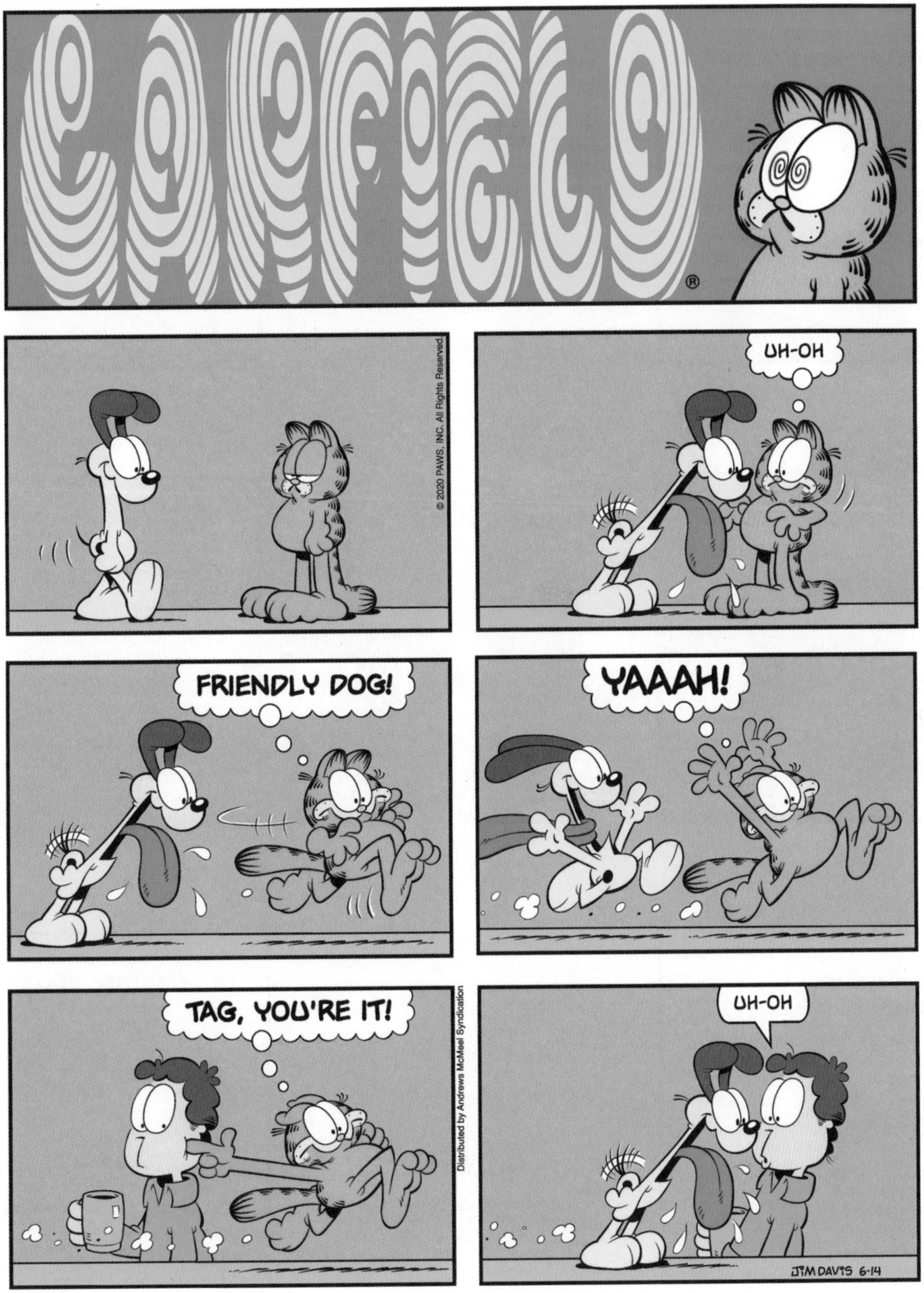
© 2020 PAWS, INC. All Rights Reserved.
UH-OH
FRIENDLY DOG!
YAAAH!
TAG, YOU'RE IT!
Distributed by Andrews McMeel Syndication
UH-OH
JIM DAVIS 6-14

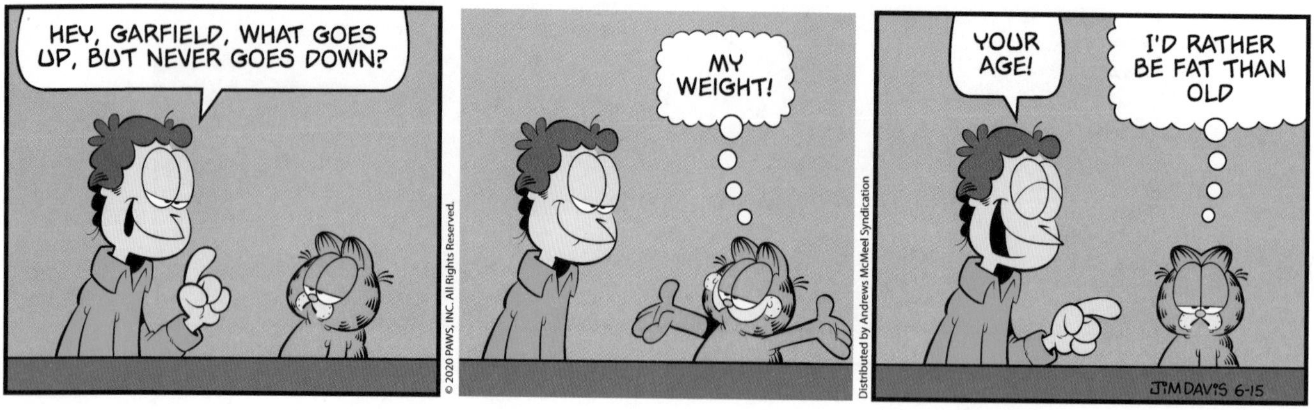
HEY, GARFIELD, WHAT GOES UP, BUT NEVER GOES DOWN?
MY WEIGHT!
YOUR AGE!
I'D RATHER BE FAT THAN OLD
JIM DAVIS 6-15
© 2020 PAWS, INC. All Rights Reserved.
Distributed by Andrews McMeel Syndication

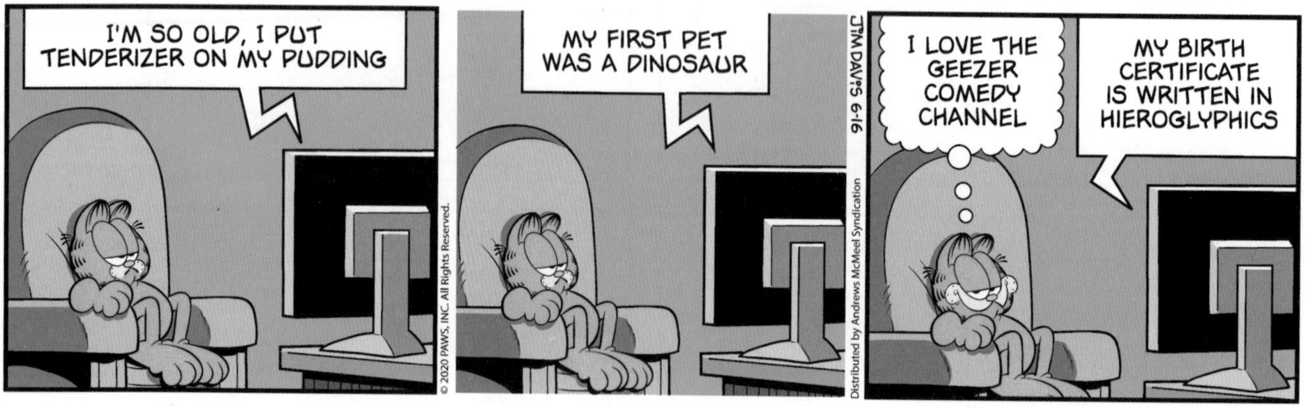
I'M SO OLD, I PUT TENDERIZER ON MY PUDDING
MY FIRST PET WAS A DINOSAUR
I LOVE THE GEEZER COMEDY CHANNEL
MY BIRTH CERTIFICATE IS WRITTEN IN HIEROGLYPHICS
JIM DAVIS 6-16
© 2020 PAWS, INC. All Rights Reserved.
Distributed by Andrews McMeel Syndication

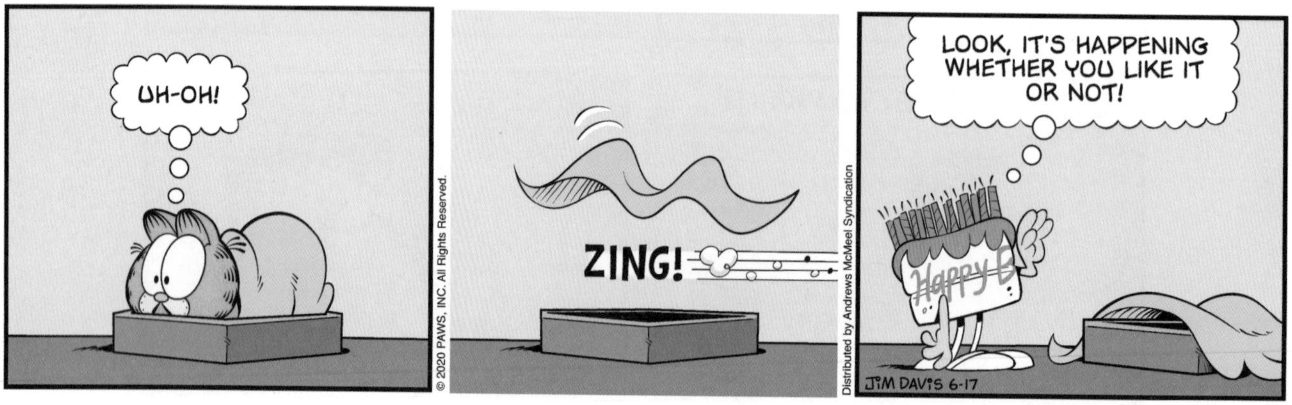
UH-OH!
ZING!
LOOK, IT'S HAPPENING WHETHER YOU LIKE IT OR NOT!
Happy B
JIM DAVIS 6-17
© 2020 PAWS, INC. All Rights Reserved.
Distributed by Andrews McMeel Syndication

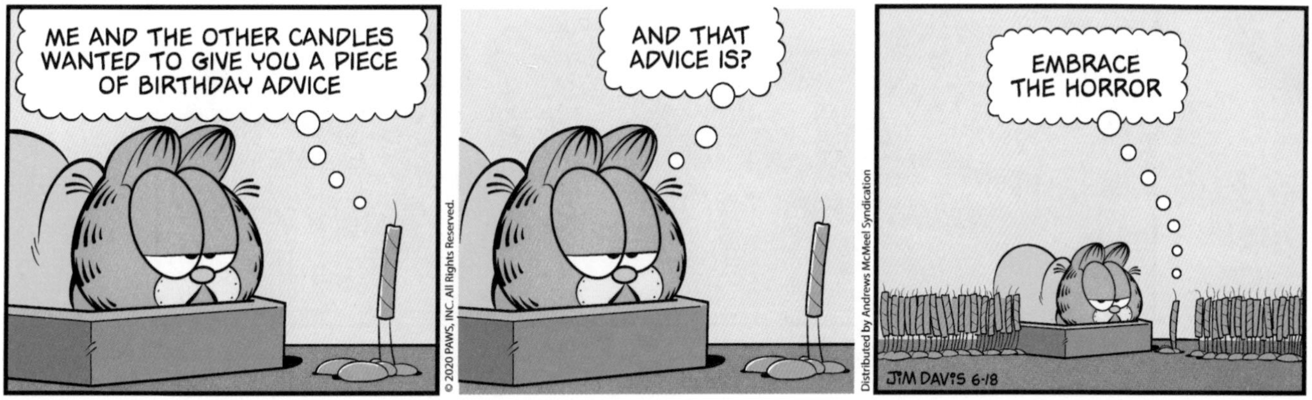
ME AND THE OTHER CANDLES WANTED TO GIVE YOU A PIECE OF BIRTHDAY ADVICE
AND THAT ADVICE IS?
EMBRACE THE HORROR
JIM DAVIS 6-18

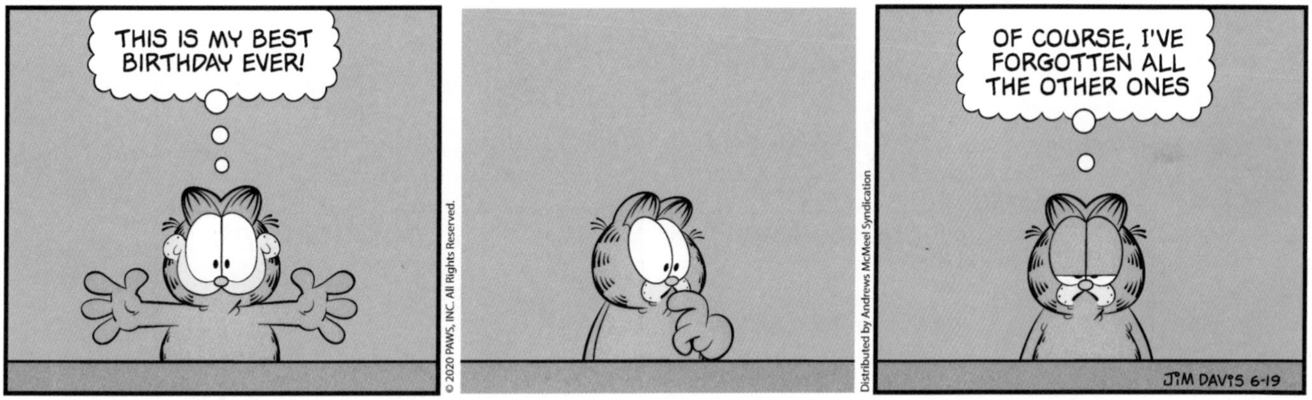
THIS IS MY BEST BIRTHDAY EVER!
OF COURSE, I'VE FORGOTTEN ALL THE OTHER ONES
JIM DAVIS 6-19

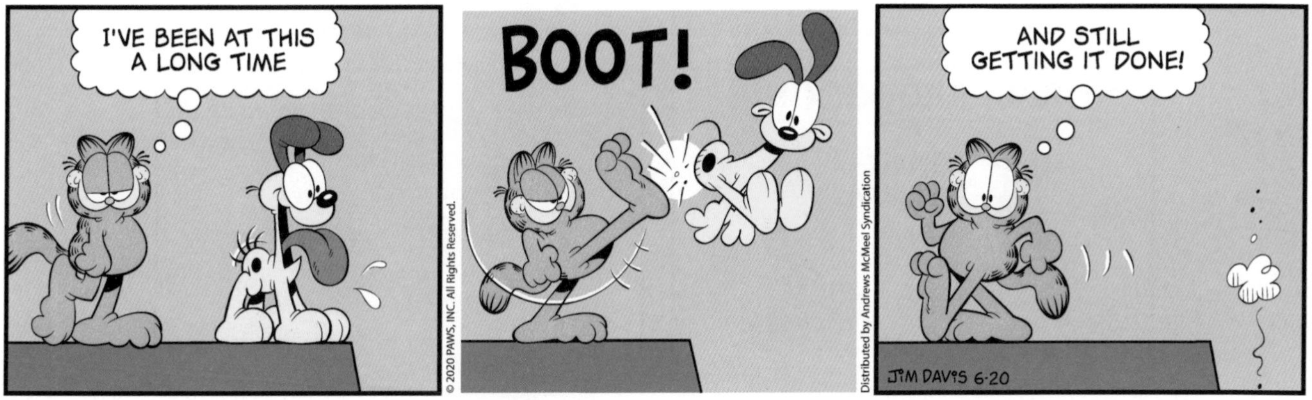
I'VE BEEN AT THIS A LONG TIME
BOOT!
AND STILL GETTING IT DONE!
JIM DAVIS 6-20

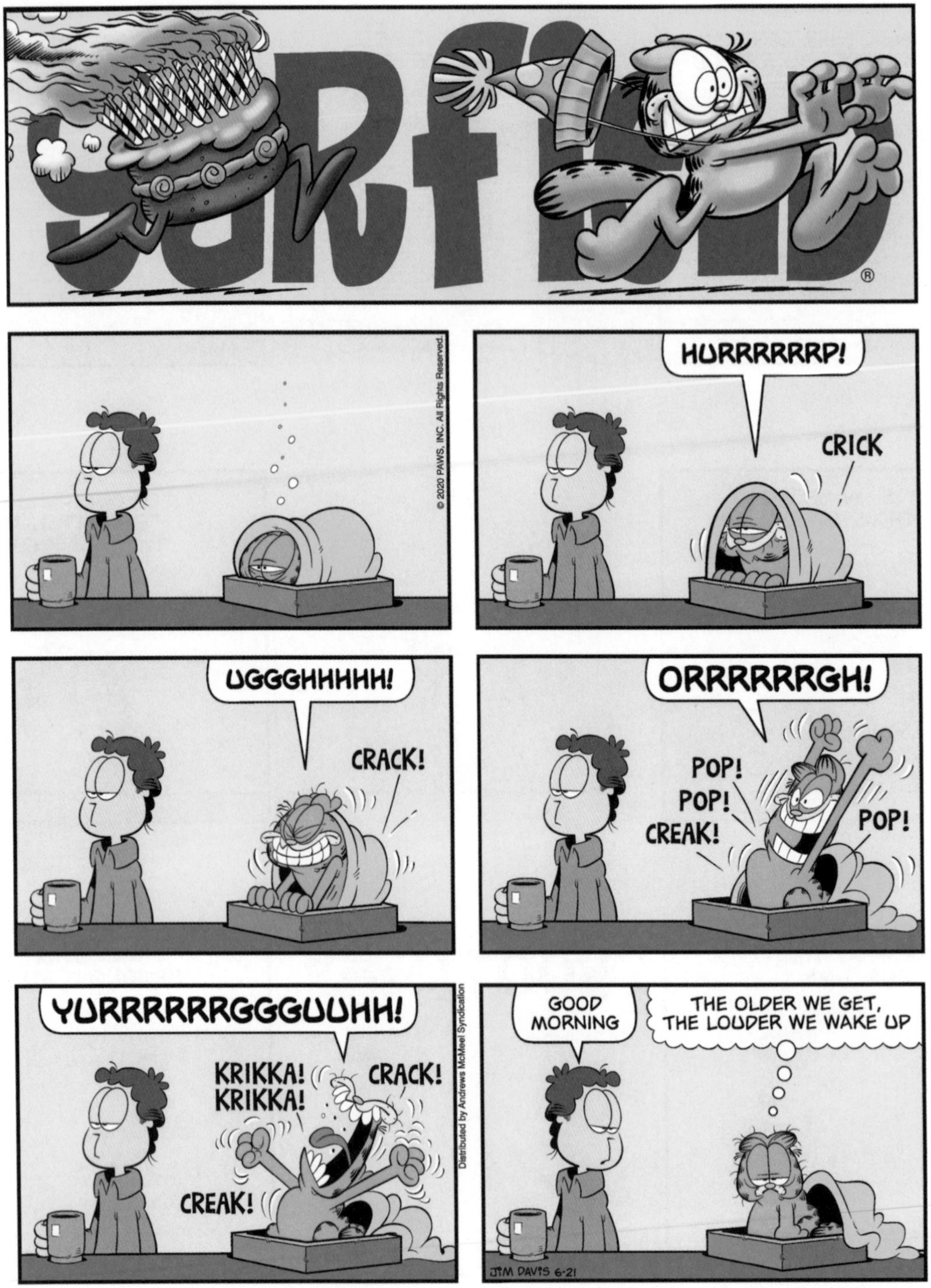
© 2020 PAWS, INC. All Rights Reserved.
HURRRRRRP!
CRICK
UGGGHHHHH!
CRACK!
ORRRRRRGH!
POP!
POP!
CREAK!
POP!
YURRRRRRGGGUUHH!
KRIKKA!
KRIKKA!
CRACK!
CREAK!
Distributed by Andrews McMeel Syndication
GOOD MORNING
THE OLDER WE GET, THE LOUDER WE WAKE UP
JIM DAVIS 6-21

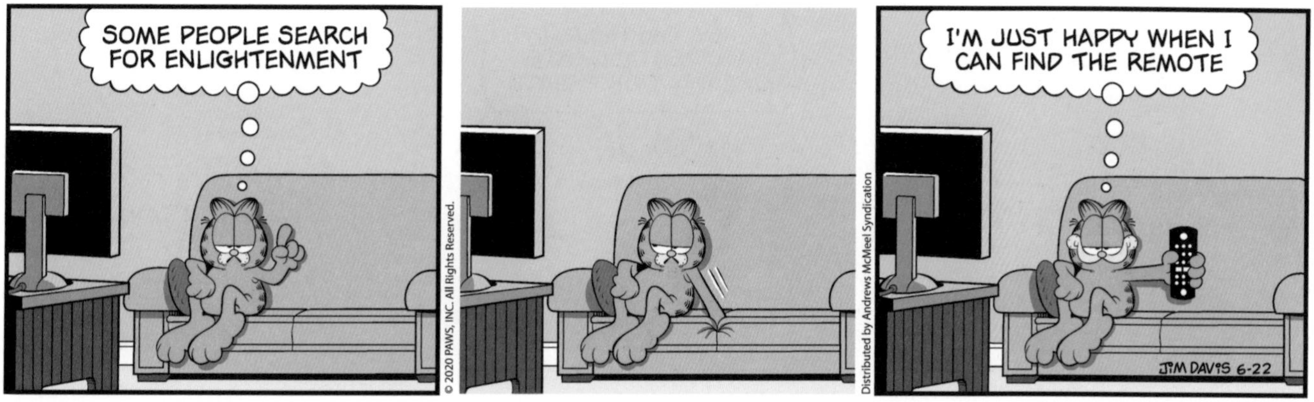
SOME PEOPLE SEARCH FOR ENLIGHTENMENT
© 2020 PAWS, INC. All Rights Reserved.
Distributed by Andrews McMeel Syndication
I'M JUST HAPPY WHEN I CAN FIND THE REMOTE
JIM DAVIS 6-22

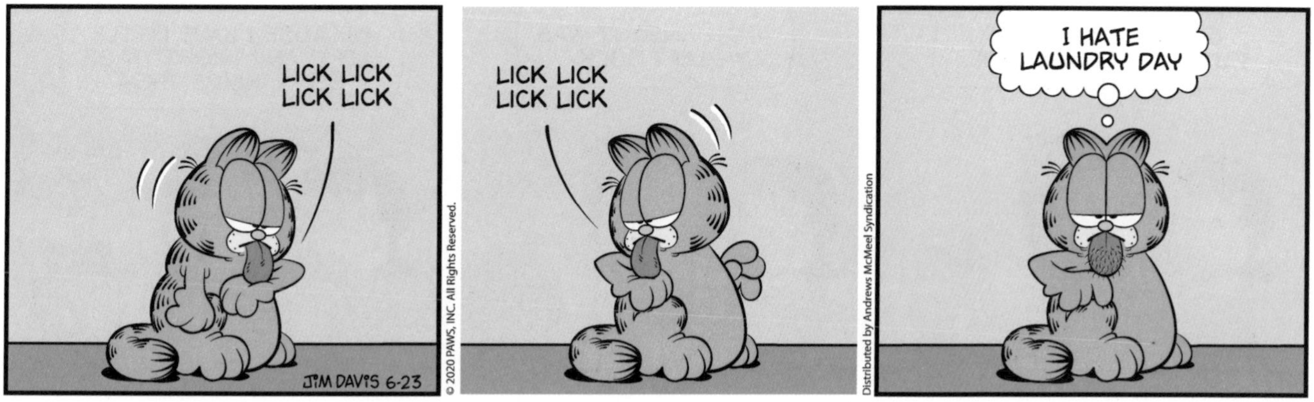
LICK LICK LICK LICK
JIM DAVIS 6-23
© 2020 PAWS, INC. All Rights Reserved.
LICK LICK LICK LICK
Distributed by Andrews McMeel Syndication
I HATE LAUNDRY DAY

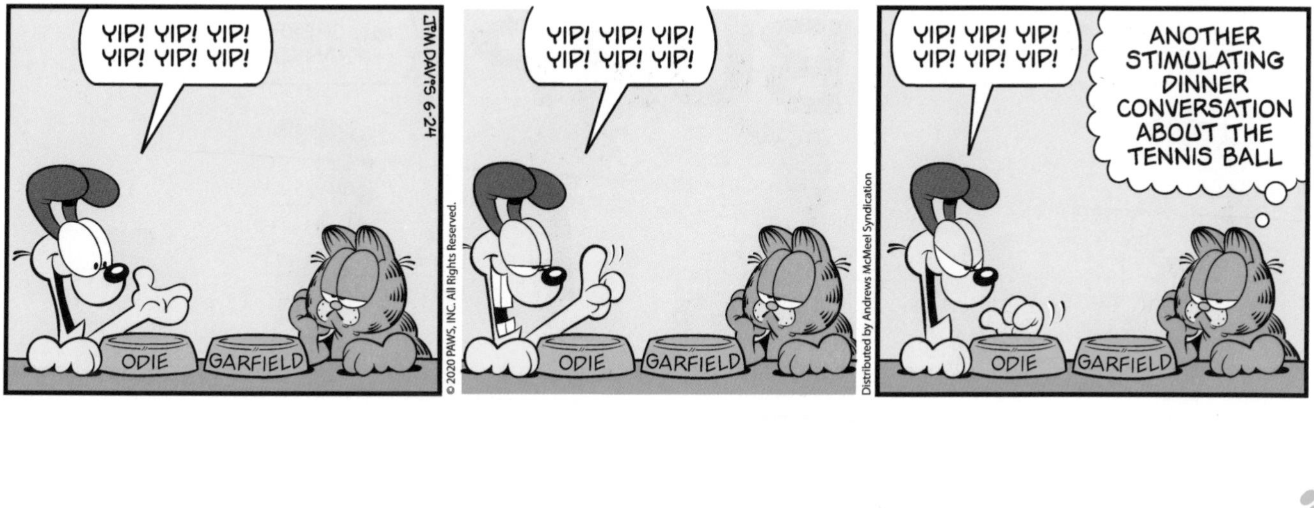
YIP! YIP! YIP! YIP! YIP! YIP!
JIM DAVIS 6-24
ODIE
GARFIELD
© 2020 PAWS, INC. All Rights Reserved.
YIP! YIP! YIP! YIP! YIP! YIP!
ODIE
GARFIELD
Distributed by Andrews McMeel Syndication
YIP! YIP! YIP! YIP! YIP! YIP!
ANOTHER STIMULATING DINNER CONVERSATION ABOUT THE TENNIS BALL
ODIE
GARFIELD

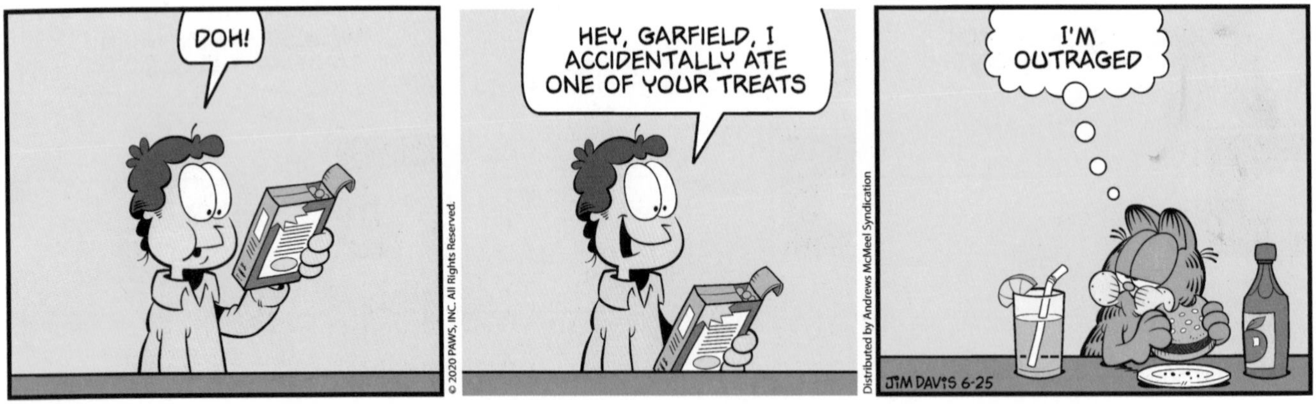
DOH!
HEY, GARFIELD, I ACCIDENTALLY ATE ONE OF YOUR TREATS
I'M OUTRAGED
© 2020 PAWS, INC. All Rights Reserved.
Distributed by Andrews McMeel Syndication
JIM DAVIS 6-25

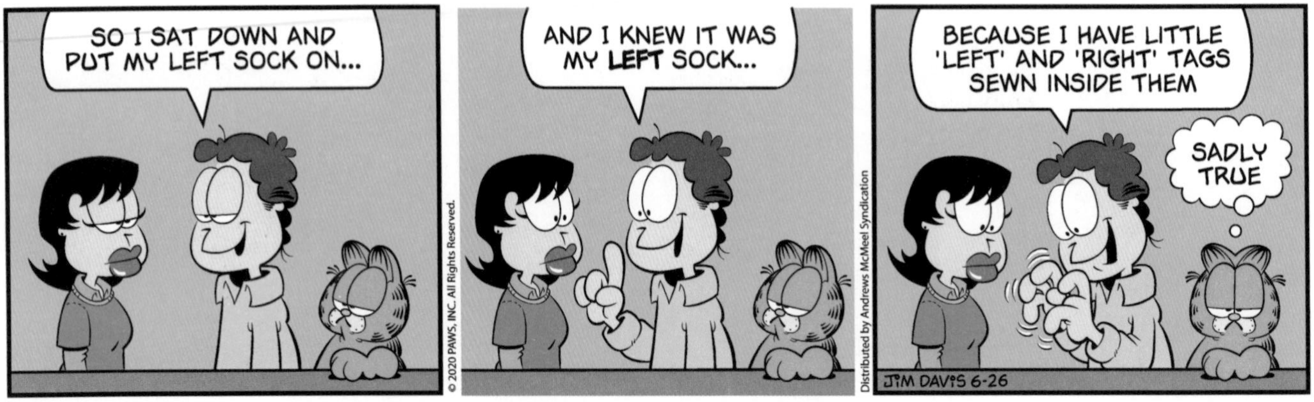
SO I SAT DOWN AND PUT MY LEFT SOCK ON...
AND I KNEW IT WAS MY **LEFT** SOCK...
BECAUSE I HAVE LITTLE 'LEFT' AND 'RIGHT' TAGS SEWN INSIDE THEM
SADLY TRUE
© 2020 PAWS, INC. All Rights Reserved.
Distributed by Andrews McMeel Syndication
JIM DAVIS 6-26

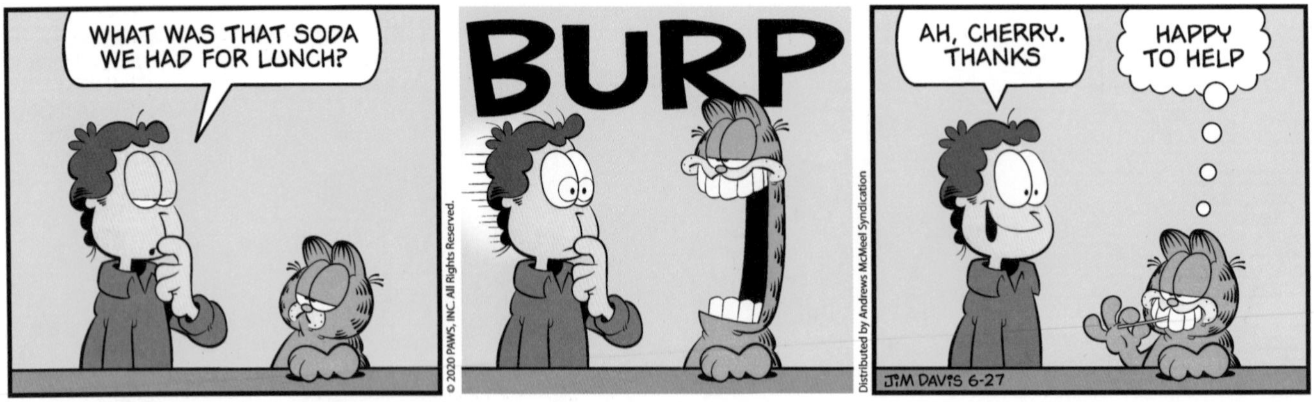
WHAT WAS THAT SODA WE HAD FOR LUNCH?
BURP
AH, CHERRY. THANKS
HAPPY TO HELP
© 2020 PAWS, INC. All Rights Reserved.
Distributed by Andrews McMeel Syndication
JIM DAVIS 6-27

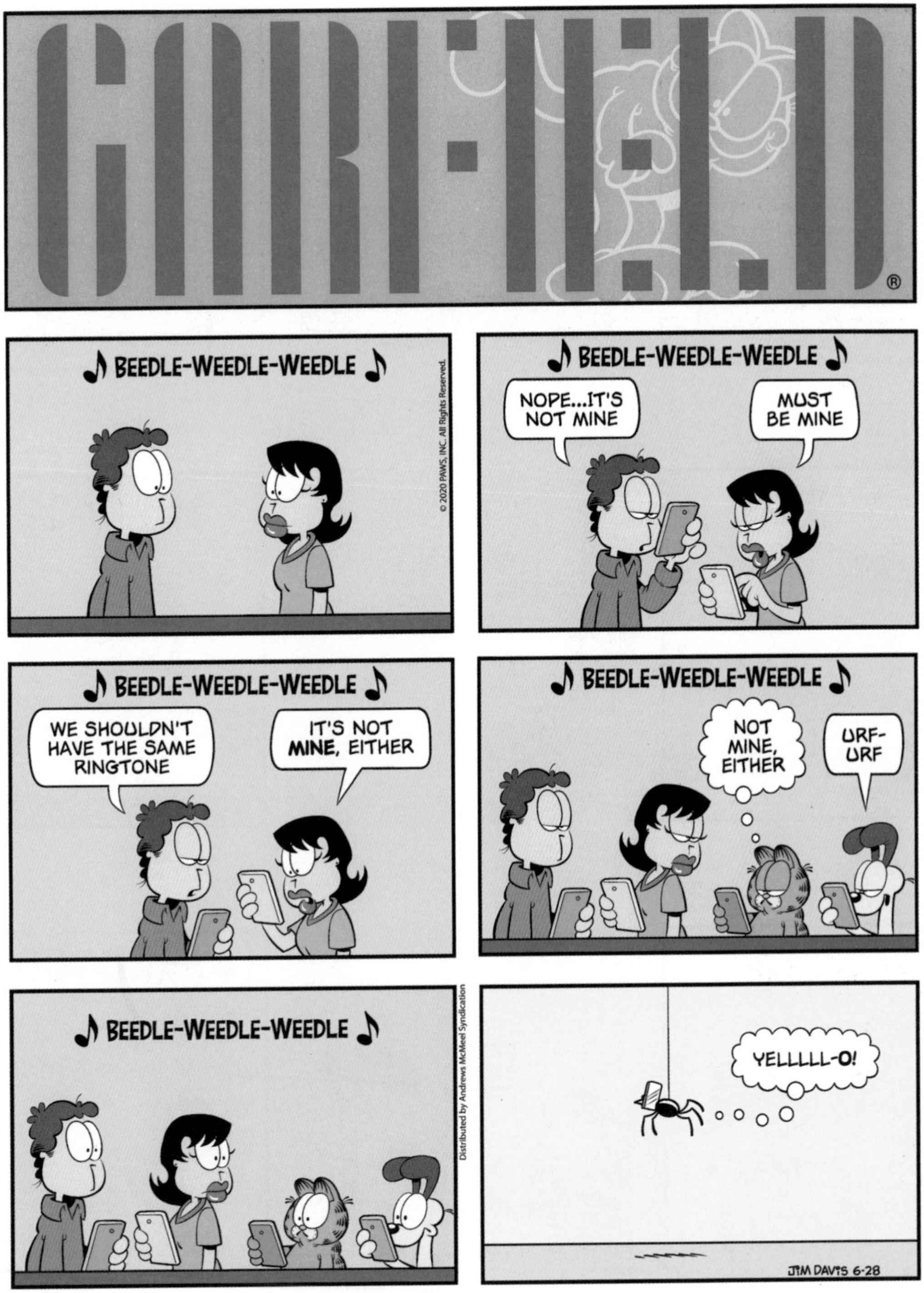
GARFIELD®
♪ BEEDLE-WEEDLE-WEEDLE ♪
© 2020 PAWS, INC. All Rights Reserved.
♪ BEEDLE-WEEDLE-WEEDLE ♪
NOPE...IT'S NOT MINE
MUST BE MINE
♪ BEEDLE-WEEDLE-WEEDLE ♪
WE SHOULDN'T HAVE THE SAME RINGTONE
IT'S NOT **MINE**, EITHER
♪ BEEDLE-WEEDLE-WEEDLE ♪
NOT MINE, EITHER
URF-URF
♪ BEEDLE-WEEDLE-WEEDLE ♪
Distributed by Andrews McMeel Syndication
YELLLLL-**O**!
JIM DAVIS 6-28

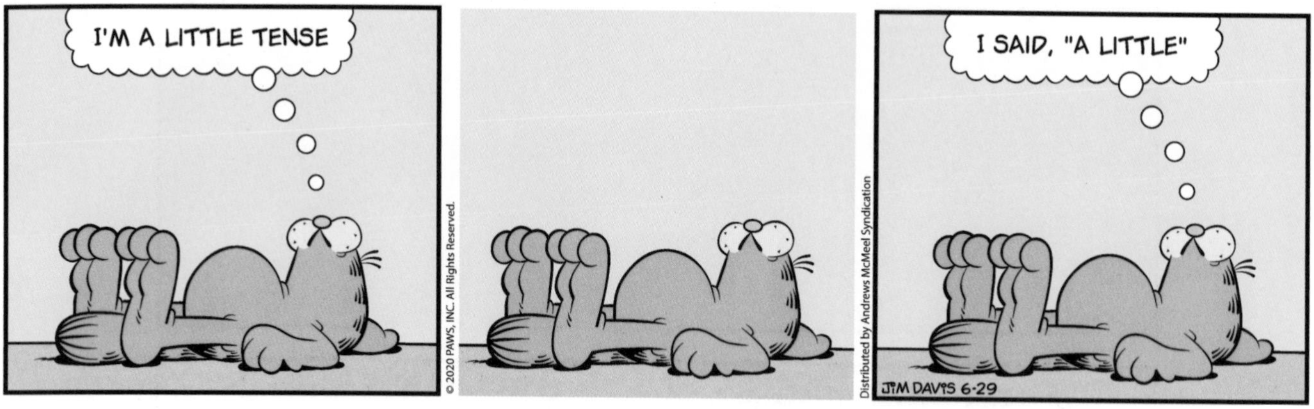
I'M A LITTLE TENSE
© 2020 PAWS, INC. All Rights Reserved.
Distributed by Andrews McMeel Syndication
I SAID, "A LITTLE"
JIM DAVIS 6-29

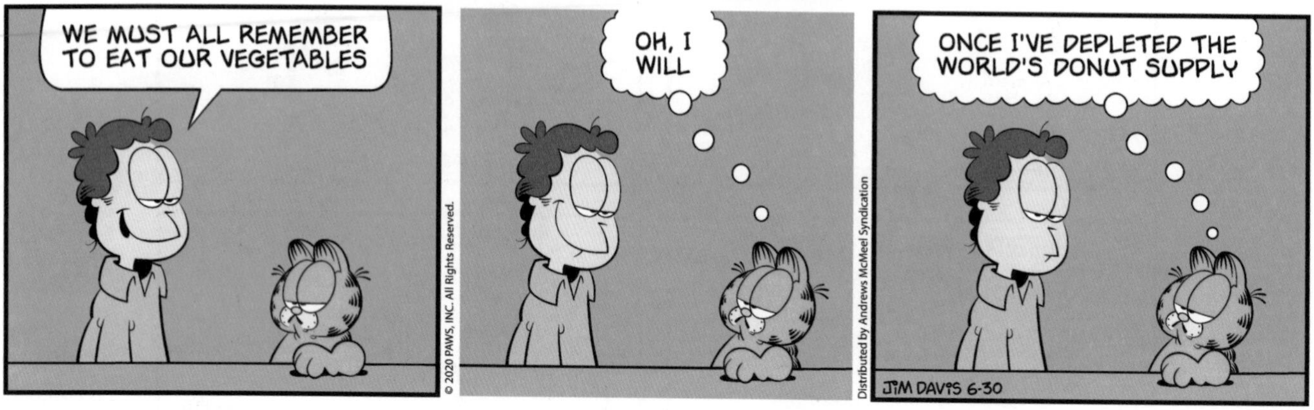
WE MUST ALL REMEMBER TO EAT OUR VEGETABLES
© 2020 PAWS, INC. All Rights Reserved.
OH, I WILL
Distributed by Andrews McMeel Syndication
ONCE I'VE DEPLETED THE WORLD'S DONUT SUPPLY
JIM DAVIS 6-30

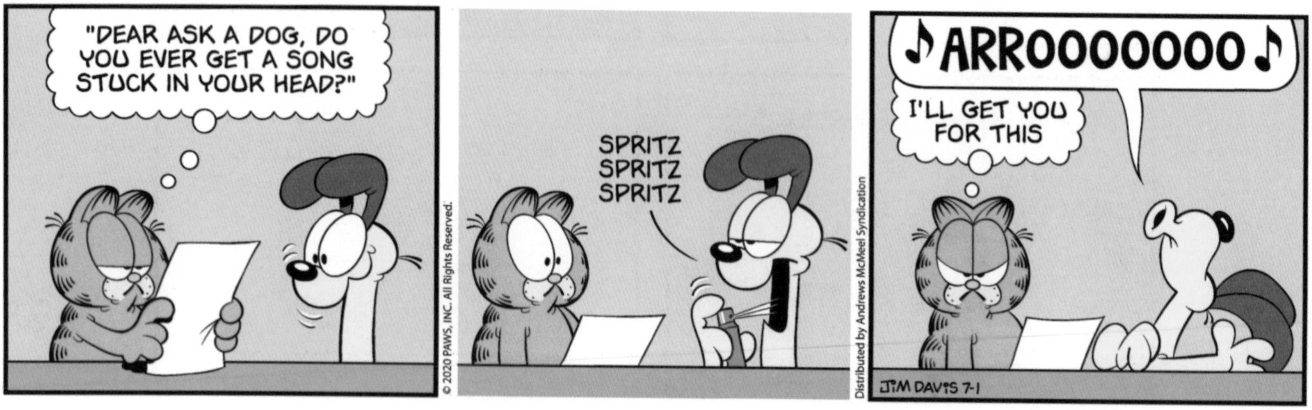
"DEAR ASK A DOG, DO YOU EVER GET A SONG STUCK IN YOUR HEAD?"
© 2020 PAWS, INC. All Rights Reserved.
SPRITZ SPRITZ SPRITZ
Distributed by Andrews McMeel Syndication
♪ ARROOOOOOO ♪
I'LL GET YOU FOR THIS
JIM DAVIS 7-1

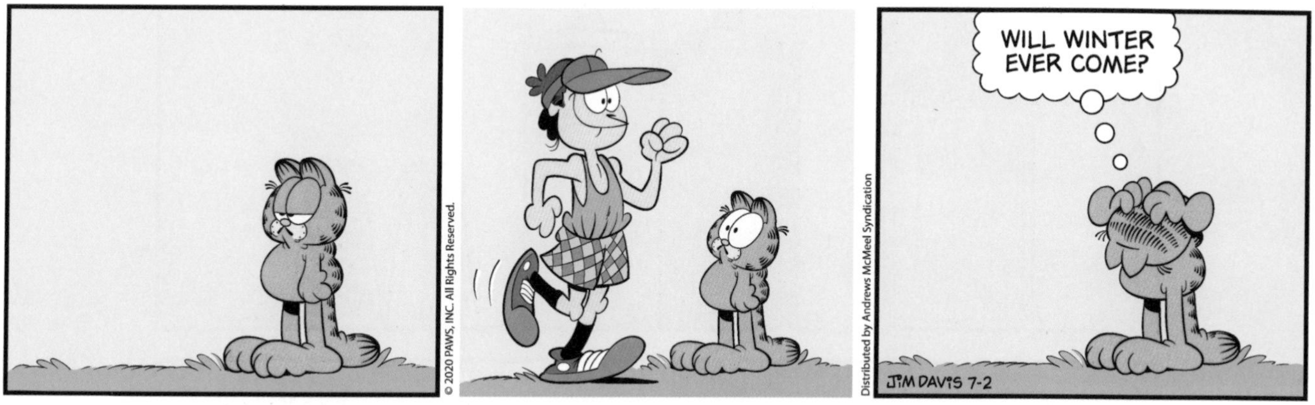
© 2020 PAWS, INC. All Rights Reserved.
Distributed by Andrews McMeel Syndication
WILL WINTER EVER COME?
JIM DAVIS 7-2

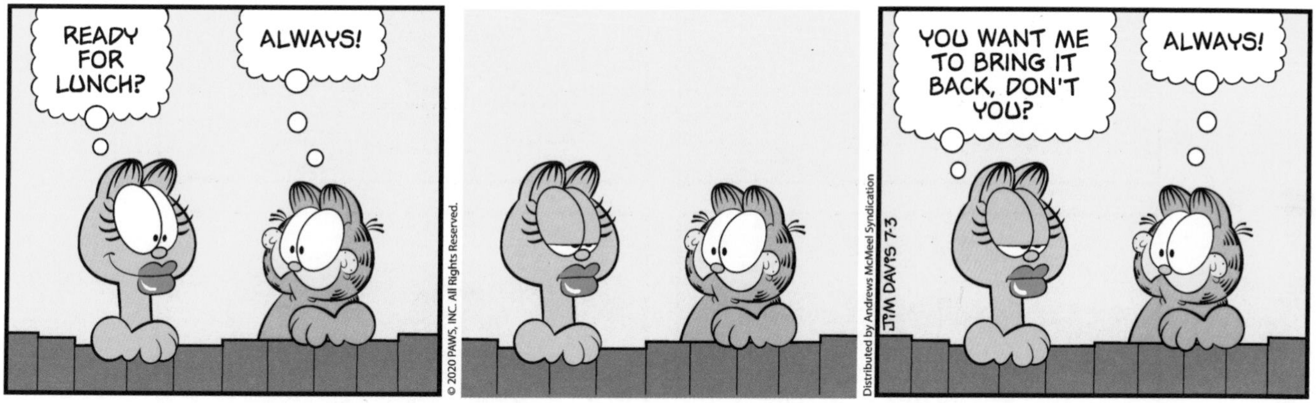
READY FOR LUNCH?
ALWAYS!
© 2020 PAWS, INC. All Rights Reserved.
Distributed by Andrews McMeel Syndication
JIM DAVIS 7-3
YOU WANT ME TO BRING IT BACK, DON'T YOU?
ALWAYS!

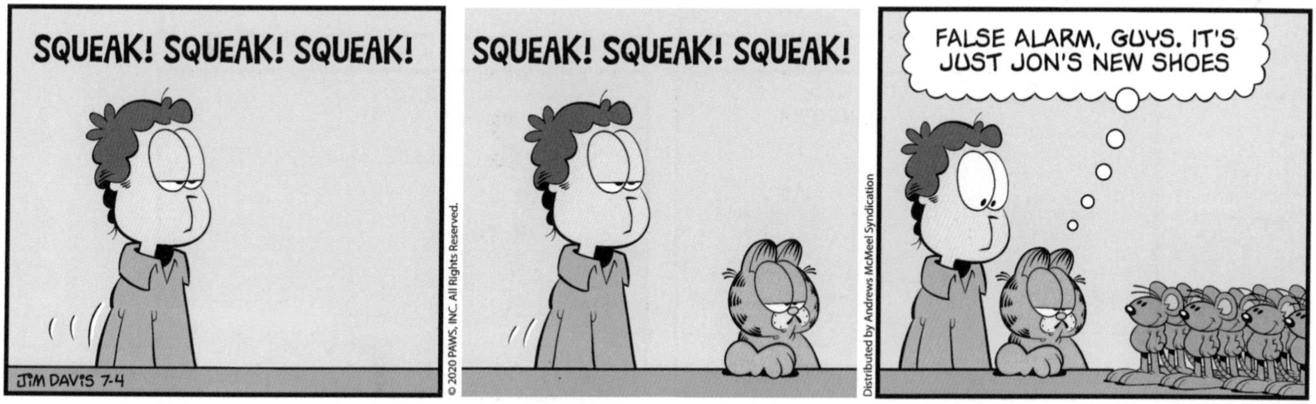
SQUEAK! SQUEAK! SQUEAK!
JIM DAVIS 7-4
© 2020 PAWS, INC. All Rights Reserved.
SQUEAK! SQUEAK! SQUEAK!
Distributed by Andrews McMeel Syndication
FALSE ALARM, GUYS. IT'S JUST JON'S NEW SHOES

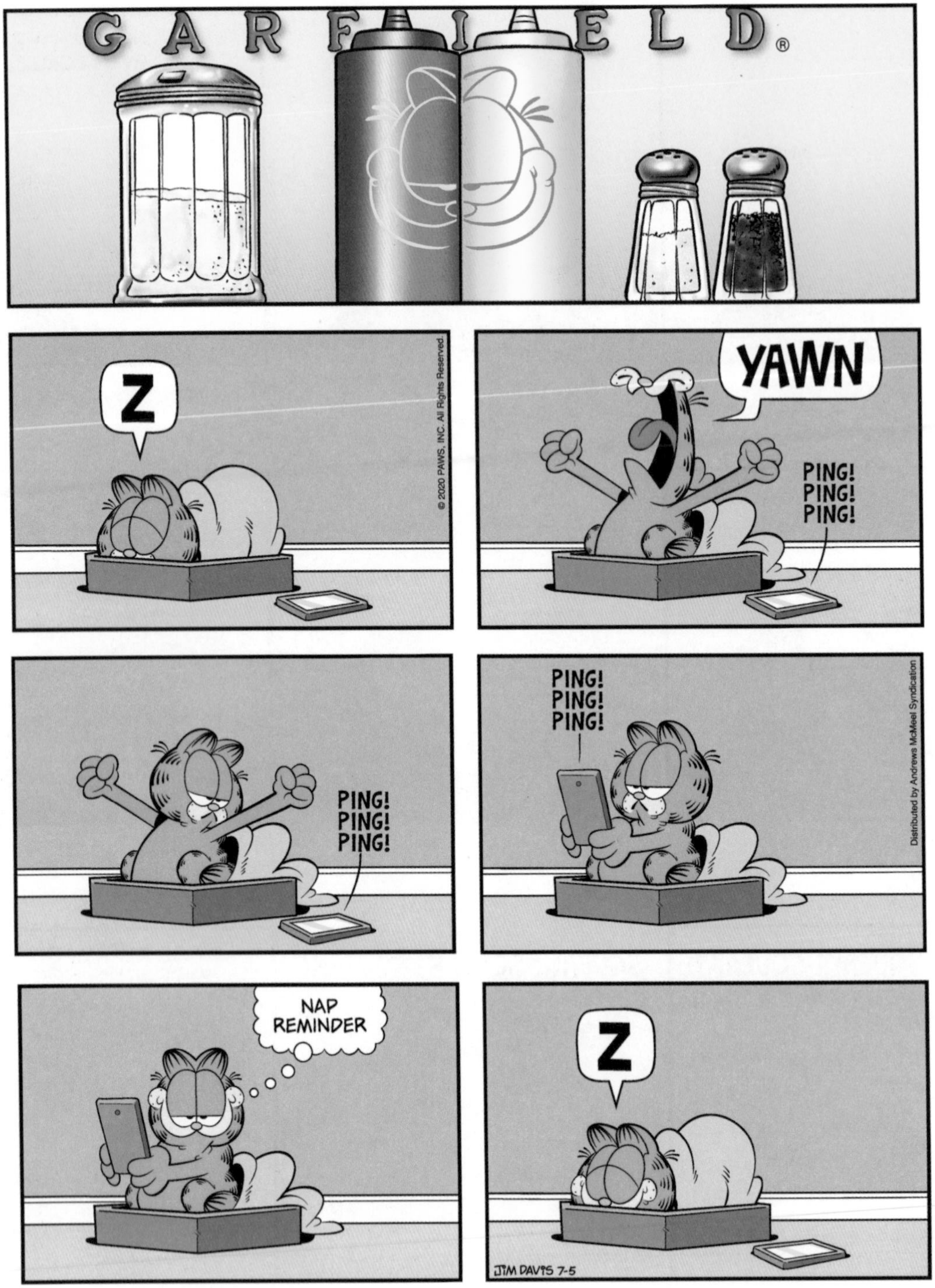
GARFIELD®
Z
© 2020 PAWS, INC. All Rights Reserved.
YAWN
PING! PING! PING!
PING! PING! PING!
PING! PING! PING!
Distributed by Andrews McMeel Syndication
NAP REMINDER
Z
JIM DAVIS 7-5

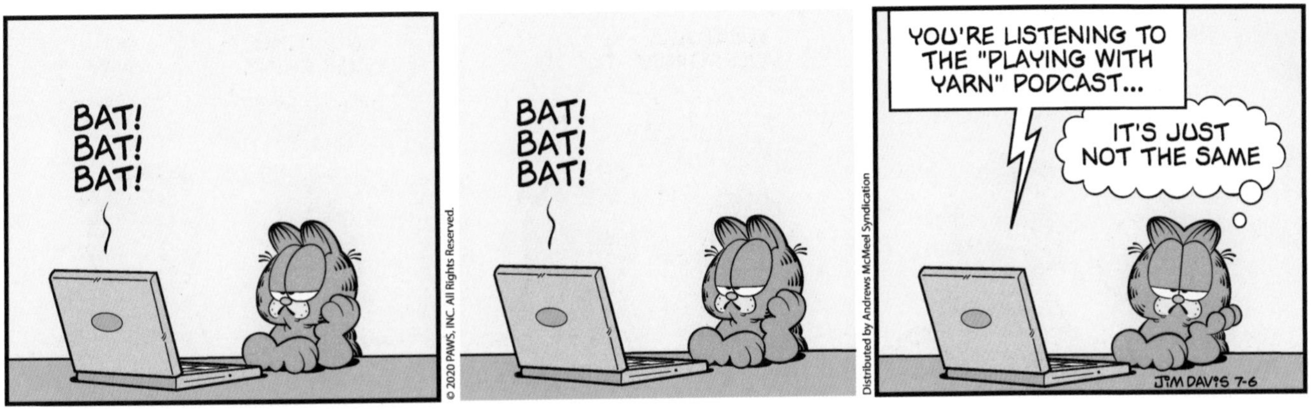
BAT!
BAT!
BAT!
© 2020 PAWS, INC. All Rights Reserved.
BAT!
BAT!
BAT!
Distributed by Andrews McMeel Syndication
YOU'RE LISTENING TO THE "PLAYING WITH YARN" PODCAST...
IT'S JUST NOT THE SAME
JIM DAVIS 7-6

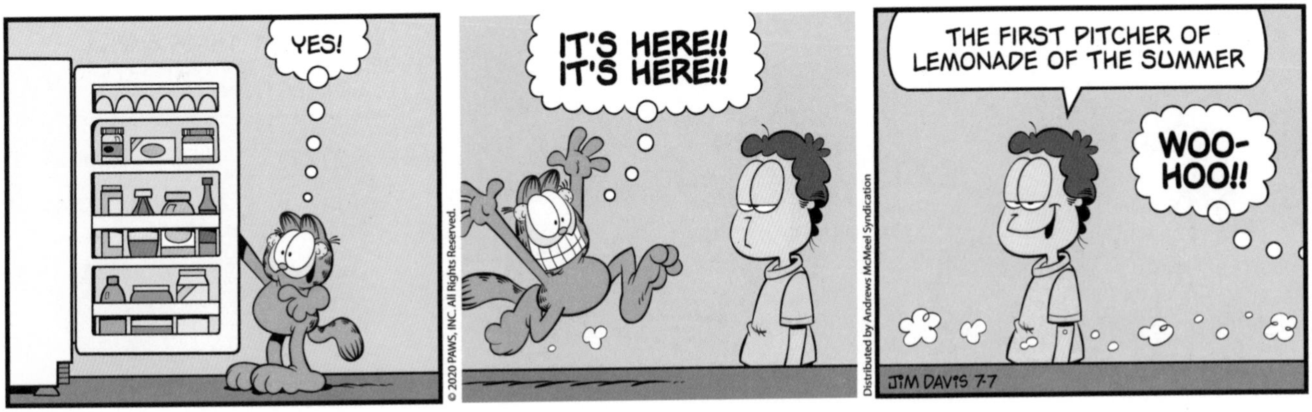
YES!
© 2020 PAWS, INC. All Rights Reserved.
IT'S HERE!! IT'S HERE!!
Distributed by Andrews McMeel Syndication
THE FIRST PITCHER OF LEMONADE OF THE SUMMER
WOO-HOO!!
JIM DAVIS 7-7

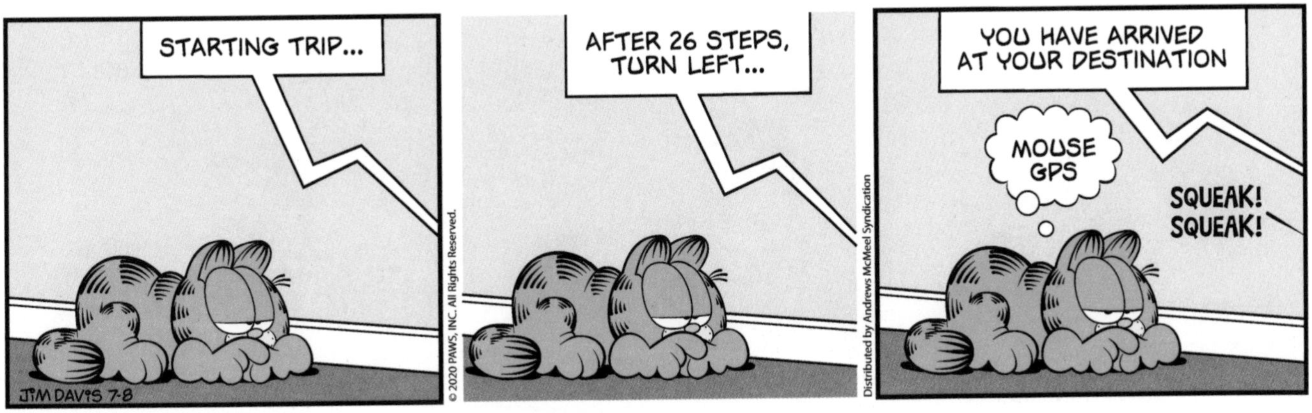
STARTING TRIP...
JIM DAVIS 7-8
© 2020 PAWS, INC. All Rights Reserved.
AFTER 26 STEPS, TURN LEFT...
Distributed by Andrews McMeel Syndication
YOU HAVE ARRIVED AT YOUR DESTINATION
MOUSE GPS
SQUEAK! SQUEAK!

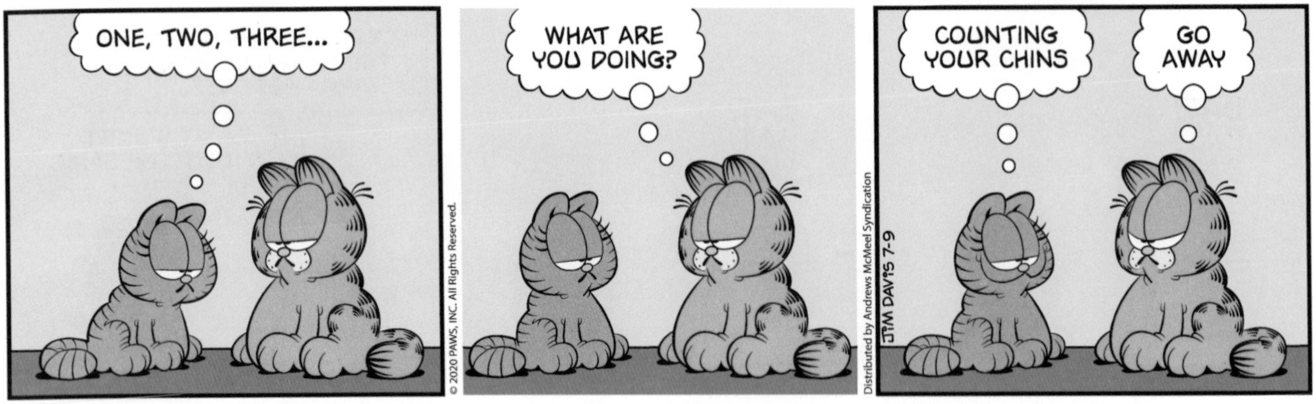
ONE, TWO, THREE...
© 2020 PAWS, INC. All Rights Reserved.
WHAT ARE YOU DOING?
Distributed by Andrews McMeel Syndication
JIM DAVIS 7-9
COUNTING YOUR CHINS
GO AWAY

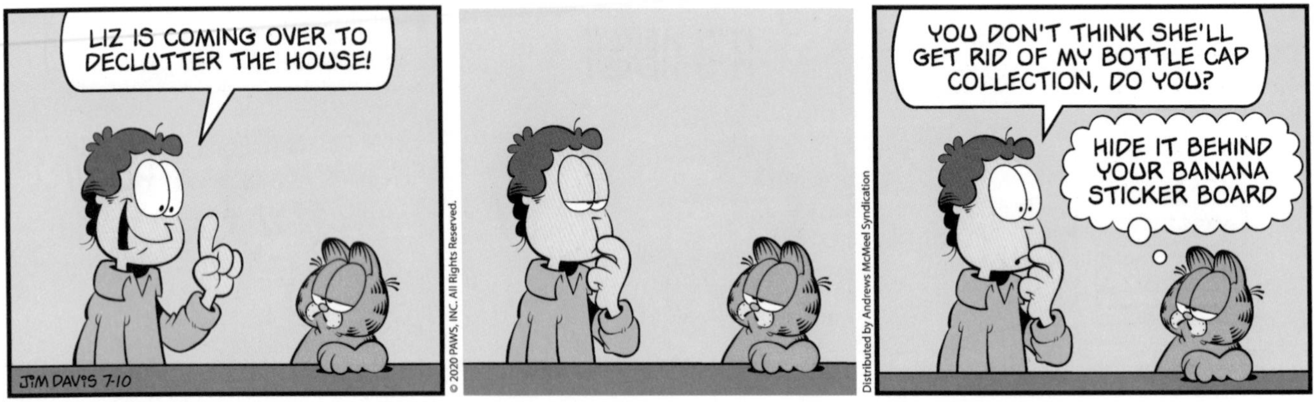
LIZ IS COMING OVER TO DECLUTTER THE HOUSE!
JIM DAVIS 7-10
© 2020 PAWS, INC. All Rights Reserved.
Distributed by Andrews McMeel Syndication
YOU DON'T THINK SHE'LL GET RID OF MY BOTTLE CAP COLLECTION, DO YOU?
HIDE IT BEHIND YOUR BANANA STICKER BOARD

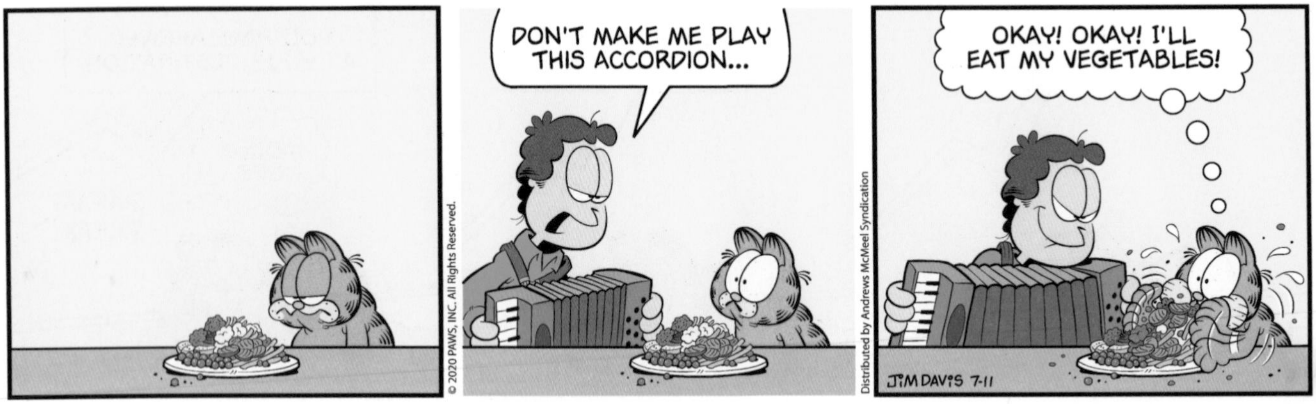
© 2020 PAWS, INC. All Rights Reserved.
DON'T MAKE ME PLAY THIS ACCORDION...
Distributed by Andrews McMeel Syndication
OKAY! OKAY! I'LL EAT MY VEGETABLES!
JIM DAVIS 7-11

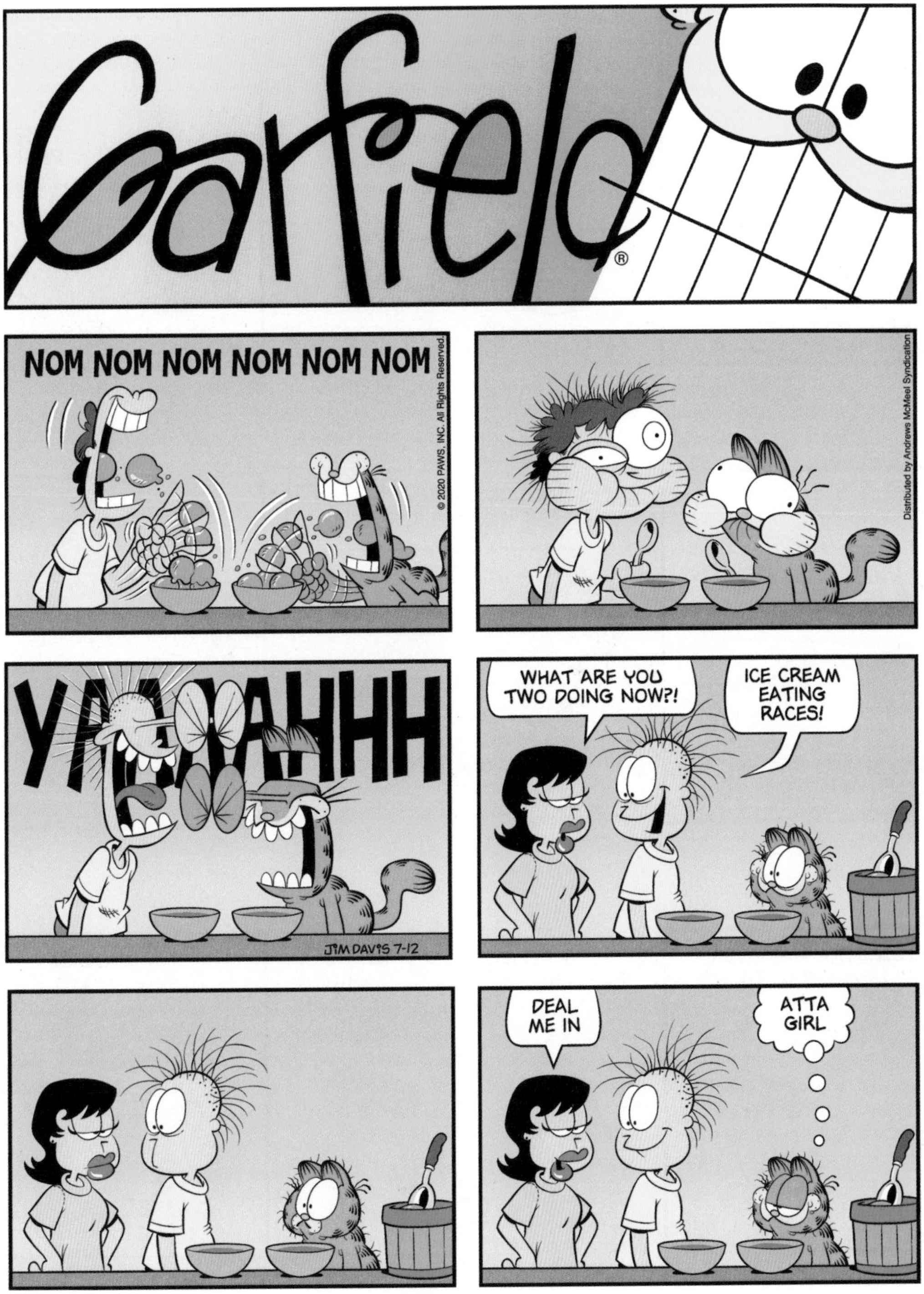
Garfield®
NOM NOM NOM NOM NOM NOM
© 2020 PAWS, INC. All Rights Reserved.
Distributed by Andrews McMeel Syndication
YA AHHH
JIM DAVIS 7-12
WHAT ARE YOU TWO DOING NOW?!
ICE CREAM EATING RACES!
DEAL ME IN
ATTA GIRL

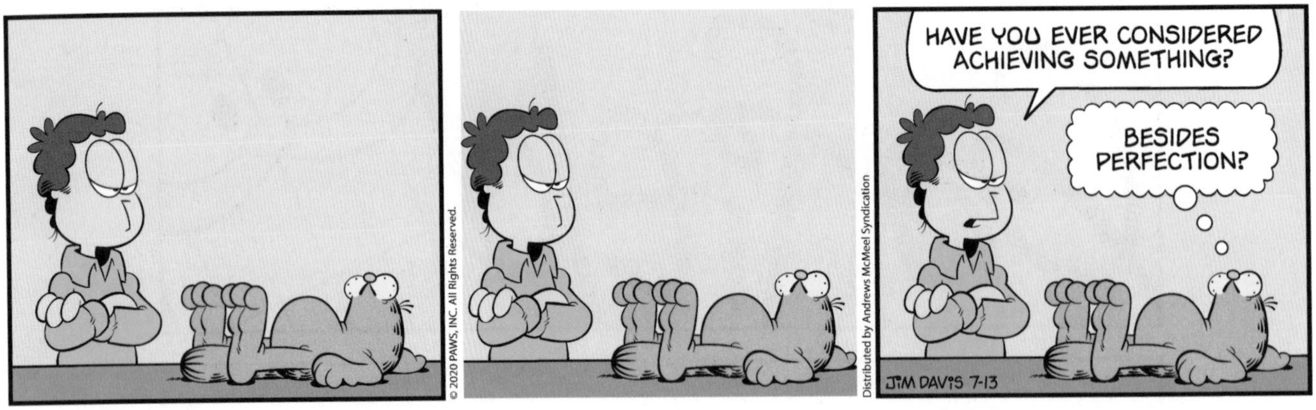
© 2020 PAWS, INC. All Rights Reserved.
HAVE YOU EVER CONSIDERED ACHIEVING SOMETHING?
BESIDES PERFECTION?
Distributed by Andrews McMeel Syndication
JIM DAVIS 7-13

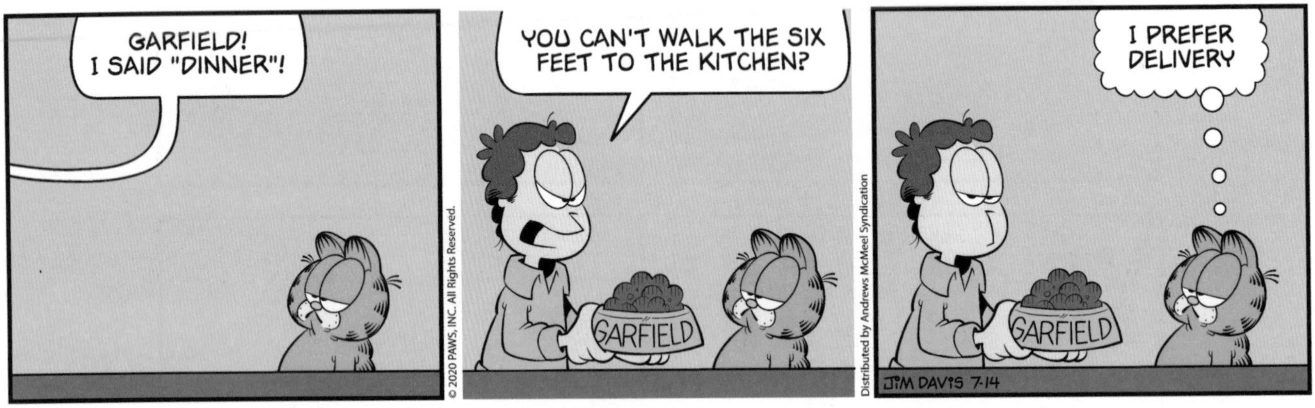
GARFIELD! I SAID "DINNER"!
© 2020 PAWS, INC. All Rights Reserved.
YOU CAN'T WALK THE SIX FEET TO THE KITCHEN?
GARFIELD
I PREFER DELIVERY
GARFIELD
Distributed by Andrews McMeel Syndication
JIM DAVIS 7-14

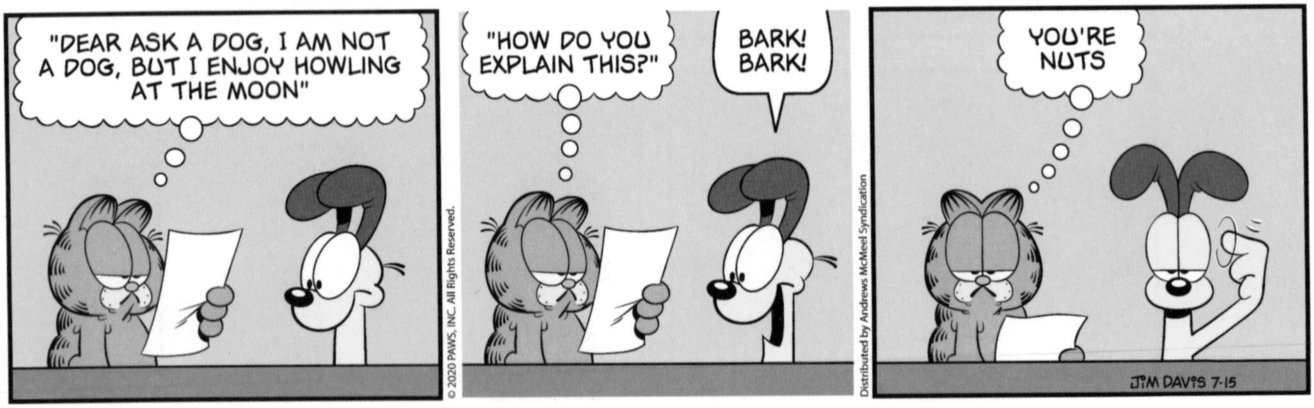
"DEAR ASK A DOG, I AM NOT A DOG, BUT I ENJOY HOWLING AT THE MOON"
© 2020 PAWS, INC. All Rights Reserved.
"HOW DO YOU EXPLAIN THIS?"
BARK! BARK!
Distributed by Andrews McMeel Syndication
YOU'RE NUTS
JIM DAVIS 7-15

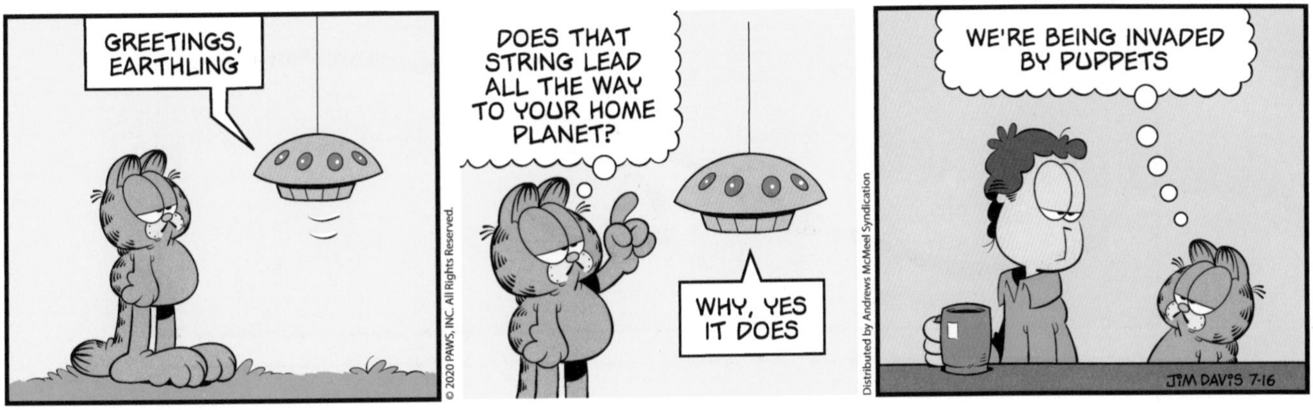
GREETINGS, EARTHLING
DOES THAT STRING LEAD ALL THE WAY TO YOUR HOME PLANET?
WHY, YES IT DOES
WE'RE BEING INVADED BY PUPPETS
© 2020 PAWS, INC. All Rights Reserved.
Distributed by Andrews McMeel Syndication
JIM DAVIS 7-16

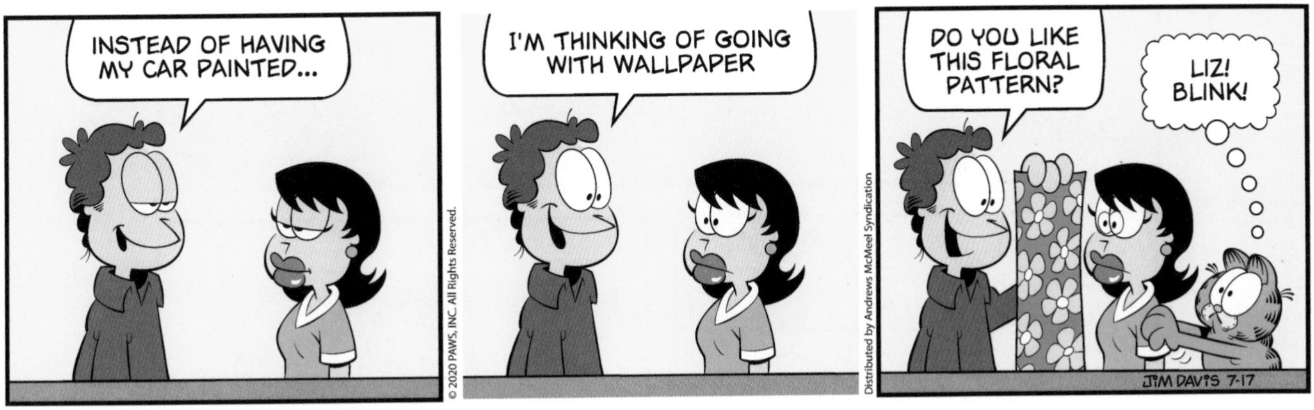
INSTEAD OF HAVING MY CAR PAINTED...
I'M THINKING OF GOING WITH WALLPAPER
DO YOU LIKE THIS FLORAL PATTERN?
LIZ! BLINK!
© 2020 PAWS, INC. All Rights Reserved.
Distributed by Andrews McMeel Syndication
JIM DAVIS 7-17

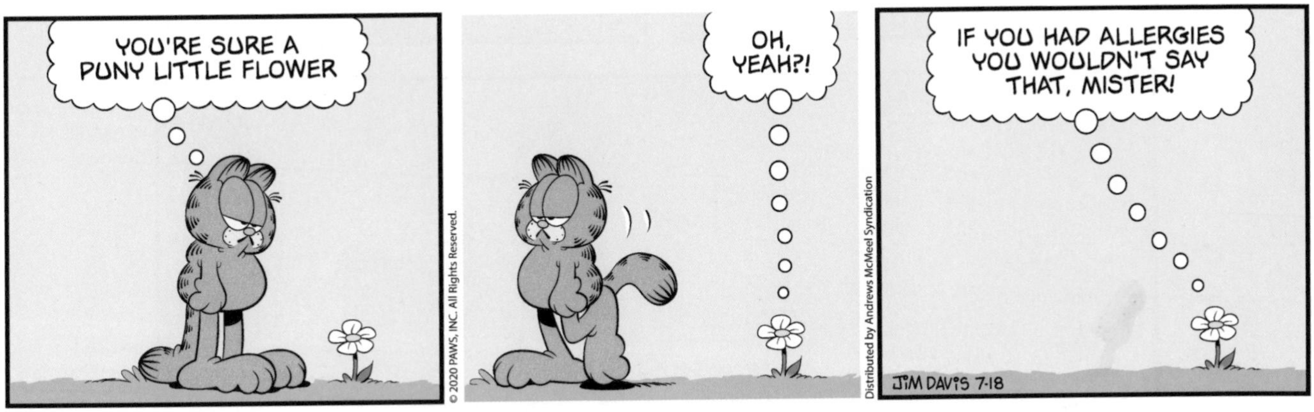
YOU'RE SURE A PUNY LITTLE FLOWER
OH, YEAH?!
IF YOU HAD ALLERGIES YOU WOULDN'T SAY THAT, MISTER!
© 2020 PAWS, INC. All Rights Reserved.
Distributed by Andrews McMeel Syndication
JIM DAVIS 7-18

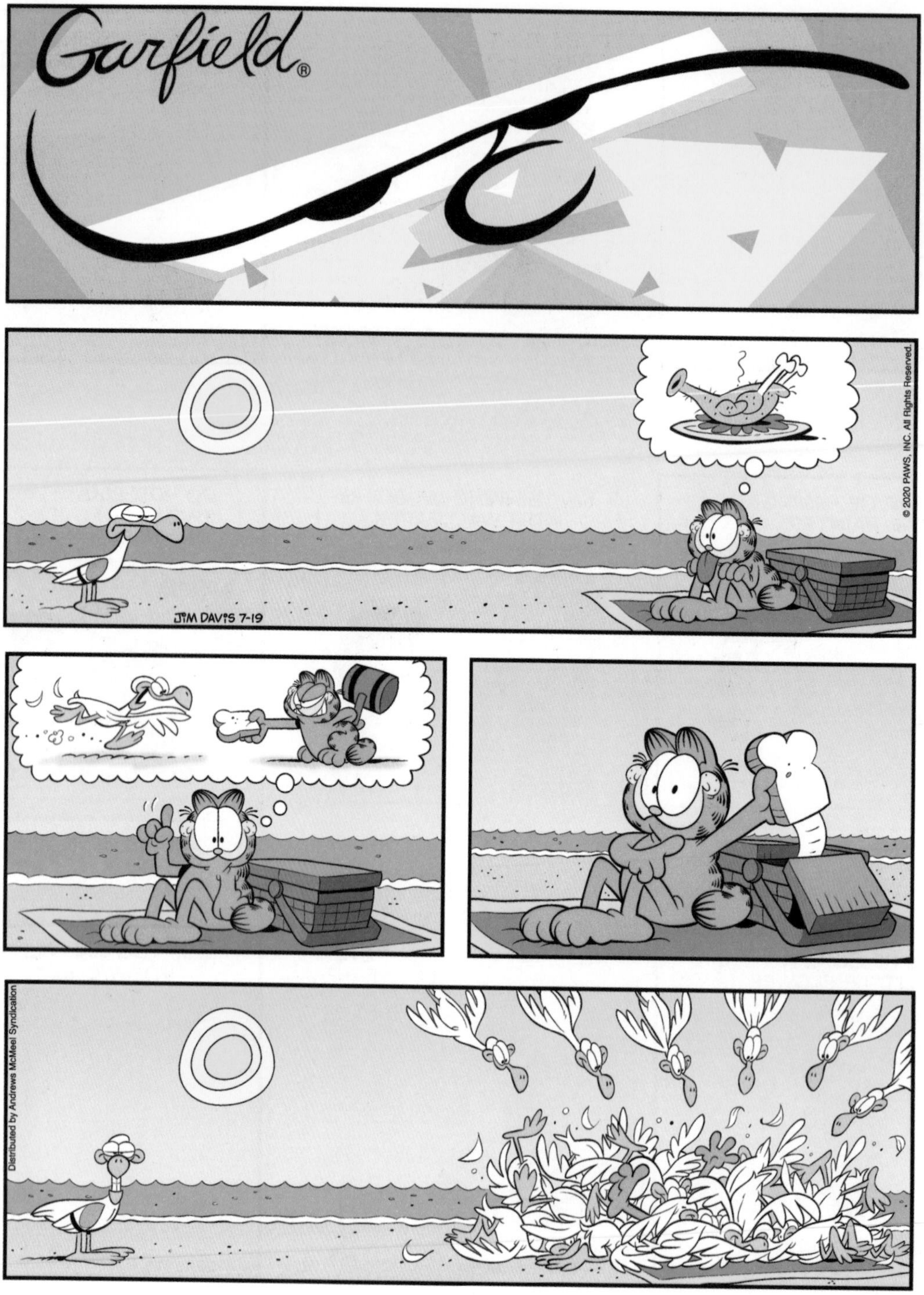
Garfield®
JIM DAVIS 7-19
© 2020 PAWS, INC. All Rights Reserved.
Distributed by Andrews McMeel Syndication

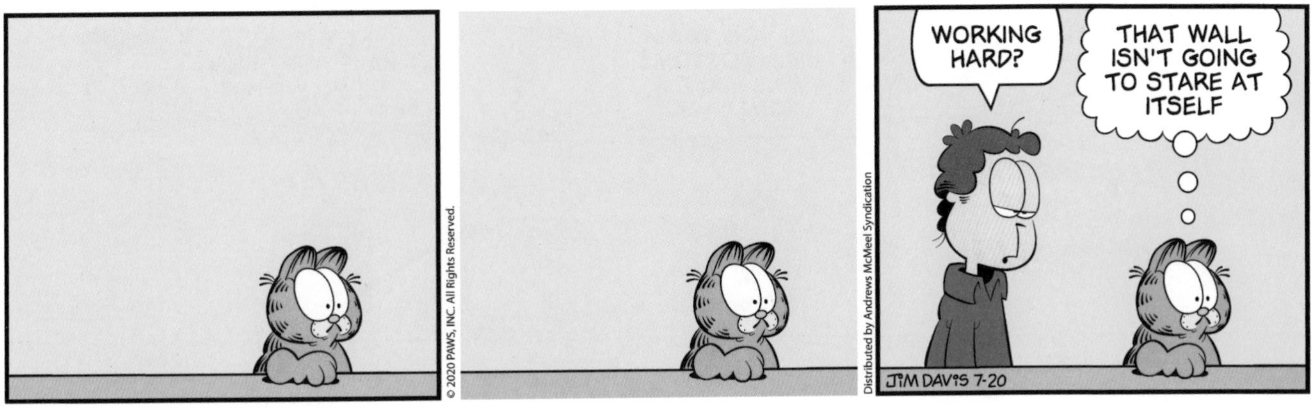
WORKING HARD?
THAT WALL ISN'T GOING TO STARE AT ITSELF
© 2020 PAWS, INC. All Rights Reserved.
Distributed by Andrews McMeel Syndication
JIM DAVIS 7-20

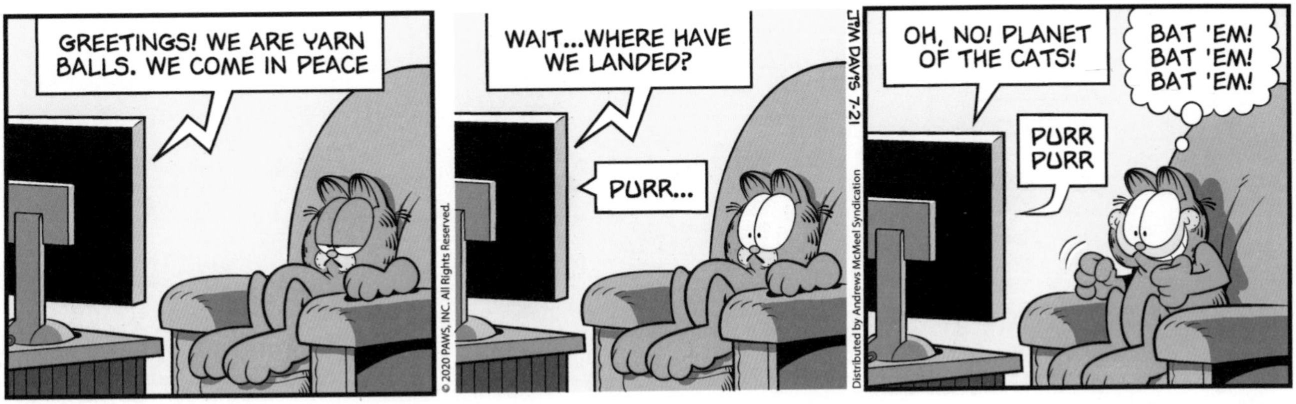
GREETINGS! WE ARE YARN BALLS. WE COME IN PEACE
WAIT...WHERE HAVE WE LANDED?
PURR...
OH, NO! PLANET OF THE CATS!
PURR PURR
BAT 'EM! BAT 'EM! BAT 'EM!
© 2020 PAWS, INC. All Rights Reserved.
Distributed by Andrews McMeel Syndication
JIM DAVIS 7-21

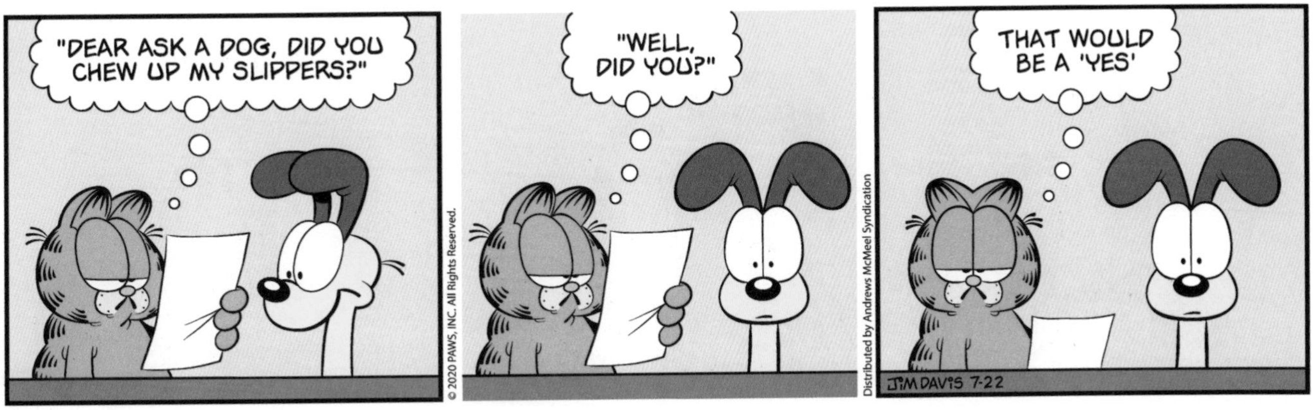
"DEAR ASK A DOG, DID YOU CHEW UP MY SLIPPERS?"
"WELL, DID YOU?"
THAT WOULD BE A 'YES'
© 2020 PAWS, INC. All Rights Reserved.
Distributed by Andrews McMeel Syndication
JIM DAVIS 7-22

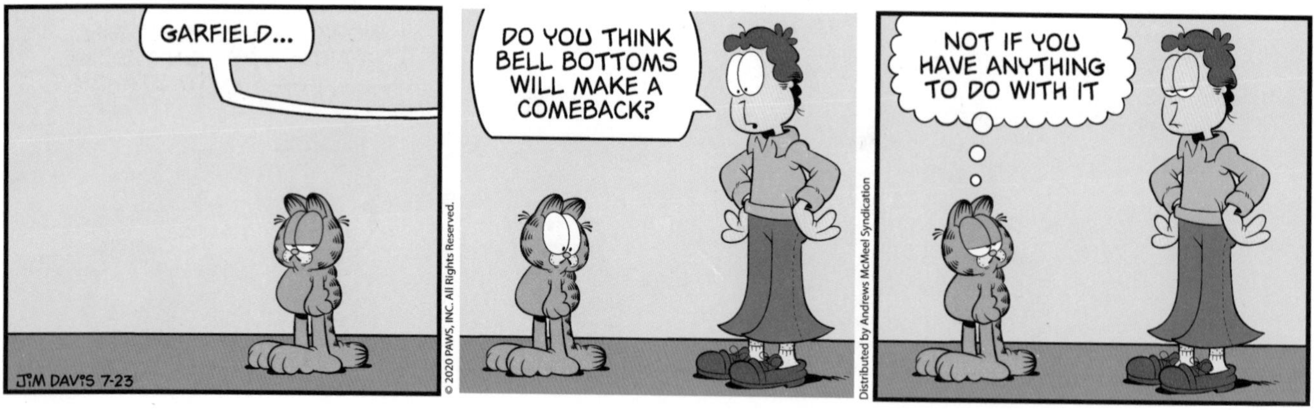
GARFIELD...
JIM DAVIS 7-23
© 2020 PAWS, INC. All Rights Reserved.
DO YOU THINK BELL BOTTOMS WILL MAKE A COMEBACK?
Distributed by Andrews McMeel Syndication
NOT IF YOU HAVE ANYTHING TO DO WITH IT

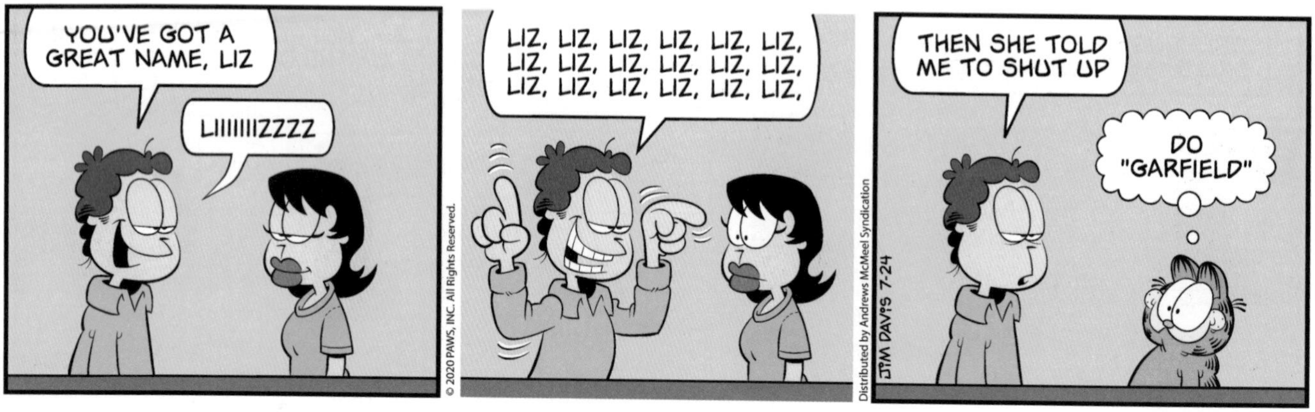
YOU'VE GOT A GREAT NAME, LIZ
LIIIIIIZZZZ
© 2020 PAWS, INC. All Rights Reserved.
LIZ, LIZ, LIZ, LIZ, LIZ, LIZ, LIZ, LIZ, LIZ, LIZ, LIZ, LIZ, LIZ, LIZ, LIZ, LIZ, LIZ, LIZ,
Distributed by Andrews McMeel Syndication
JIM DAVIS 7-24
THEN SHE TOLD ME TO SHUT UP
DO "GARFIELD"

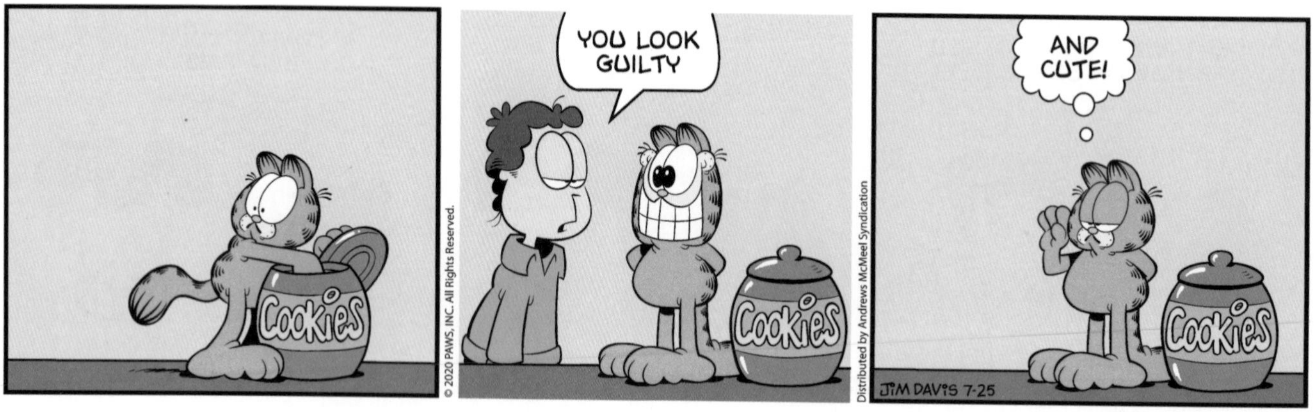
COOKIES
© 2020 PAWS, INC. All Rights Reserved.
YOU LOOK GUILTY
COOKIES
Distributed by Andrews McMeel Syndication
AND CUTE!
COOKIES
JIM DAVIS 7-25

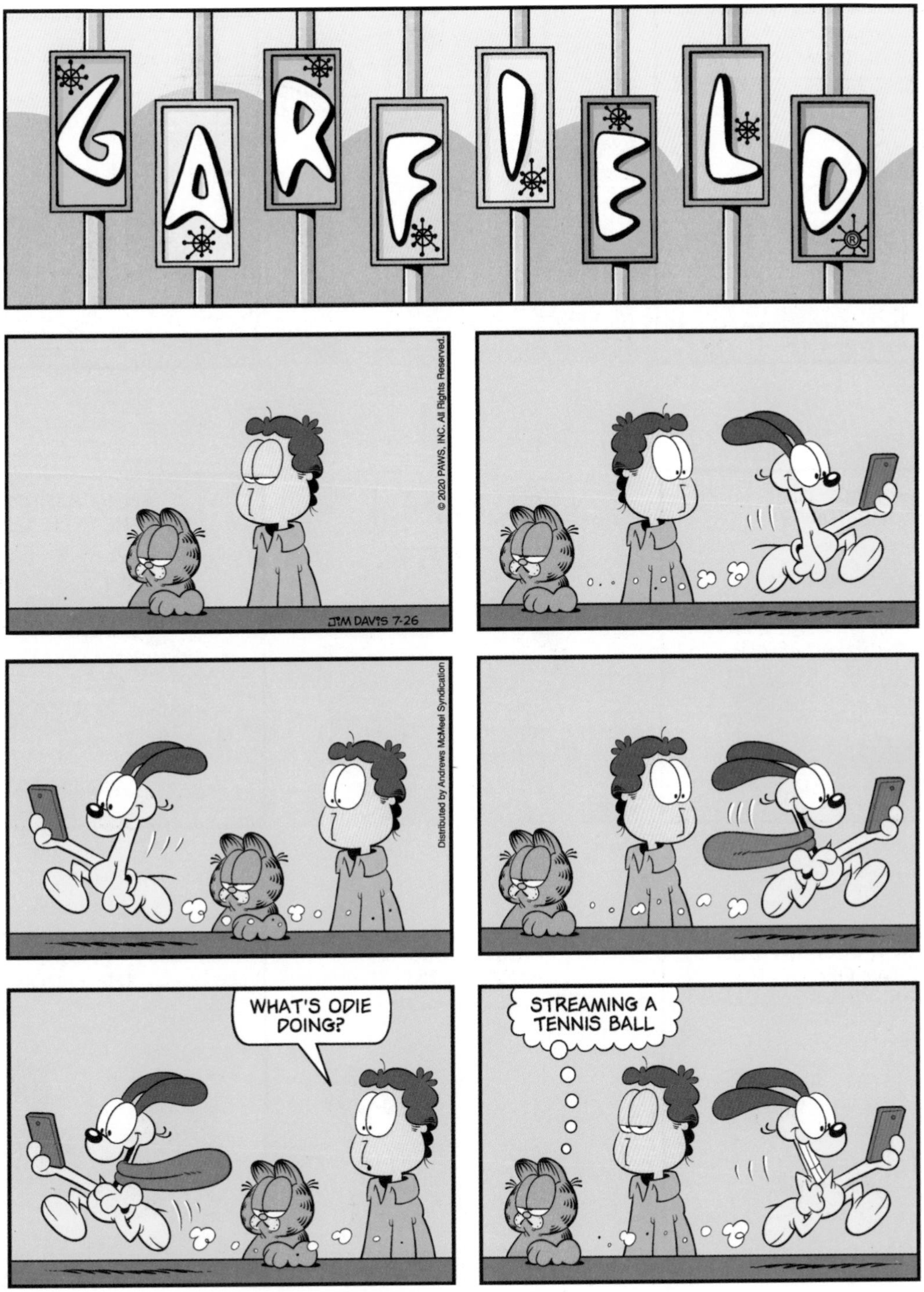
GARFIELD
© 2020 PAWS, INC. All Rights Reserved.
JIM DAVIS 7-26
Distributed by Andrews McMeel Syndication
WHAT'S ODIE DOING?
STREAMING A TENNIS BALL

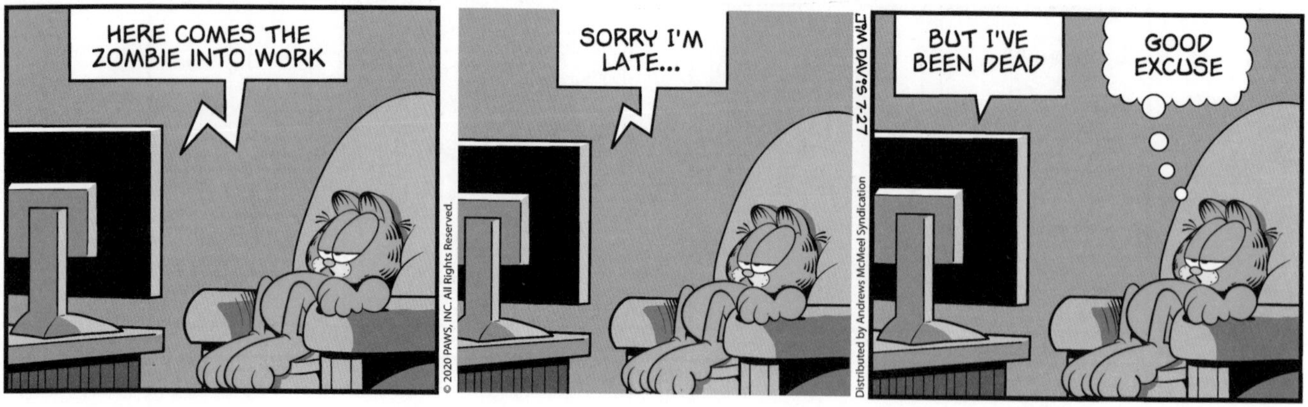
HERE COMES THE ZOMBIE INTO WORK
SORRY I'M LATE...
BUT I'VE BEEN DEAD
GOOD EXCUSE
JIM DAVIS 7-27
© 2020 PAWS, INC. All Rights Reserved.
Distributed by Andrews McMeel Syndication

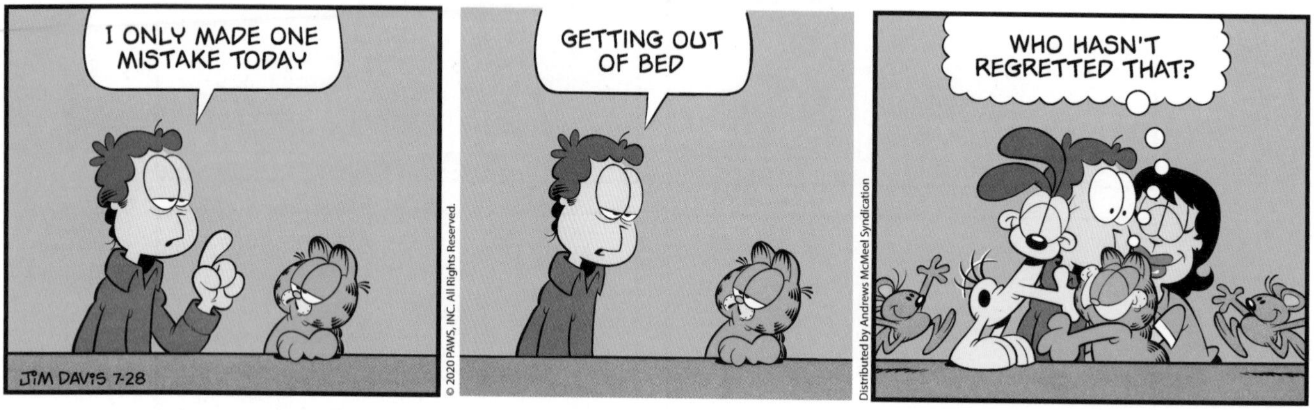
I ONLY MADE ONE MISTAKE TODAY
GETTING OUT OF BED
WHO HASN'T REGRETTED THAT?
JIM DAVIS 7-28
© 2020 PAWS, INC. All Rights Reserved.
Distributed by Andrews McMeel Syndication

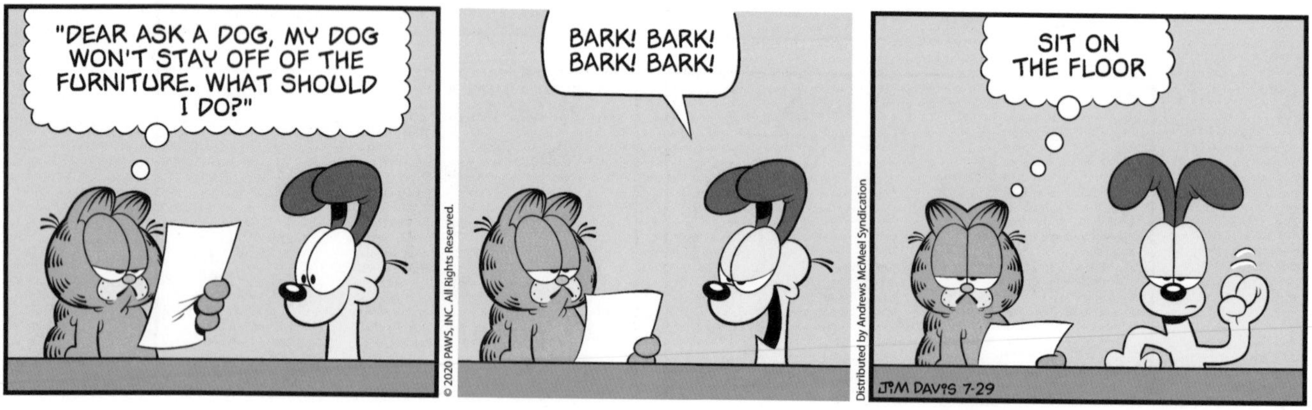
"DEAR ASK A DOG, MY DOG WON'T STAY OFF OF THE FURNITURE. WHAT SHOULD I DO?"
BARK! BARK! BARK! BARK!
SIT ON THE FLOOR
JIM DAVIS 7-29
© 2020 PAWS, INC. All Rights Reserved.
Distributed by Andrews McMeel Syndication

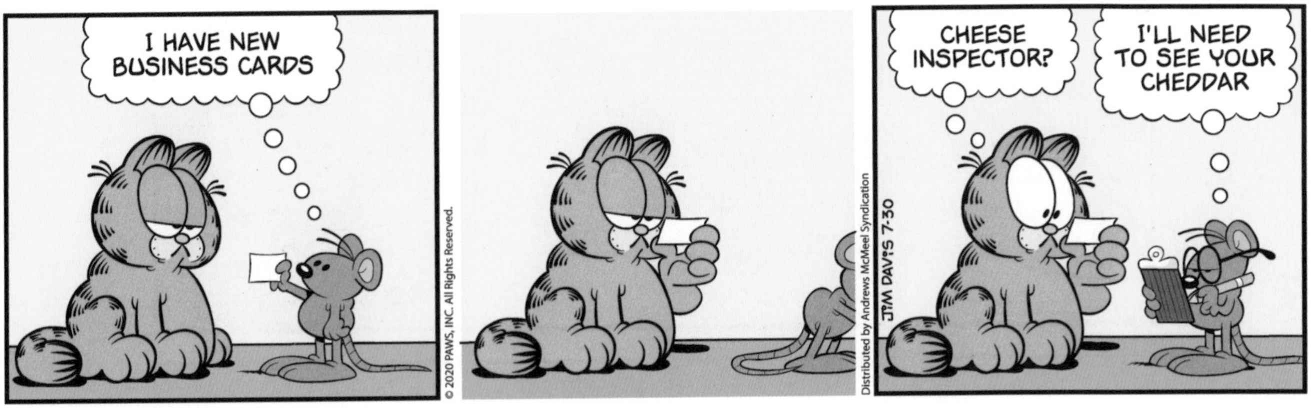
I HAVE NEW BUSINESS CARDS
© 2020 PAWS, INC. All Rights Reserved.
Distributed by Andrews McMeel Syndication
JIM DAVIS 7-30
CHEESE INSPECTOR?
I'LL NEED TO SEE YOUR CHEDDAR

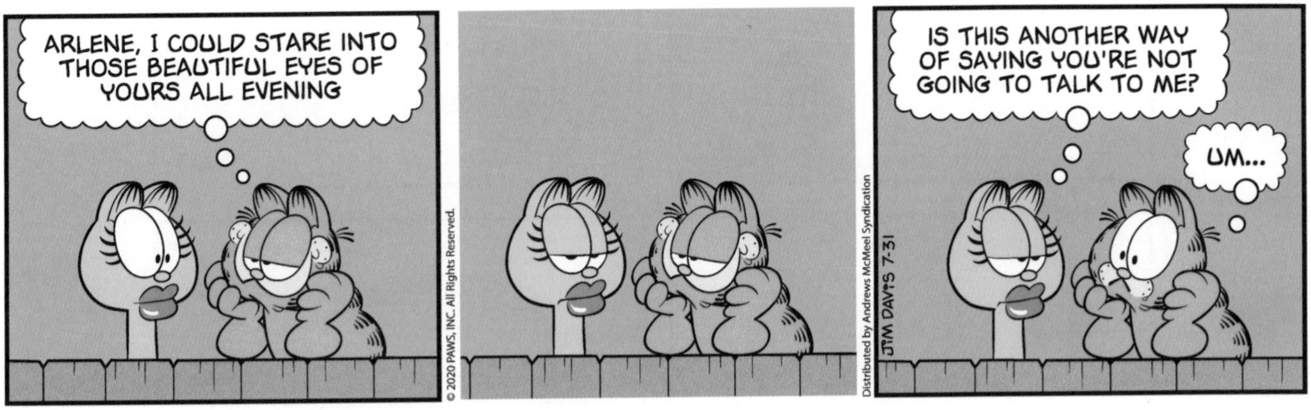
ARLENE, I COULD STARE INTO THOSE BEAUTIFUL EYES OF YOURS ALL EVENING
© 2020 PAWS, INC. All Rights Reserved.
Distributed by Andrews McMeel Syndication
JIM DAVIS 7-31
IS THIS ANOTHER WAY OF SAYING YOU'RE NOT GOING TO TALK TO ME?
UM...

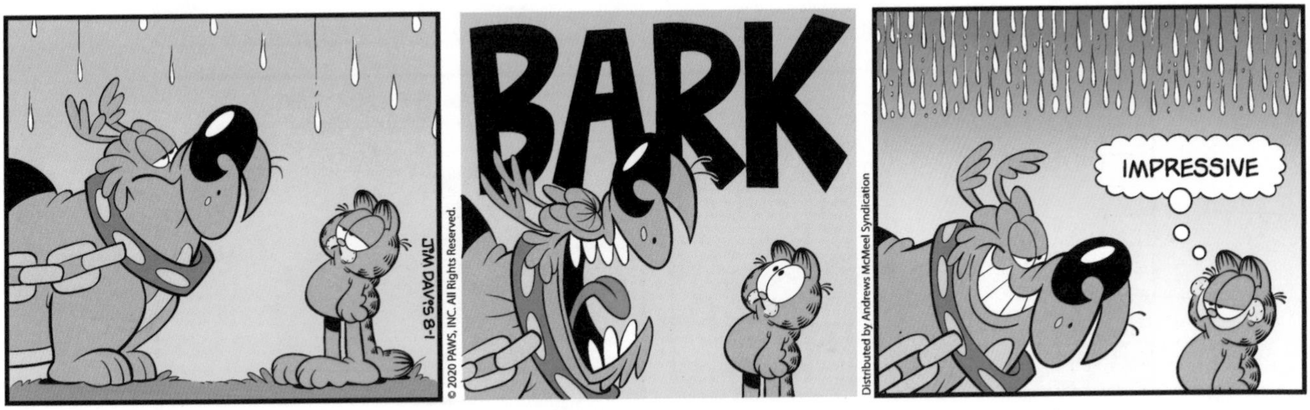
JIM DAVIS 8-1
© 2020 PAWS, INC. All Rights Reserved.
BARK
Distributed by Andrews McMeel Syndication
IMPRESSIVE

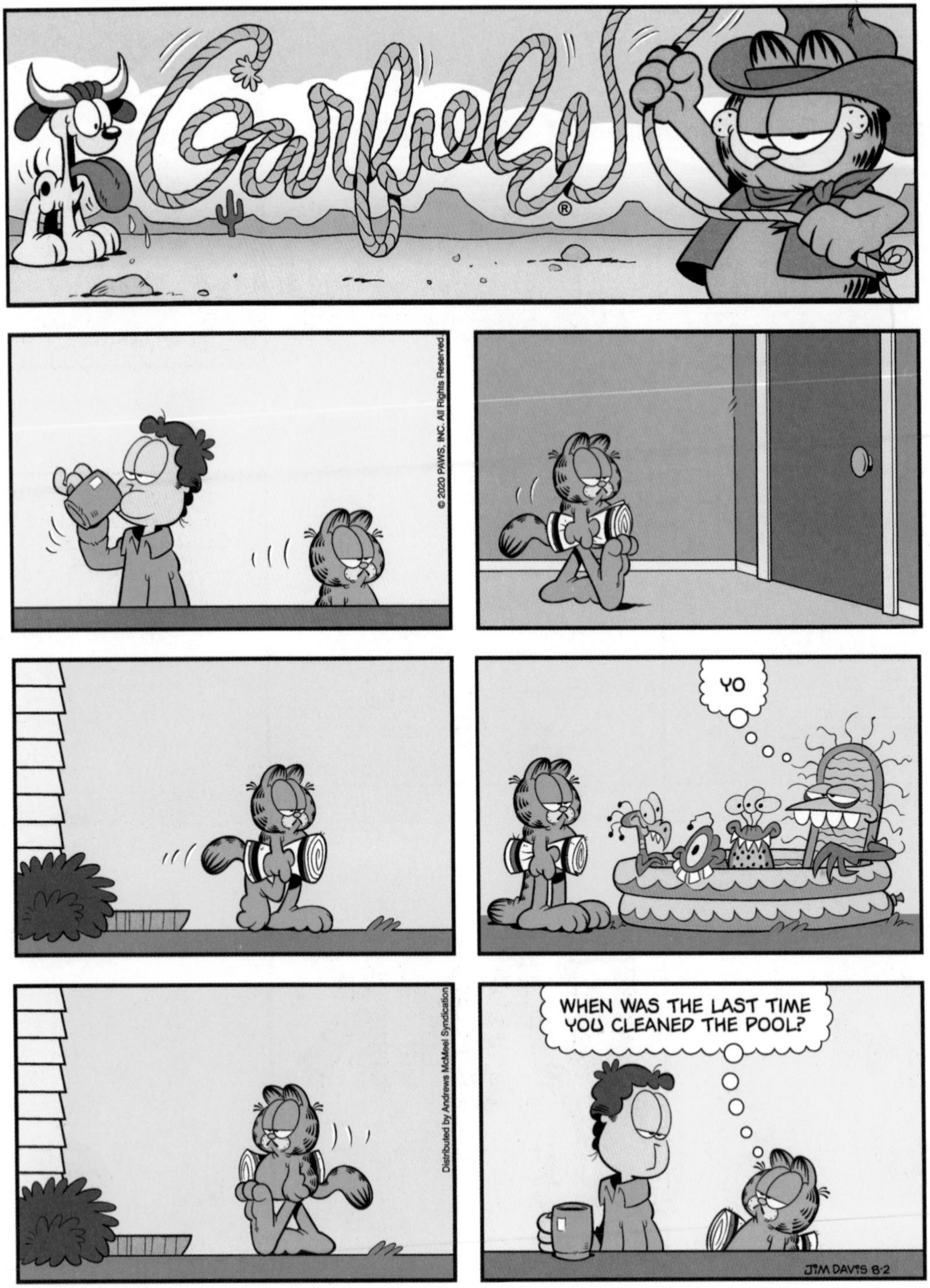
Garfield®
© 2020 PAWS, INC. All Rights Reserved
YO
Distributed by Andrews McMeel Syndication
WHEN WAS THE LAST TIME YOU CLEANED THE POOL?
JIM DAVIS 8-2

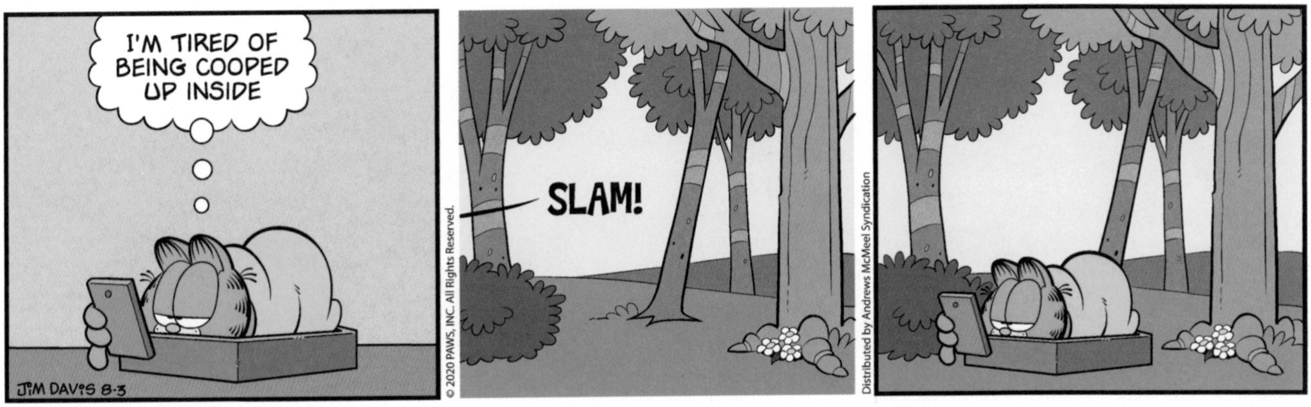
I'M TIRED OF BEING COOPED UP INSIDE
SLAM!
JIM DAVIS 8-3

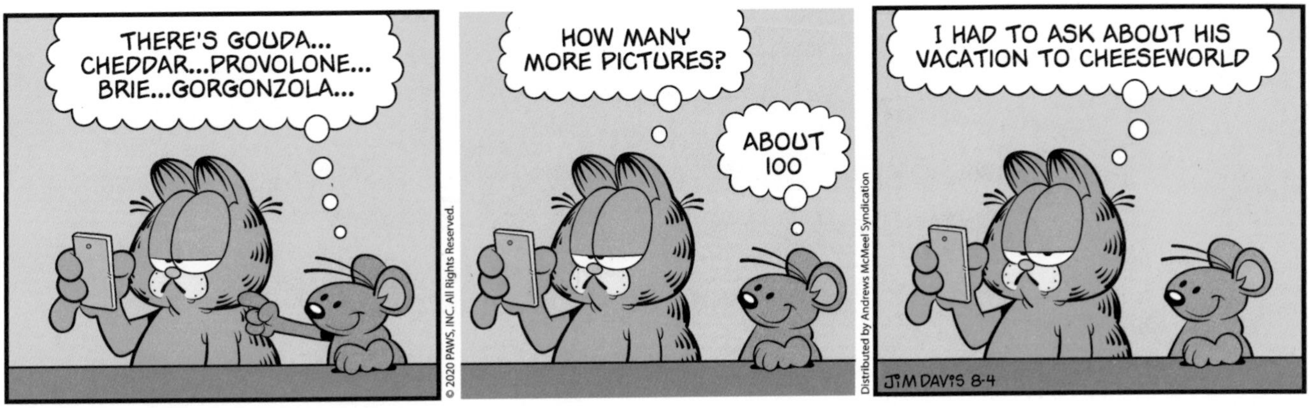
THERE'S GOUDA... CHEDDAR...PROVOLONE... BRIE...GORGONZOLA...
HOW MANY MORE PICTURES?
ABOUT 100
I HAD TO ASK ABOUT HIS VACATION TO CHEESEWORLD
JIM DAVIS 8-4

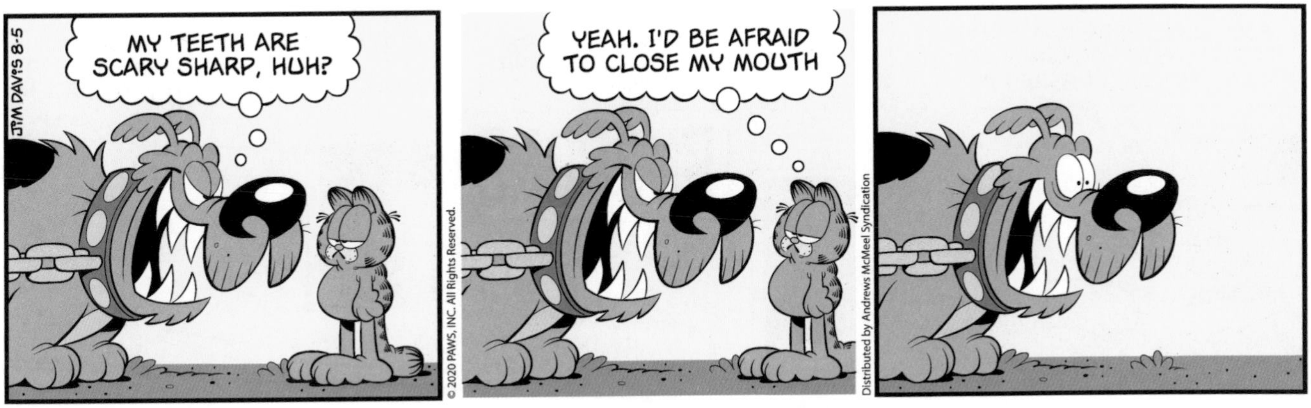
JIM DAVIS 8-5
MY TEETH ARE SCARY SHARP, HUH?
YEAH. I'D BE AFRAID TO CLOSE MY MOUTH

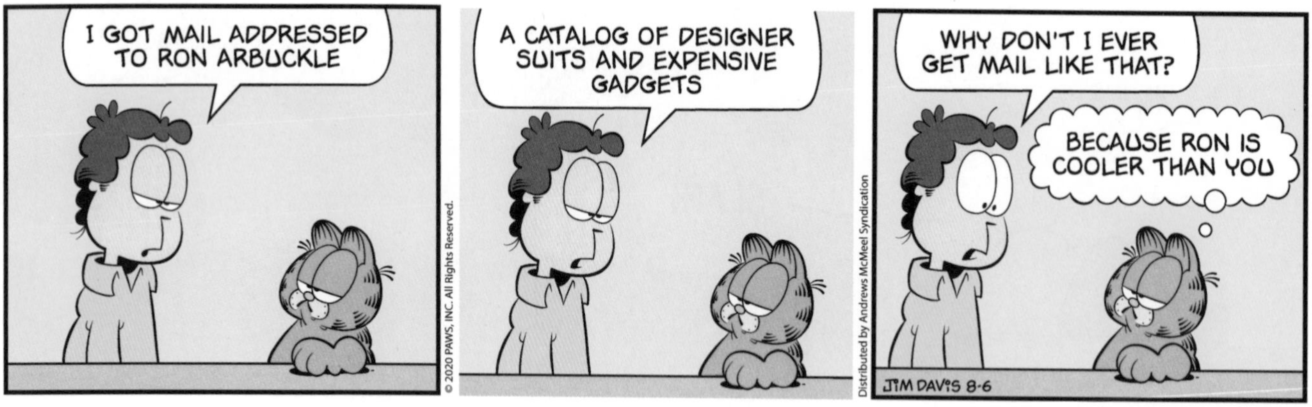
I GOT MAIL ADDRESSED TO RON ARBUCKLE
A CATALOG OF DESIGNER SUITS AND EXPENSIVE GADGETS
WHY DON'T I EVER GET MAIL LIKE THAT?
BECAUSE RON IS COOLER THAN YOU
JIM DAVIS 8-6
© 2020 PAWS, INC. All Rights Reserved.
Distributed by Andrews McMeel Syndication

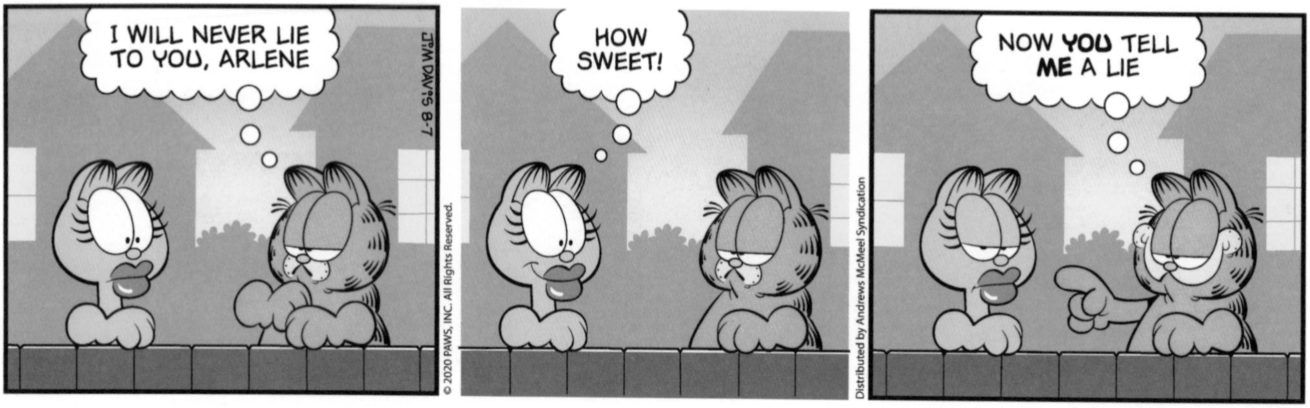
I WILL NEVER LIE TO YOU, ARLENE
JIM DAVIS 8-7
HOW SWEET!
NOW **YOU** TELL **ME** A LIE
© 2020 PAWS, INC. All Rights Reserved.
Distributed by Andrews McMeel Syndication

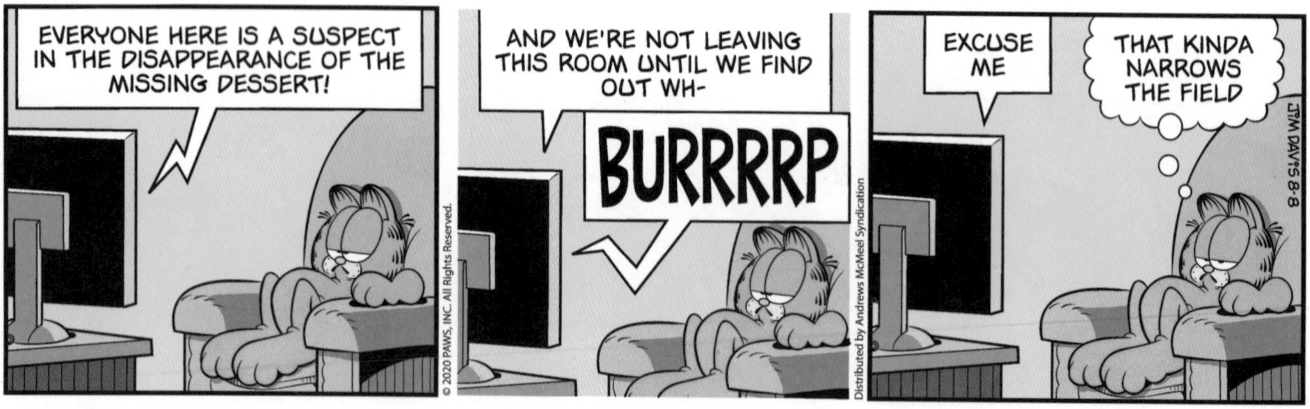
EVERYONE HERE IS A SUSPECT IN THE DISAPPEARANCE OF THE MISSING DESSERT!
AND WE'RE NOT LEAVING THIS ROOM UNTIL WE FIND OUT WH-
BURRRRP
EXCUSE ME
THAT KINDA NARROWS THE FIELD
JIM DAVIS 8-8
© 2020 PAWS, INC. All Rights Reserved.
Distributed by Andrews McMeel Syndication

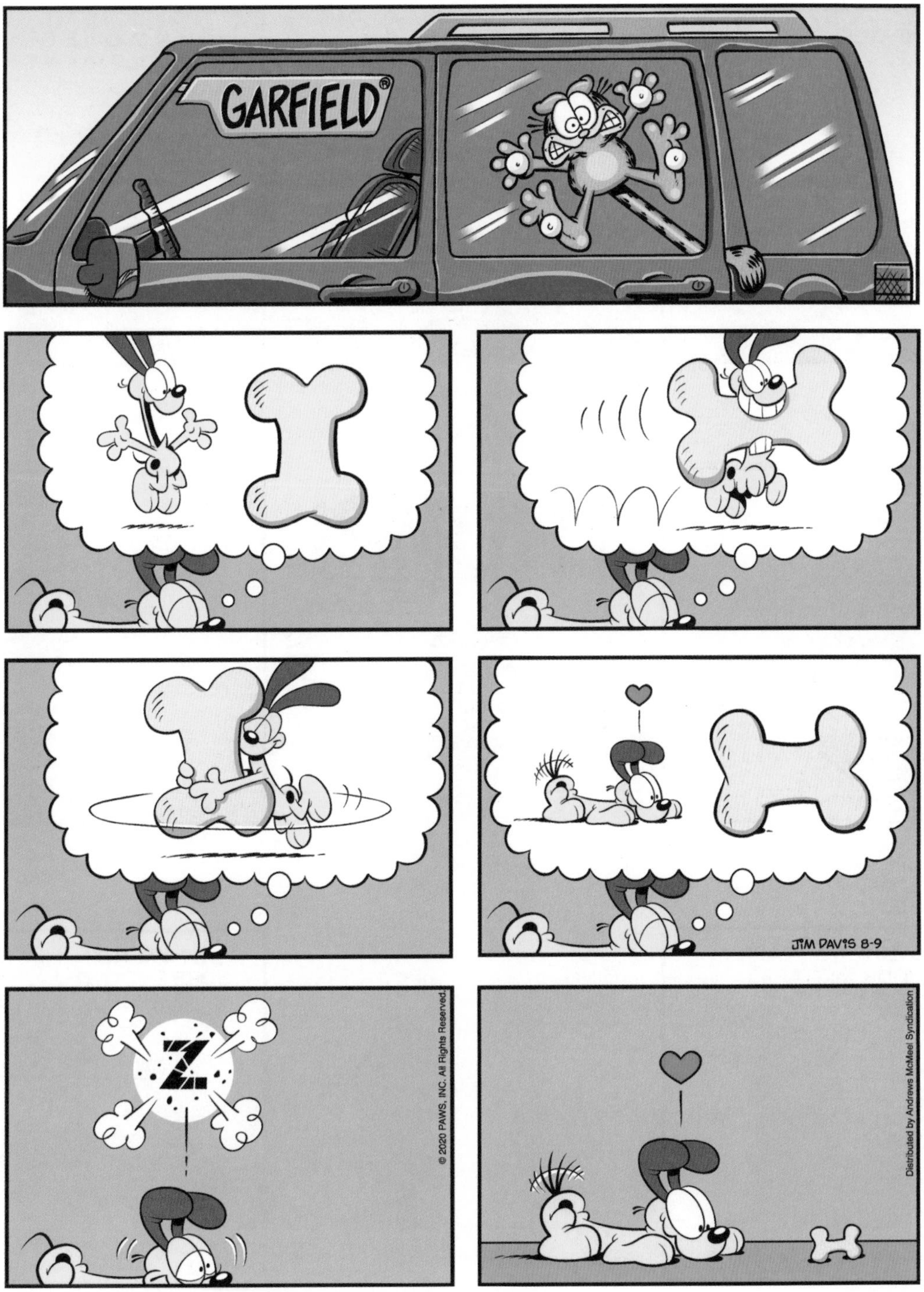
GARFIELD®
JIM DAVIS 8-9
Z
© 2020 PAWS, INC. All Rights Reserved.
Distributed by Andrews McMeel Syndication

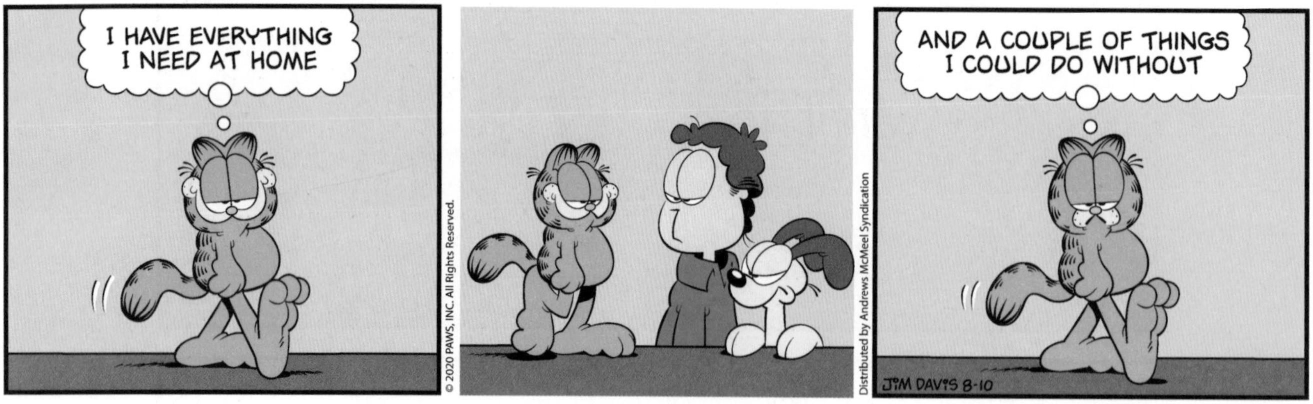
I HAVE EVERYTHING I NEED AT HOME
AND A COUPLE OF THINGS I COULD DO WITHOUT
© 2020 PAWS, INC. All Rights Reserved.
Distributed by Andrews McMeel Syndication
JIM DAVIS 8-10

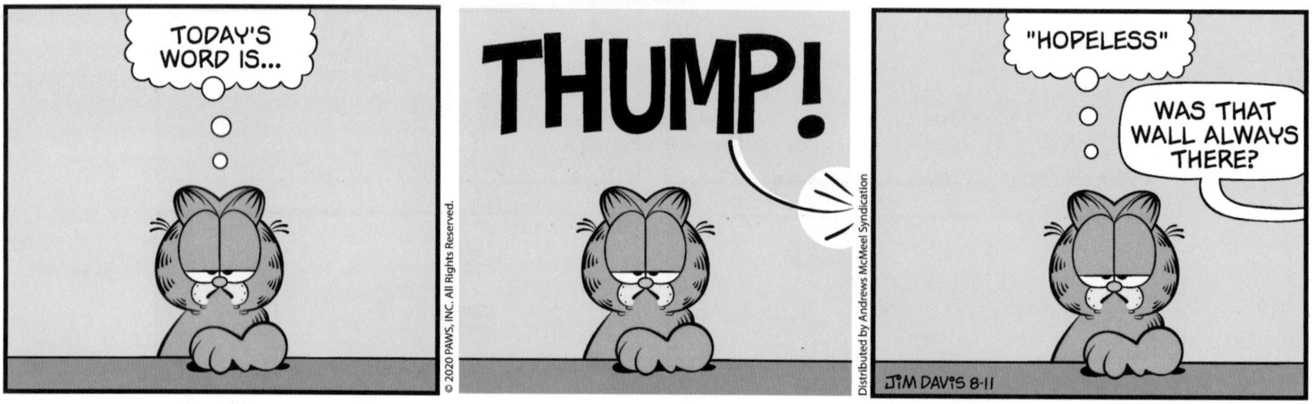
TODAY'S WORD IS...
THUMP!
"HOPELESS"
WAS THAT WALL ALWAYS THERE?
© 2020 PAWS, INC. All Rights Reserved.
Distributed by Andrews McMeel Syndication
JIM DAVIS 8-11

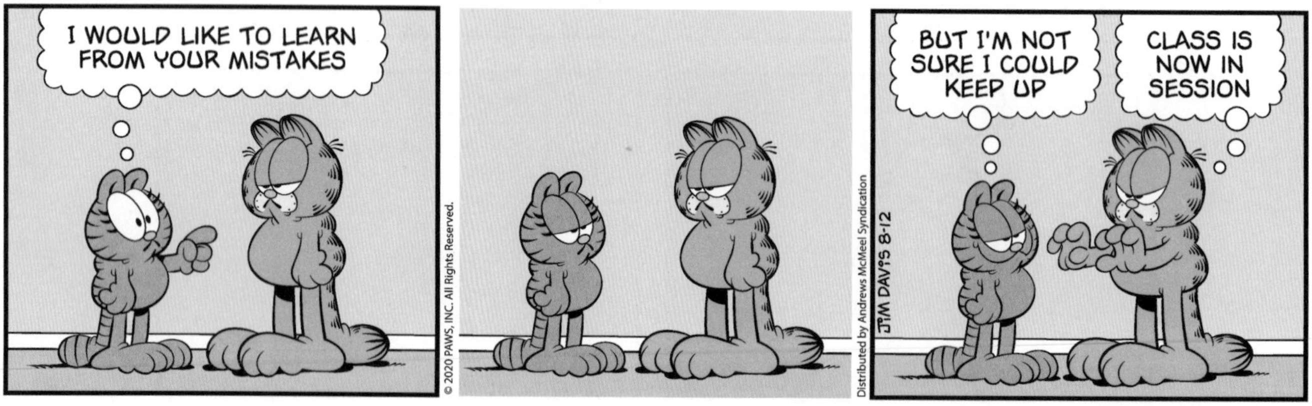
I WOULD LIKE TO LEARN FROM YOUR MISTAKES
BUT I'M NOT SURE I COULD KEEP UP
CLASS IS NOW IN SESSION
© 2020 PAWS, INC. All Rights Reserved.
Distributed by Andrews McMeel Syndication
JIM DAVIS 8-12

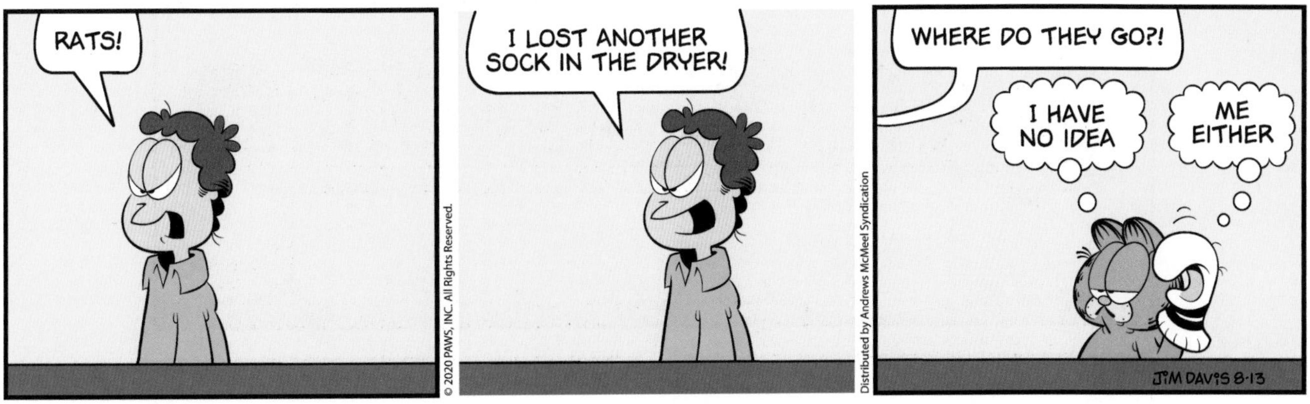
RATS!
I LOST ANOTHER SOCK IN THE DRYER!
WHERE DO THEY GO?!
I HAVE NO IDEA
ME EITHER
JIM DAVIS 8-13
© 2020 PAWS, INC. All Rights Reserved.
Distributed by Andrews McMeel Syndication

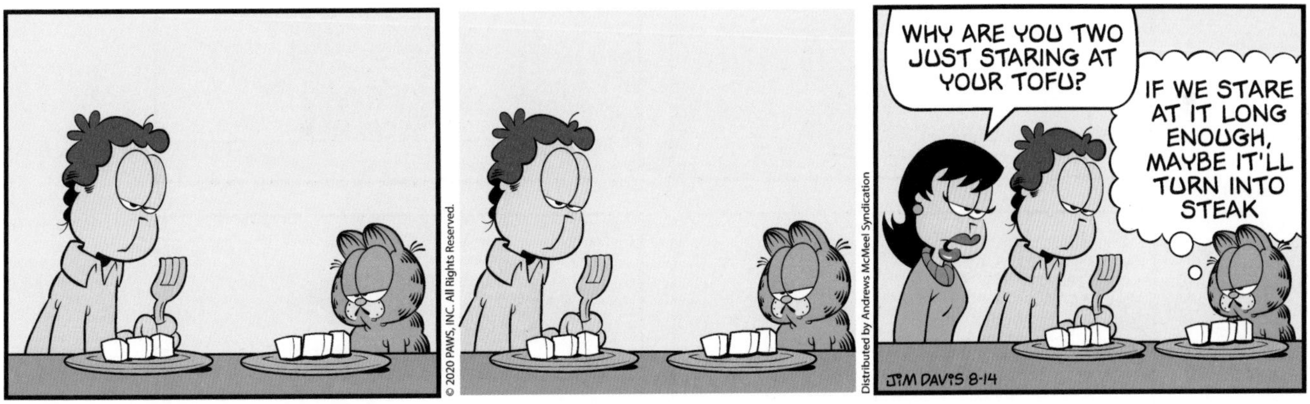
WHY ARE YOU TWO JUST STARING AT YOUR TOFU?
IF WE STARE AT IT LONG ENOUGH, MAYBE IT'LL TURN INTO STEAK
JIM DAVIS 8-14
© 2020 PAWS, INC. All Rights Reserved.
Distributed by Andrews McMeel Syndication

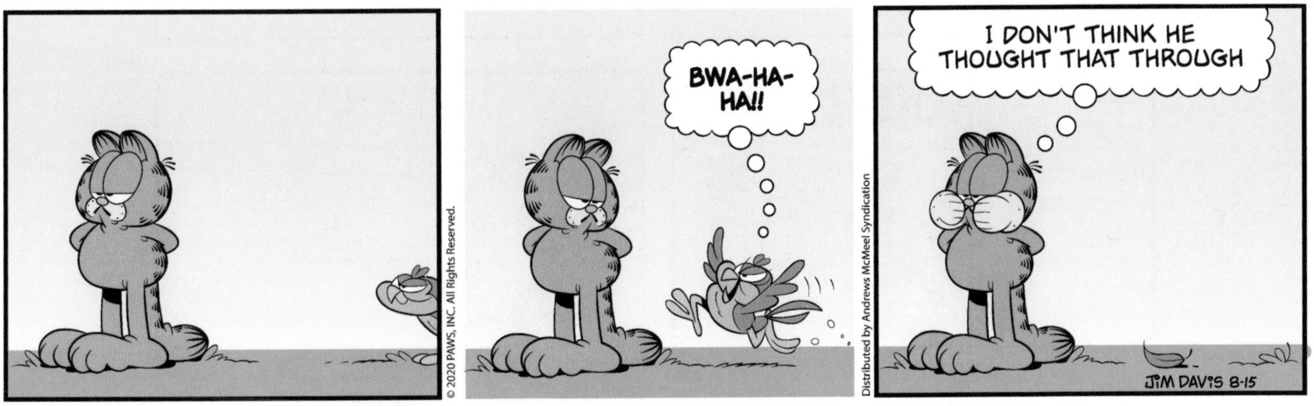
BWA-HA-HA!!
I DON'T THINK HE THOUGHT THAT THROUGH
JIM DAVIS 8-15
© 2020 PAWS, INC. All Rights Reserved.
Distributed by Andrews McMeel Syndication

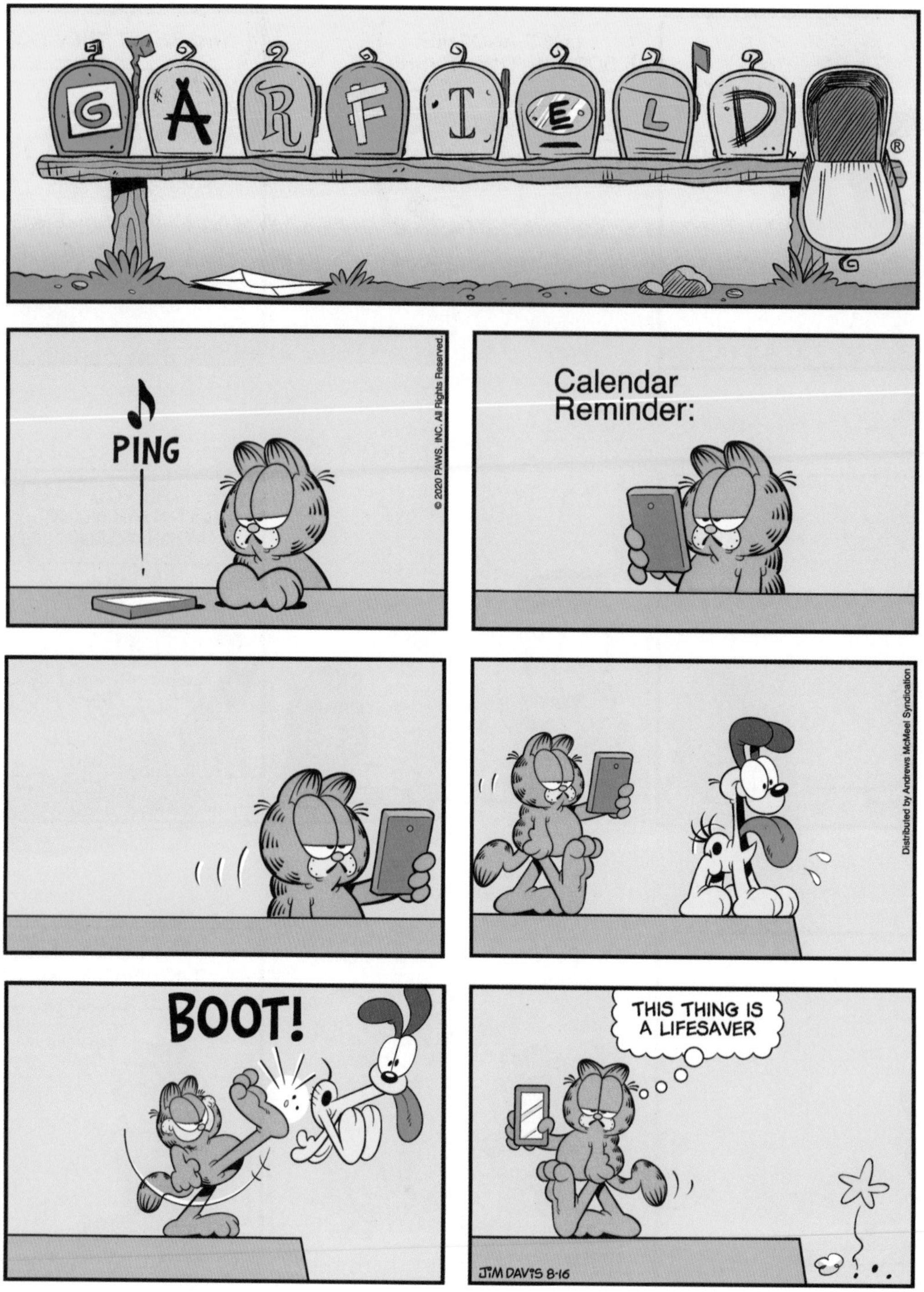

GARFIELD®
© 2020 PAWS, INC. All Rights Reserved.
PING
Calendar Reminder:
Distributed by Andrews McMeel Syndication
BOOT!
THIS THING IS A LIFESAVER
JIM DAVIS 8-16

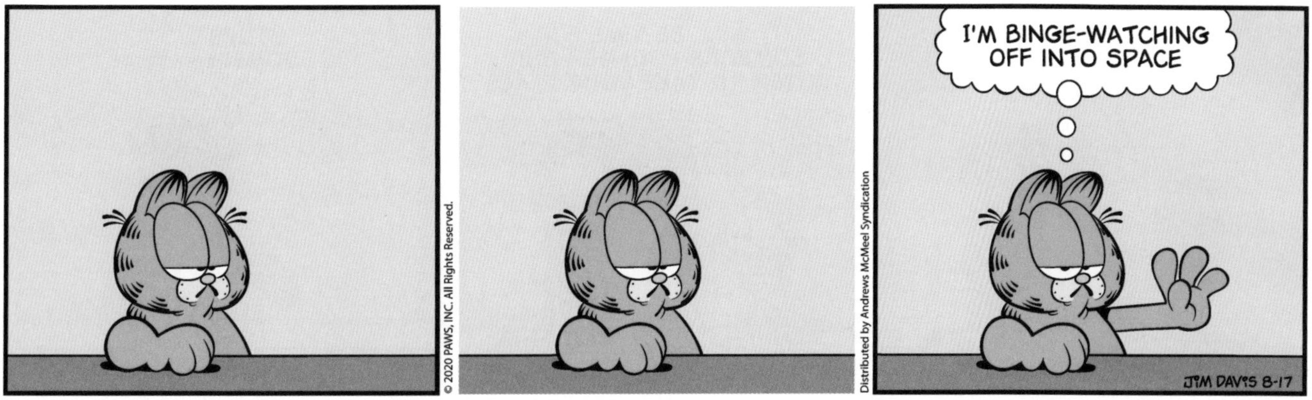
I'M BINGE-WATCHING OFF INTO SPACE
© 2020 PAWS, INC. All Rights Reserved.
Distributed by Andrews McMeel Syndication
JIM DAVIS 8-17

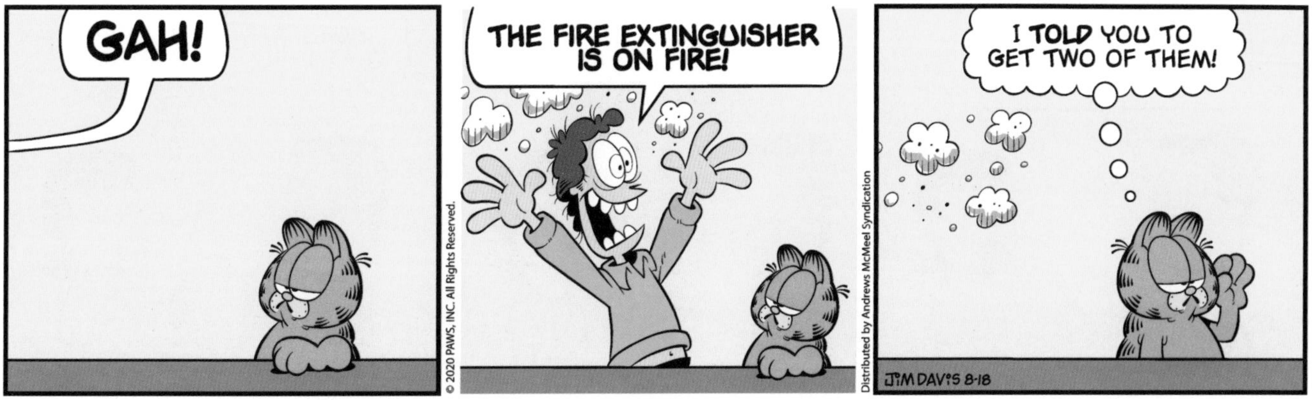
GAH!
THE FIRE EXTINGUISHER IS ON FIRE!
I TOLD YOU TO GET TWO OF THEM!
© 2020 PAWS, INC. All Rights Reserved.
Distributed by Andrews McMeel Syndication
JIM DAVIS 8-18

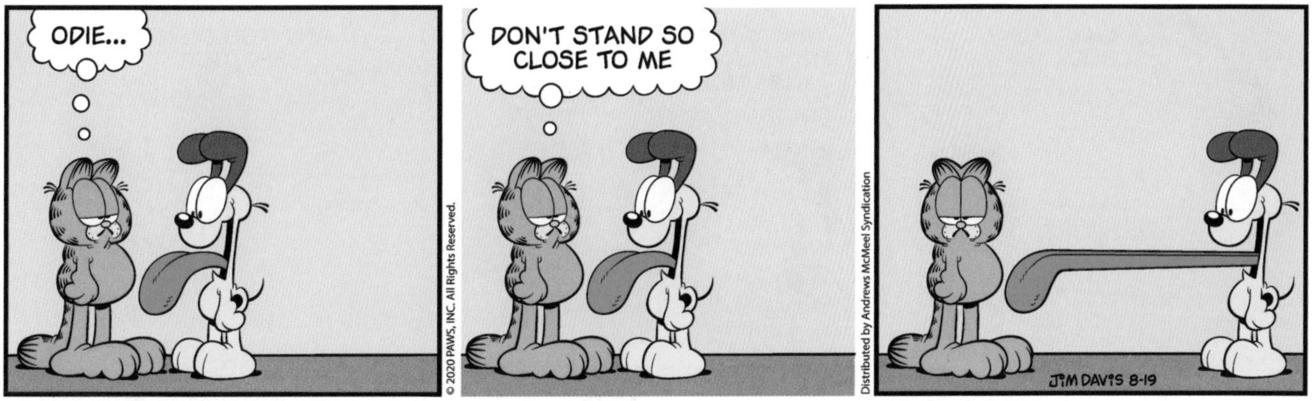
ODIE...
DON'T STAND SO CLOSE TO ME
© 2020 PAWS, INC. All Rights Reserved.
Distributed by Andrews McMeel Syndication
JIM DAVIS 8-19

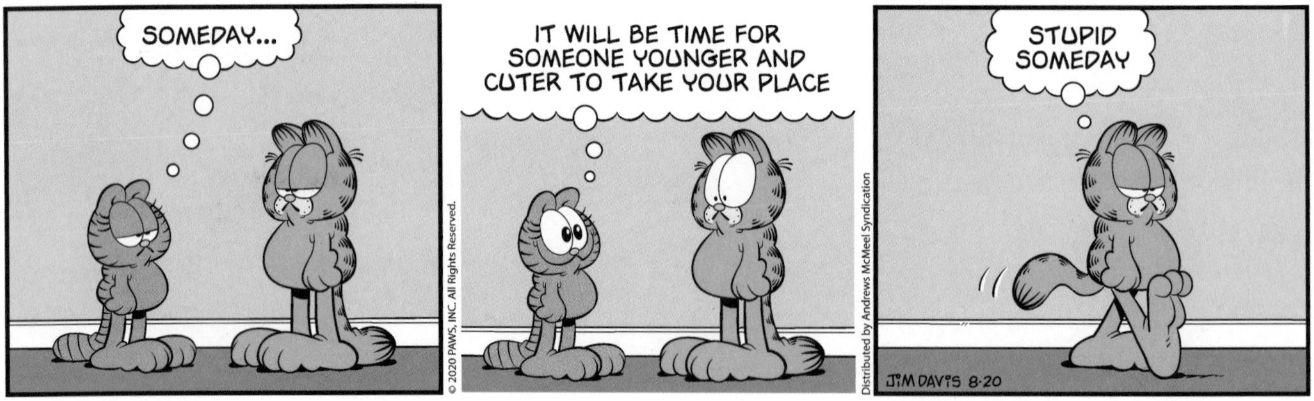
SOMEDAY...
IT WILL BE TIME FOR SOMEONE YOUNGER AND CUTER TO TAKE YOUR PLACE
STUPID SOMEDAY
© 2020 PAWS, INC. All Rights Reserved.
Distributed by Andrews McMeel Syndication
JIM DAVIS 8-20

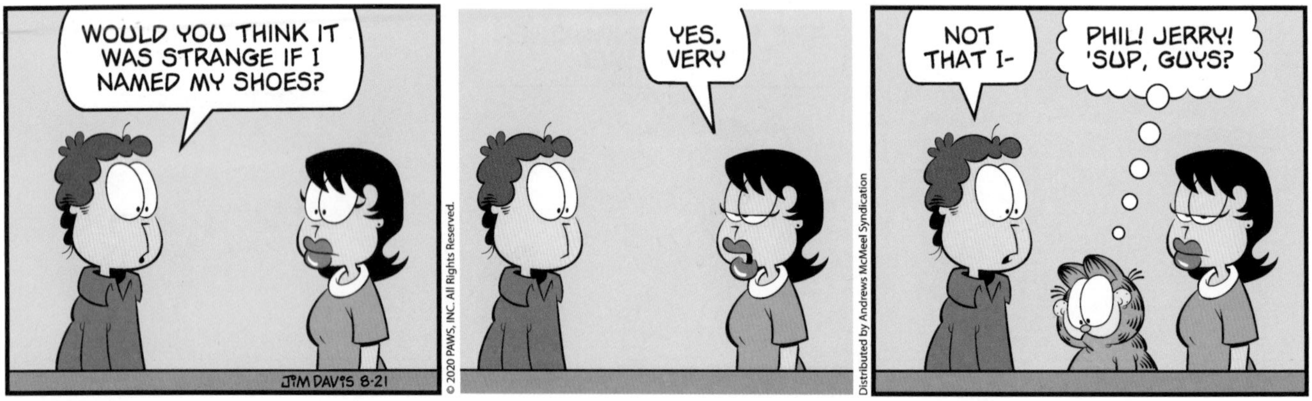
WOULD YOU THINK IT WAS STRANGE IF I NAMED MY SHOES?
YES. VERY
NOT THAT I-
PHIL! JERRY! 'SUP, GUYS?
JIM DAVIS 8-21
© 2020 PAWS, INC. All Rights Reserved.
Distributed by Andrews McMeel Syndication

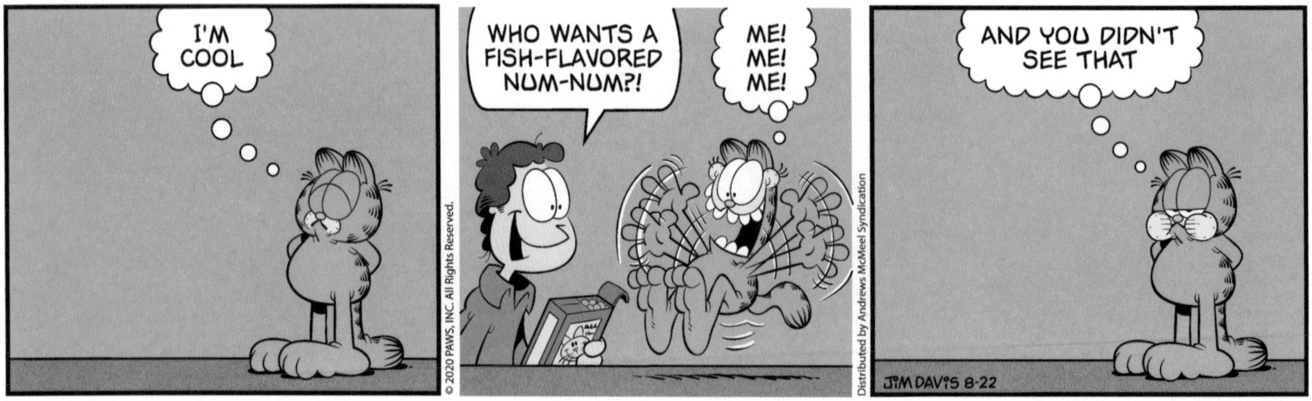
I'M COOL
WHO WANTS A FISH-FLAVORED NUM-NUM?!
ME! ME! ME!
AND YOU DIDN'T SEE THAT
© 2020 PAWS, INC. All Rights Reserved.
Distributed by Andrews McMeel Syndication
JIM DAVIS 8-22

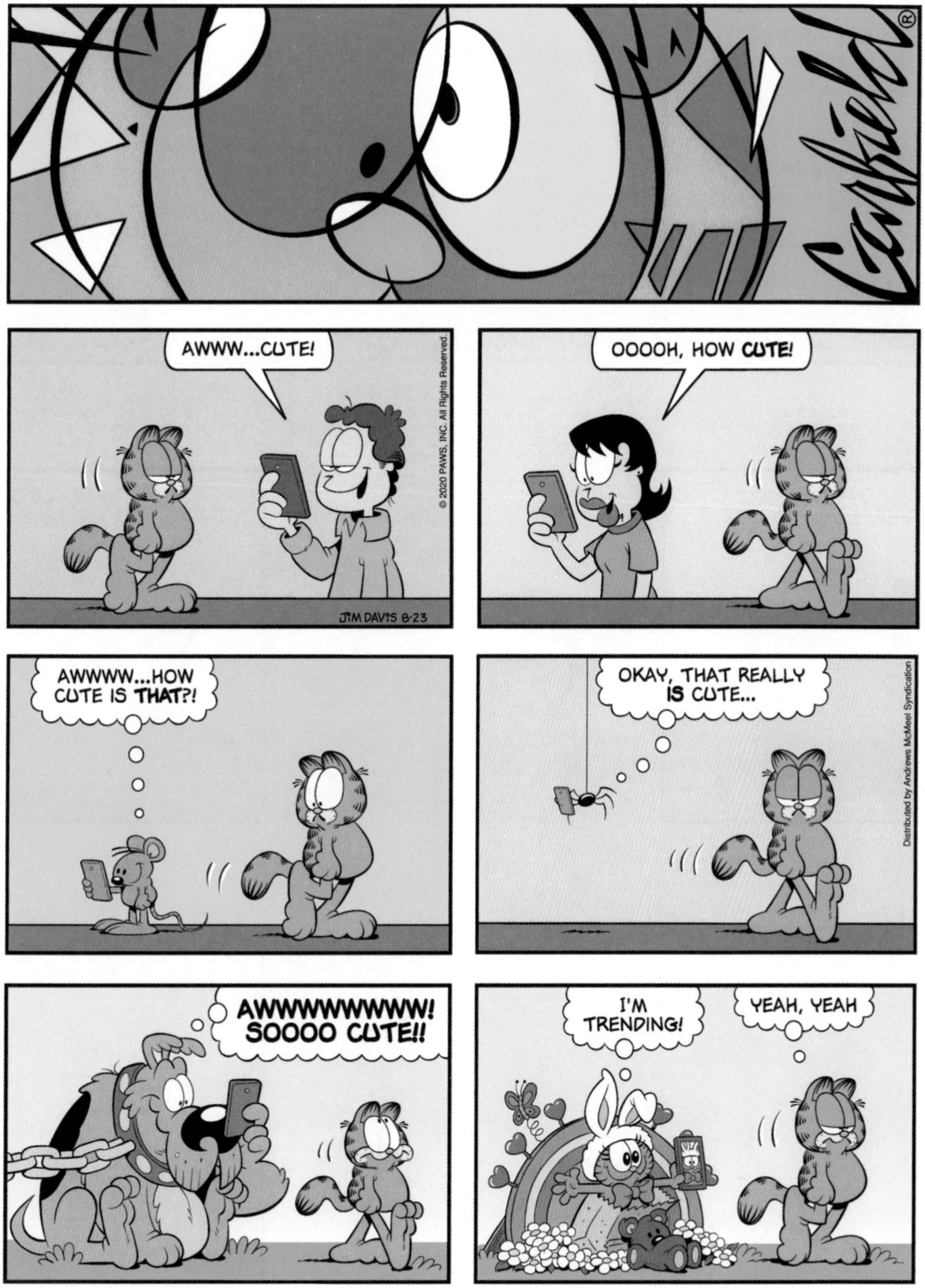
Garfield®
AWWW...CUTE!
© 2020 PAWS, INC. All Rights Reserved.
JIM DAVIS 8-23
OOOOH, HOW CUTE!
AWWWW...HOW CUTE IS THAT?!
OKAY, THAT REALLY IS CUTE...
Distributed by Andrews McMeel Syndication
AWWWWWWWW! SOOOO CUTE!!
I'M TRENDING!
YEAH, YEAH

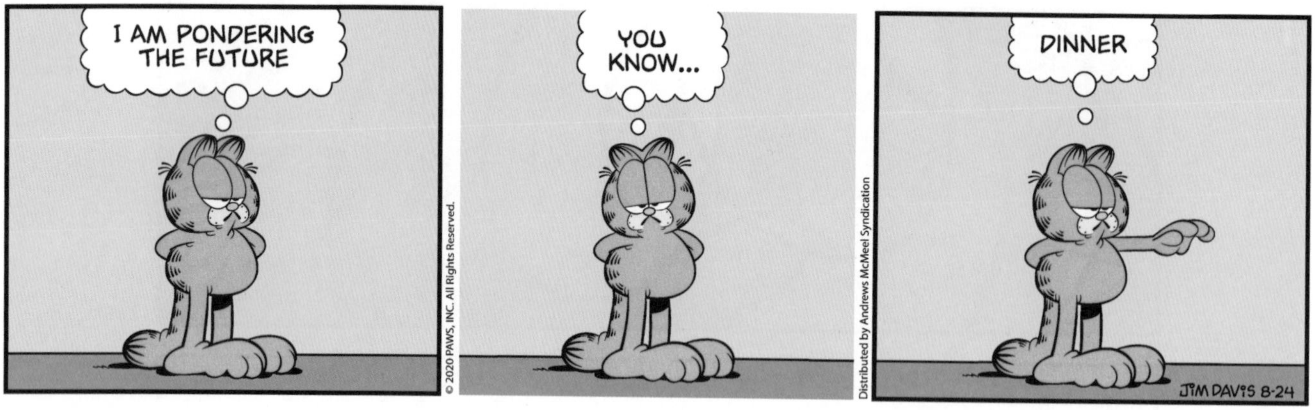
I AM PONDERING THE FUTURE
YOU KNOW...
DINNER
© 2020 PAWS, INC. All Rights Reserved.
Distributed by Andrews McMeel Syndication
JIM DAVIS 8-24

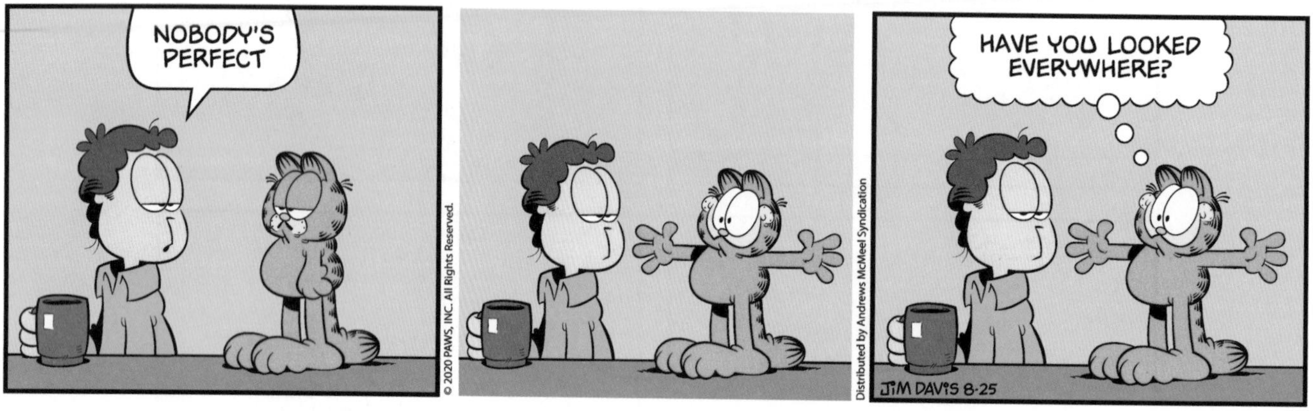
NOBODY'S PERFECT
HAVE YOU LOOKED EVERYWHERE?
© 2020 PAWS, INC. All Rights Reserved.
Distributed by Andrews McMeel Syndication
JIM DAVIS 8-25

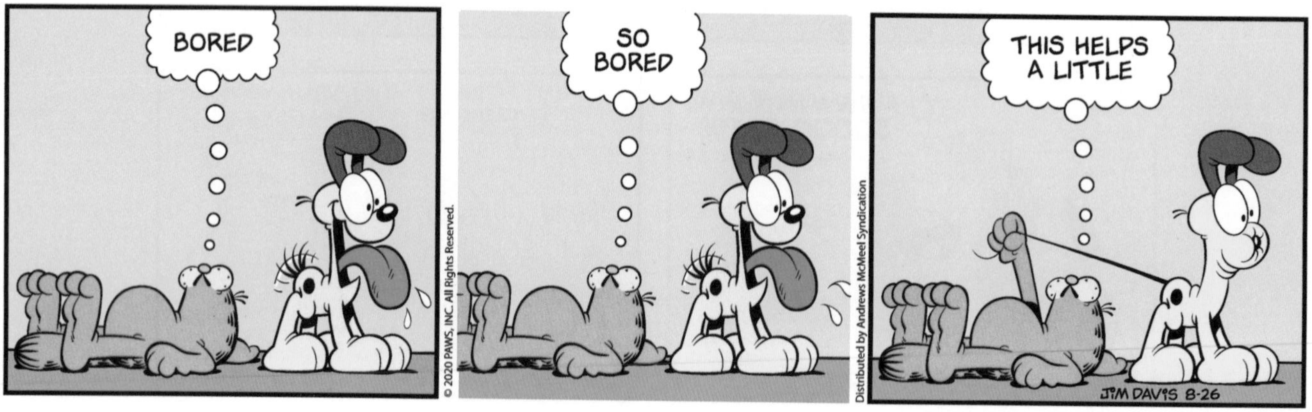
BORED
SO BORED
THIS HELPS A LITTLE
© 2020 PAWS, INC. All Rights Reserved.
Distributed by Andrews McMeel Syndication
JIM DAVIS 8-26

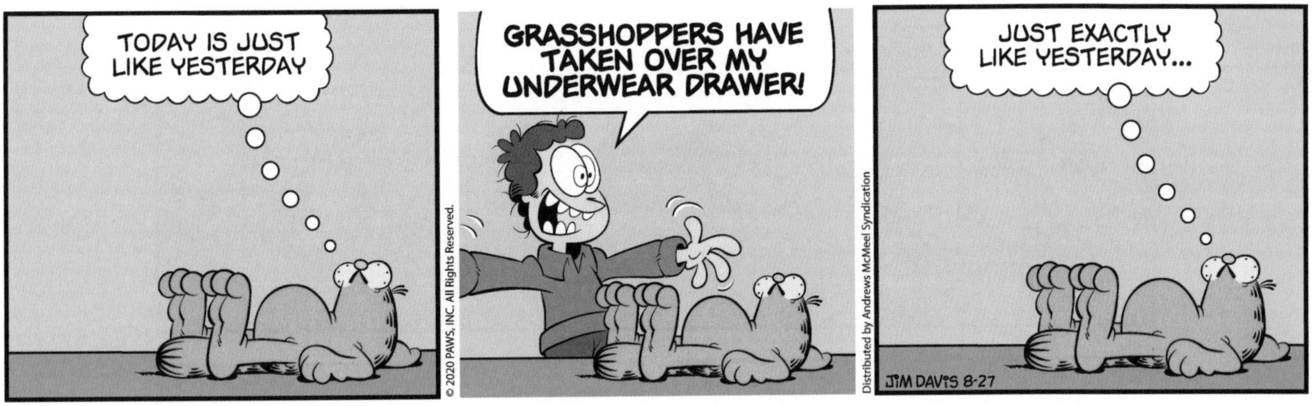
TODAY IS JUST LIKE YESTERDAY
GRASSHOPPERS HAVE TAKEN OVER MY UNDERWEAR DRAWER!
JUST EXACTLY LIKE YESTERDAY...
JIM DAVIS 8-27

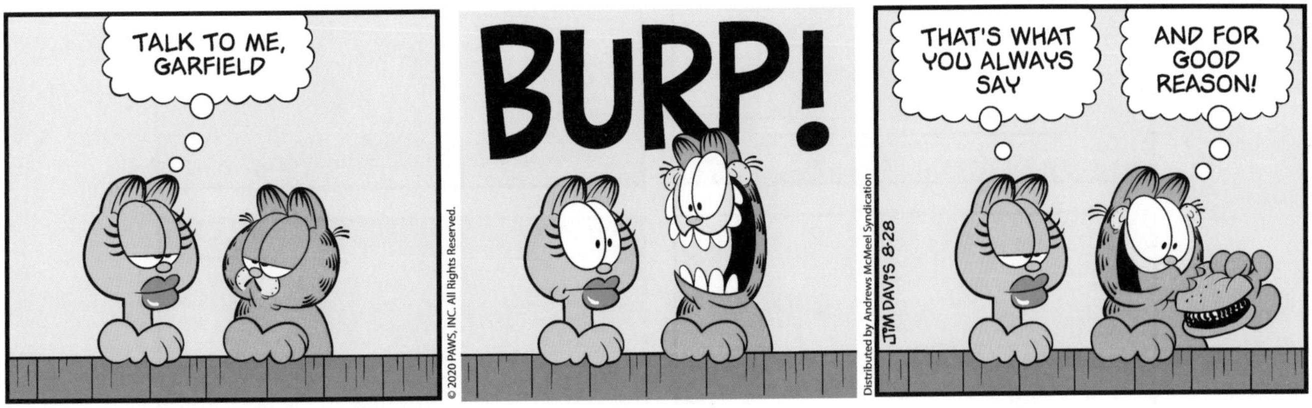
TALK TO ME, GARFIELD
BURP!
THAT'S WHAT YOU ALWAYS SAY
AND FOR GOOD REASON!
JIM DAVIS 8-28

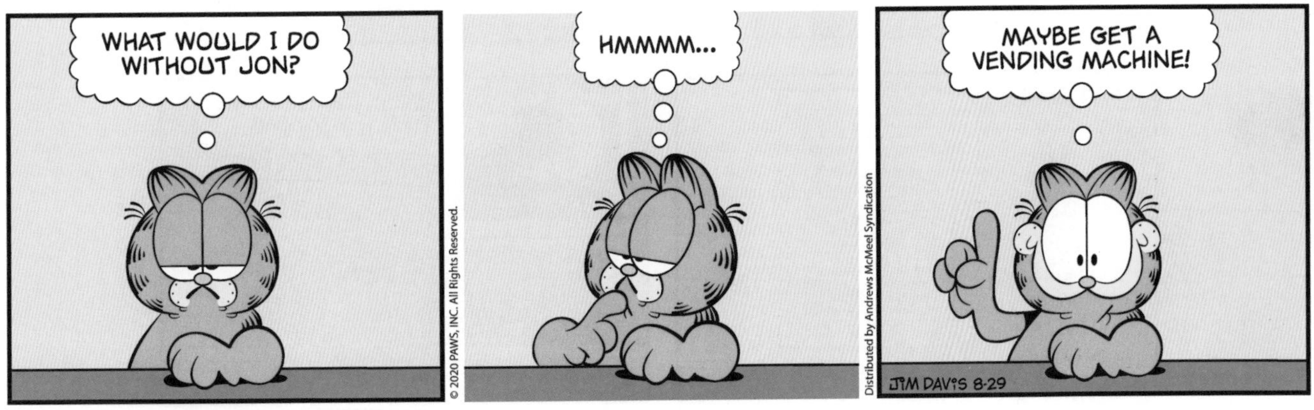
WHAT WOULD I DO WITHOUT JON?
HMMMM...
MAYBE GET A VENDING MACHINE!
JIM DAVIS 8-29

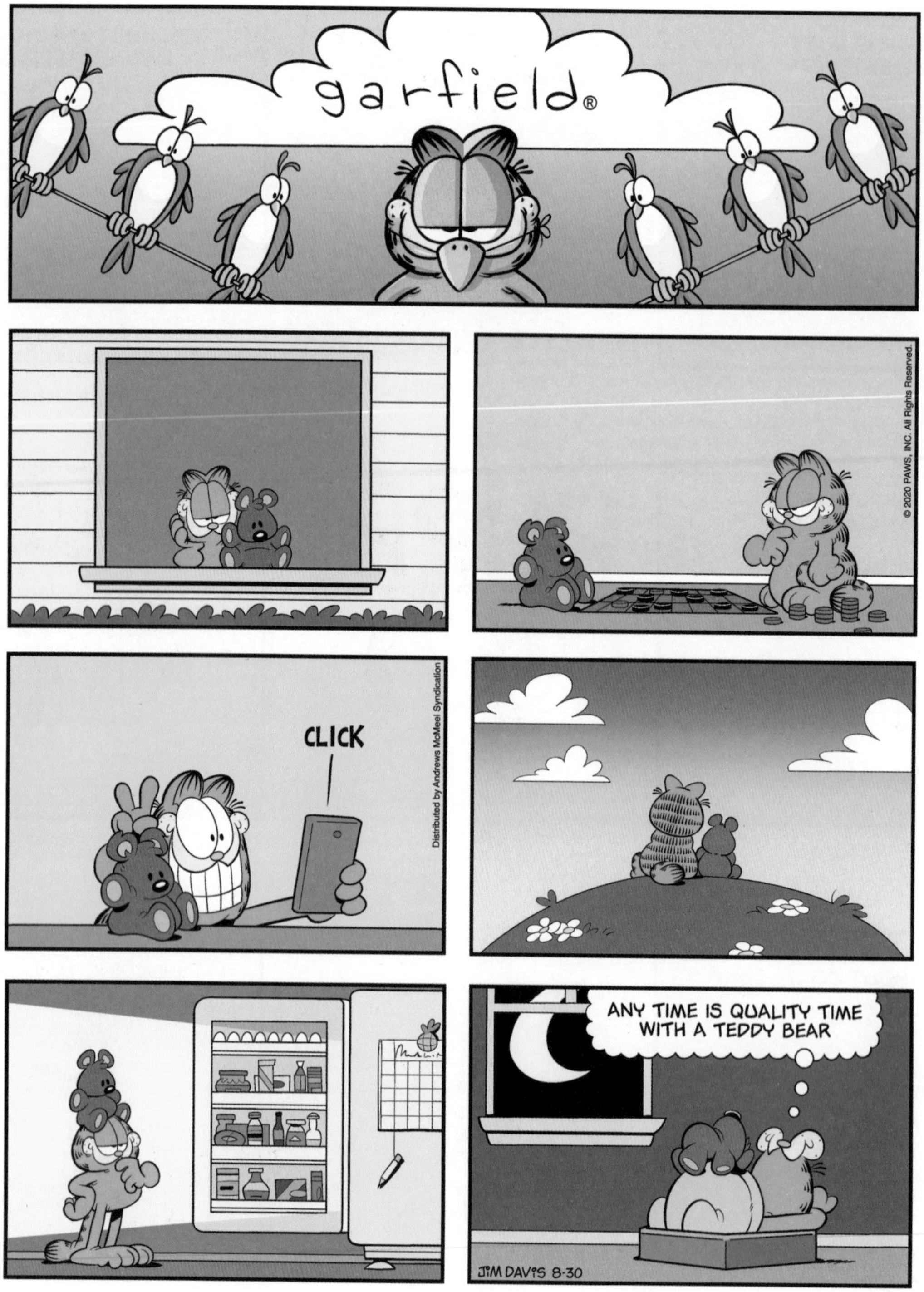
garfield®
© 2020 PAWS, INC. All Rights Reserved.
Distributed by Andrews McMeel Syndication
CLICK
ANY TIME IS QUALITY TIME WITH A TEDDY BEAR
JIM DAVIS 8-30

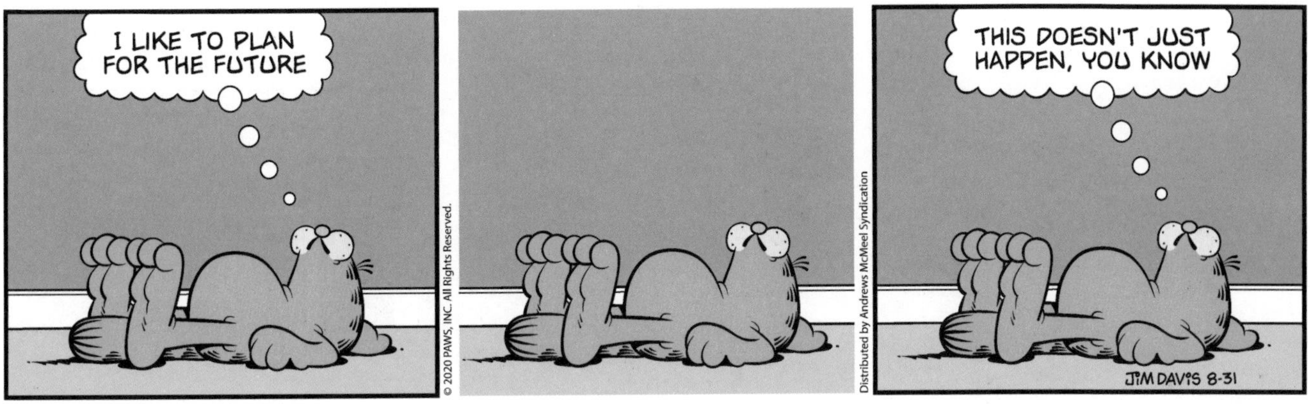
I LIKE TO PLAN FOR THE FUTURE
THIS DOESN'T JUST HAPPEN, YOU KNOW
JIM DAVIS 8-31

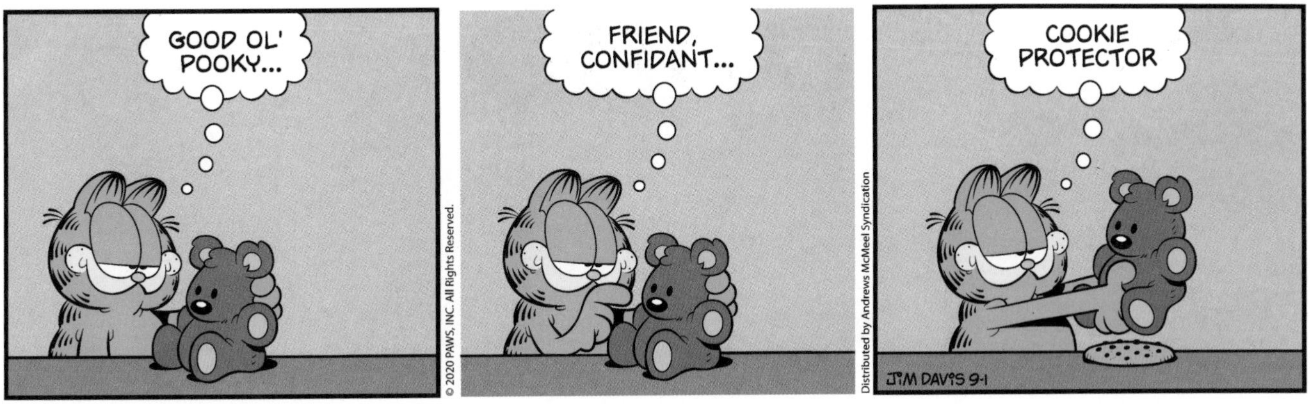
GOOD OL' POOKY...
FRIEND, CONFIDANT...
COOKIE PROTECTOR
JIM DAVIS 9-1

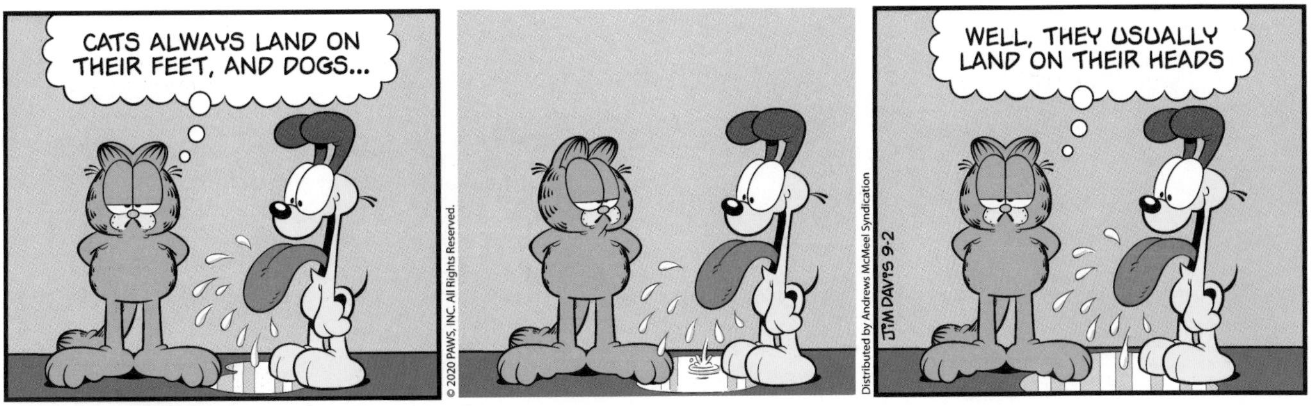
CATS ALWAYS LAND ON THEIR FEET, AND DOGS...
WELL, THEY USUALLY LAND ON THEIR HEADS
JIM DAVIS 9-2

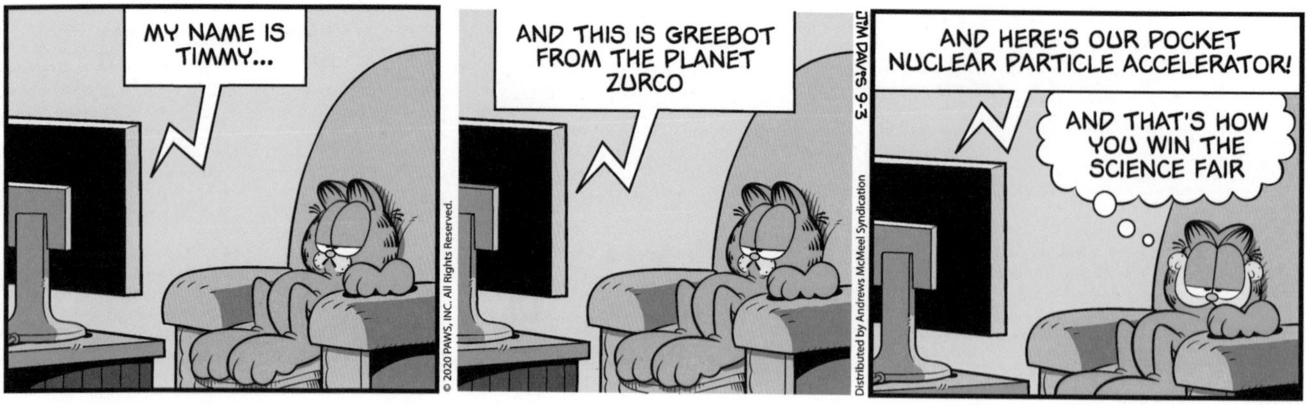

MY NAME IS TIMMY...
AND THIS IS GREEBOT FROM THE PLANET ZURCO
JIM DAVIS 9-3
© 2020 PAWS, INC. All Rights Reserved.
Distributed by Andrews McMeel Syndication
AND HERE'S OUR POCKET NUCLEAR PARTICLE ACCELERATOR!
AND THAT'S HOW YOU WIN THE SCIENCE FAIR

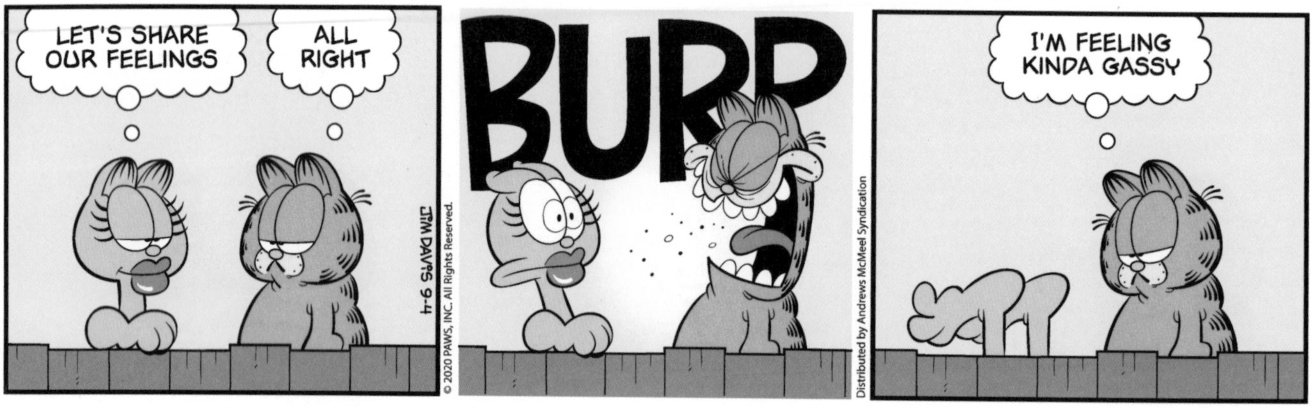

LET'S SHARE OUR FEELINGS
ALL RIGHT
JIM DAVIS 9-4
© 2020 PAWS, INC. All Rights Reserved.
BURP
Distributed by Andrews McMeel Syndication
I'M FEELING KINDA GASSY

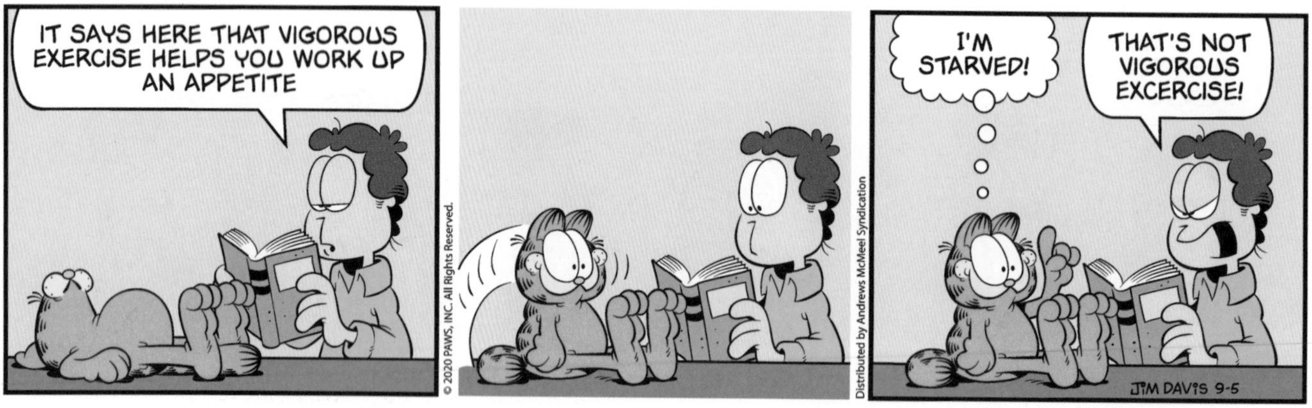

IT SAYS HERE THAT VIGOROUS EXERCISE HELPS YOU WORK UP AN APPETITE
© 2020 PAWS, INC. All Rights Reserved.
Distributed by Andrews McMeel Syndication
I'M STARVED!
THAT'S NOT VIGOROUS EXCERCISE!
JIM DAVIS 9-5

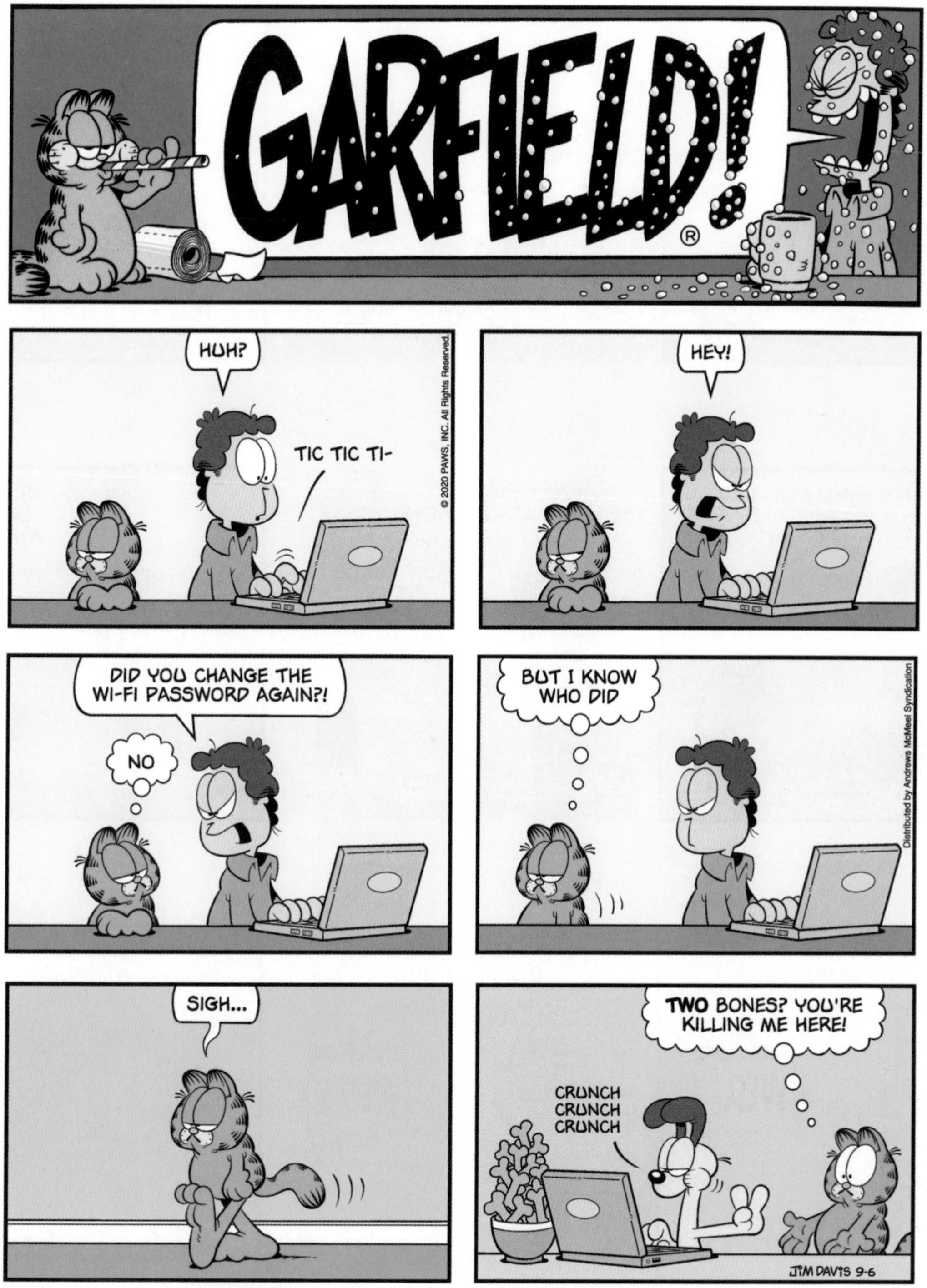
GARFIELD!
HUH?
TIC TIC TI-
© 2020 PAWS, INC. All Rights Reserved.
HEY!
DID YOU CHANGE THE WI-FI PASSWORD AGAIN?!
NO
BUT I KNOW WHO DID
Distributed by Andrews McMeel Syndication
SIGH...
CRUNCH CRUNCH CRUNCH
TWO BONES? YOU'RE KILLING ME HERE!
JIM DAVIS 9-6

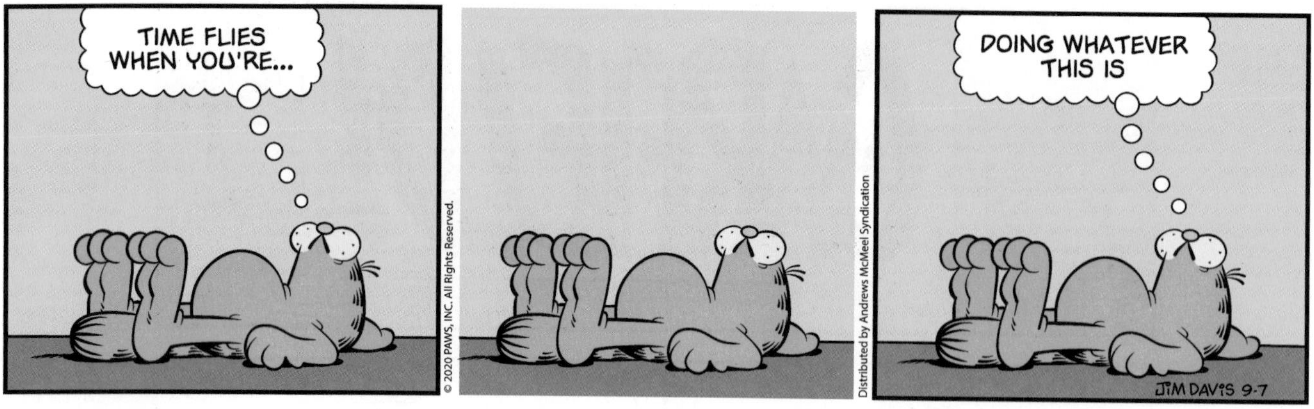
TIME FLIES WHEN YOU'RE...
© 2020 PAWS, INC. All Rights Reserved.
Distributed by Andrews McMeel Syndication
DOING WHATEVER THIS IS
JIM DAVIS 9-7

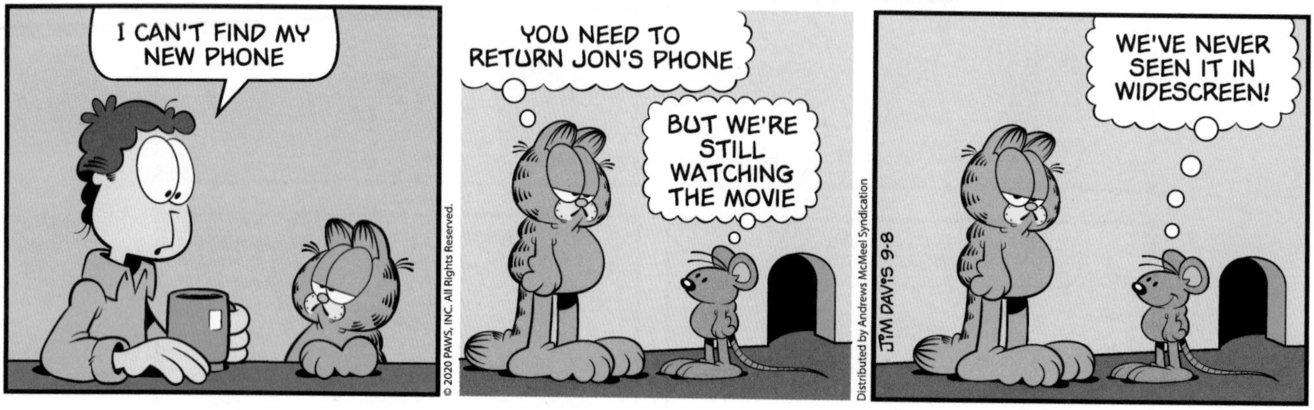
I CAN'T FIND MY NEW PHONE
© 2020 PAWS, INC. All Rights Reserved.
YOU NEED TO RETURN JON'S PHONE
BUT WE'RE STILL WATCHING THE MOVIE
JIM DAVIS 9-8
Distributed by Andrews McMeel Syndication
WE'VE NEVER SEEN IT IN WIDESCREEN!

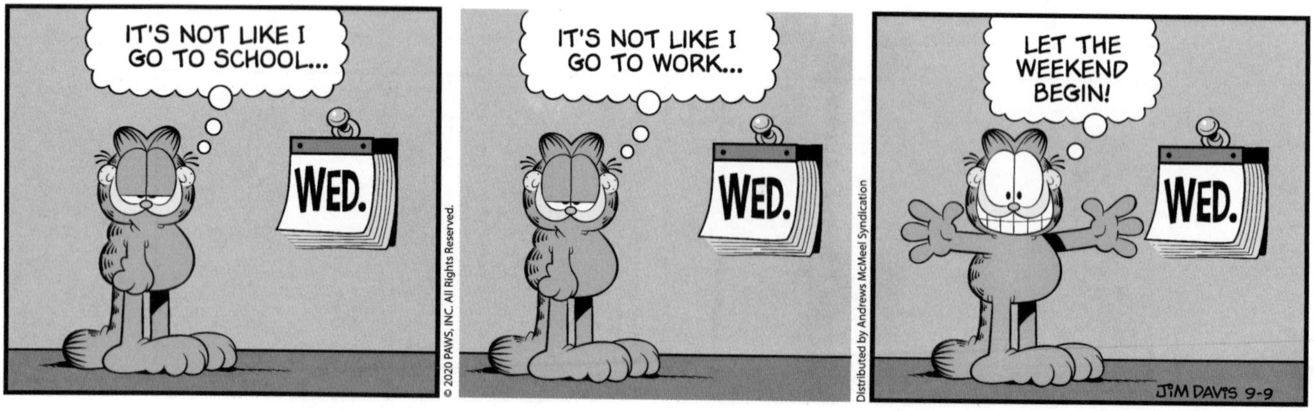
IT'S NOT LIKE I GO TO SCHOOL...
WED.
© 2020 PAWS, INC. All Rights Reserved.
IT'S NOT LIKE I GO TO WORK...
WED.
Distributed by Andrews McMeel Syndication
LET THE WEEKEND BEGIN!
WED.
JIM DAVIS 9-9

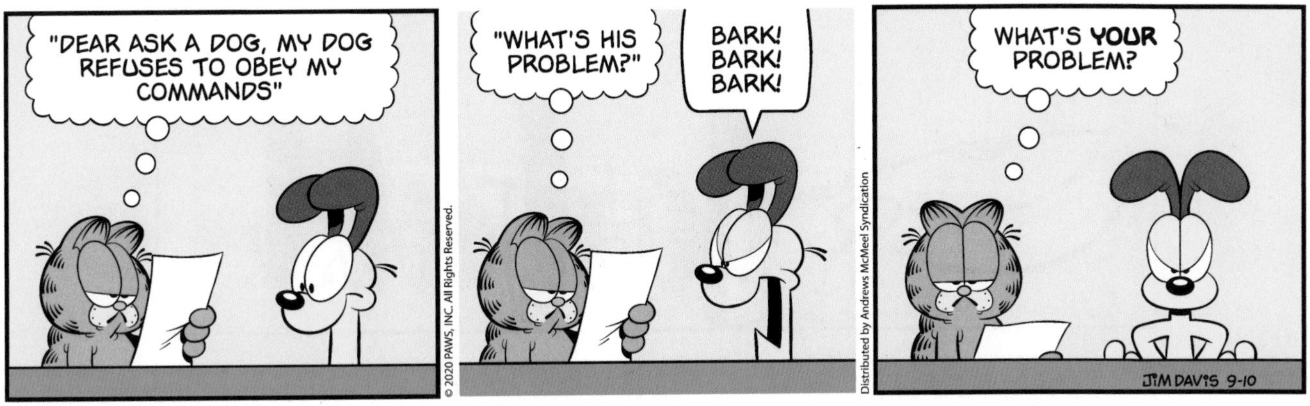
"DEAR ASK A DOG, MY DOG REFUSES TO OBEY MY COMMANDS"
© 2020 PAWS, INC. All Rights Reserved.
"WHAT'S HIS PROBLEM?"
BARK! BARK! BARK!
Distributed by Andrews McMeel Syndication
WHAT'S **YOUR** PROBLEM?
JIM DAVIS 9-10

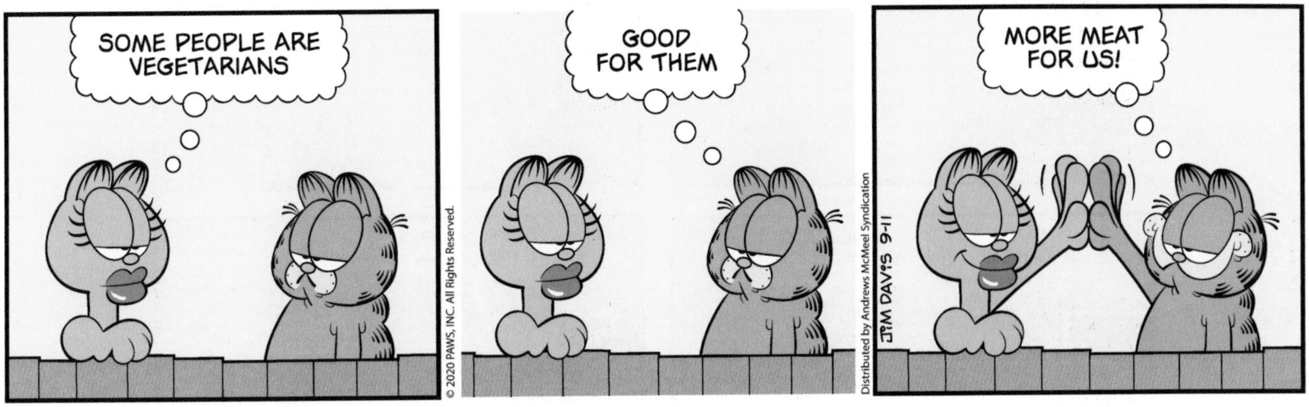
SOME PEOPLE ARE VEGETARIANS
© 2020 PAWS, INC. All Rights Reserved.
GOOD FOR THEM
Distributed by Andrews McMeel Syndication
JIM DAVIS 9-11
MORE MEAT FOR US!

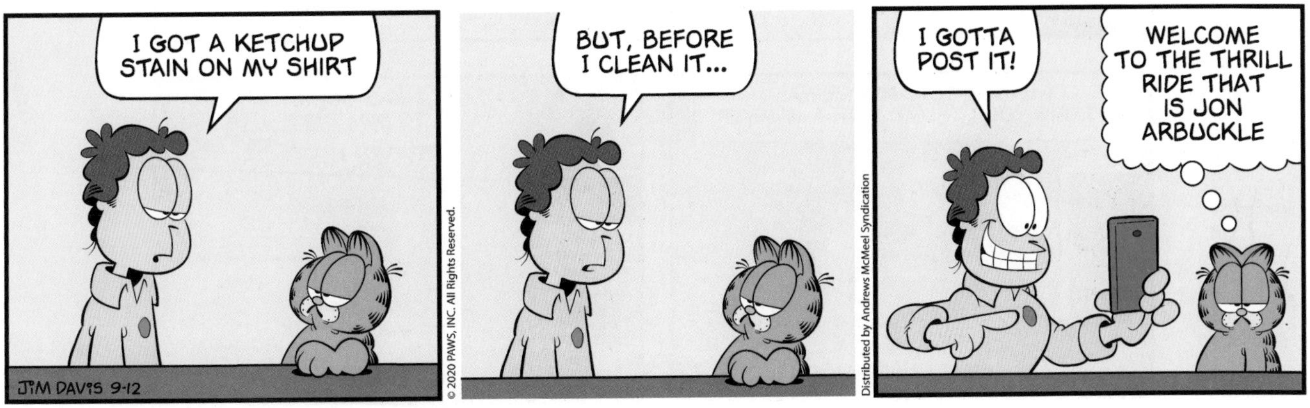
I GOT A KETCHUP STAIN ON MY SHIRT
JIM DAVIS 9-12
© 2020 PAWS, INC. All Rights Reserved.
BUT, BEFORE I CLEAN IT...
Distributed by Andrews McMeel Syndication
I GOTTA POST IT!
WELCOME TO THE THRILL RIDE THAT IS JON ARBUCKLE

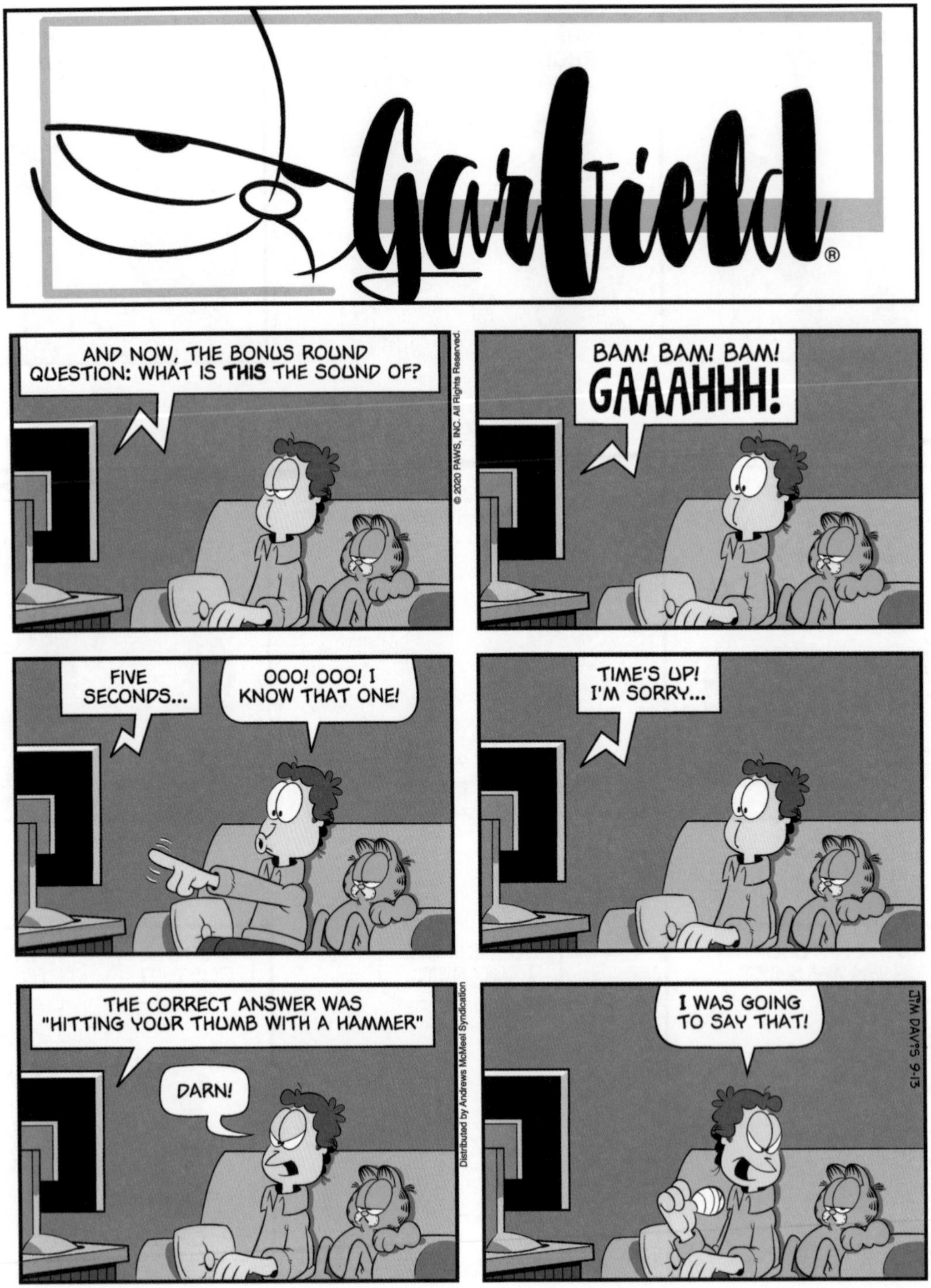
Garfield®
AND NOW, THE BONUS ROUND QUESTION: WHAT IS **THIS** THE SOUND OF?
© 2020 PAWS, INC. All Rights Reserved.
BAM! BAM! BAM! GAAAHHH!
FIVE SECONDS...
OOO! OOO! I KNOW THAT ONE!
TIME'S UP! I'M SORRY...
THE CORRECT ANSWER WAS "HITTING YOUR THUMB WITH A HAMMER"
DARN!
Distributed by Andrews McMeel Syndication
I WAS GOING TO SAY THAT!
JIM DAVIS 9-13

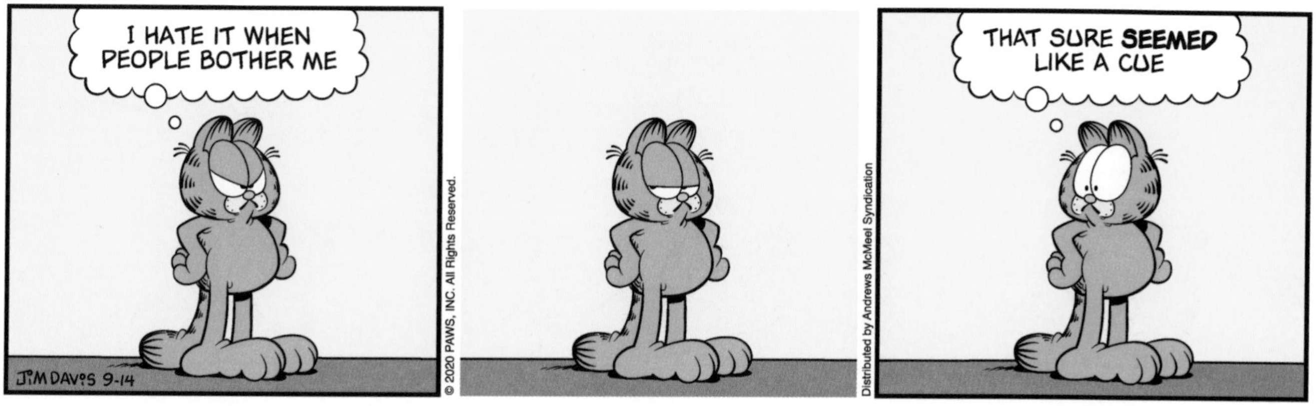
I HATE IT WHEN PEOPLE BOTHER ME
THAT SURE SEEMED LIKE A CUE
JIM DAVIS 9-14
© 2020 PAWS, INC. All Rights Reserved.
Distributed by Andrews McMeel Syndication

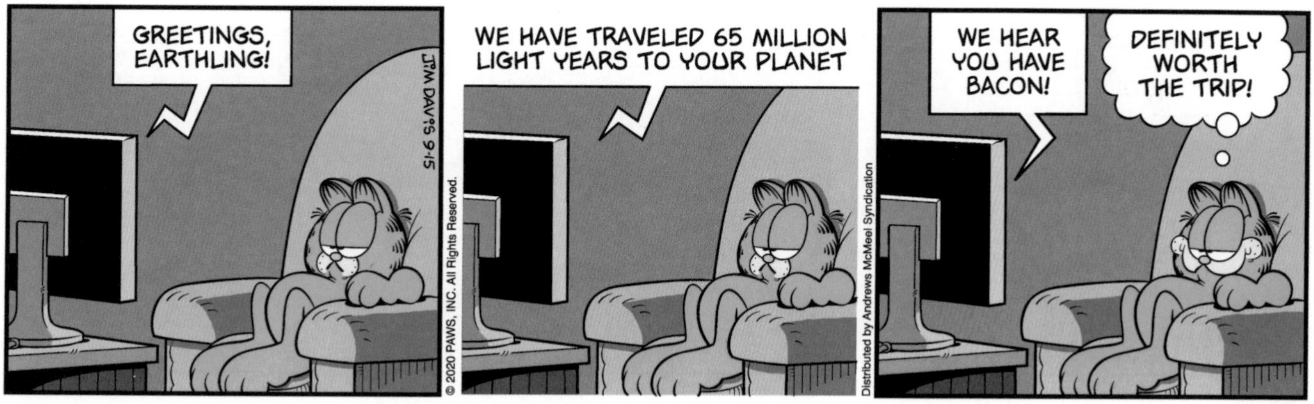
GREETINGS, EARTHLING!
WE HAVE TRAVELED 65 MILLION LIGHT YEARS TO YOUR PLANET
WE HEAR YOU HAVE BACON!
DEFINITELY WORTH THE TRIP!
JIM DAVIS 9-15
© 2020 PAWS, INC. All Rights Reserved.
Distributed by Andrews McMeel Syndication

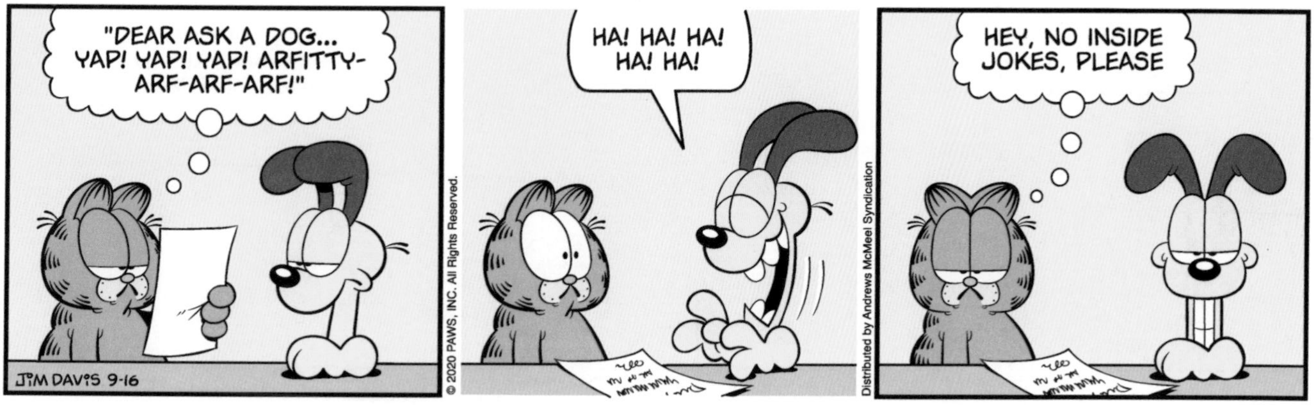
"DEAR ASK A DOG... YAP! YAP! YAP! ARFITTY-ARF-ARF-ARF!"
HA! HA! HA! HA! HA!
HEY, NO INSIDE JOKES, PLEASE
JIM DAVIS 9-16
© 2020 PAWS, INC. All Rights Reserved.
Distributed by Andrews McMeel Syndication

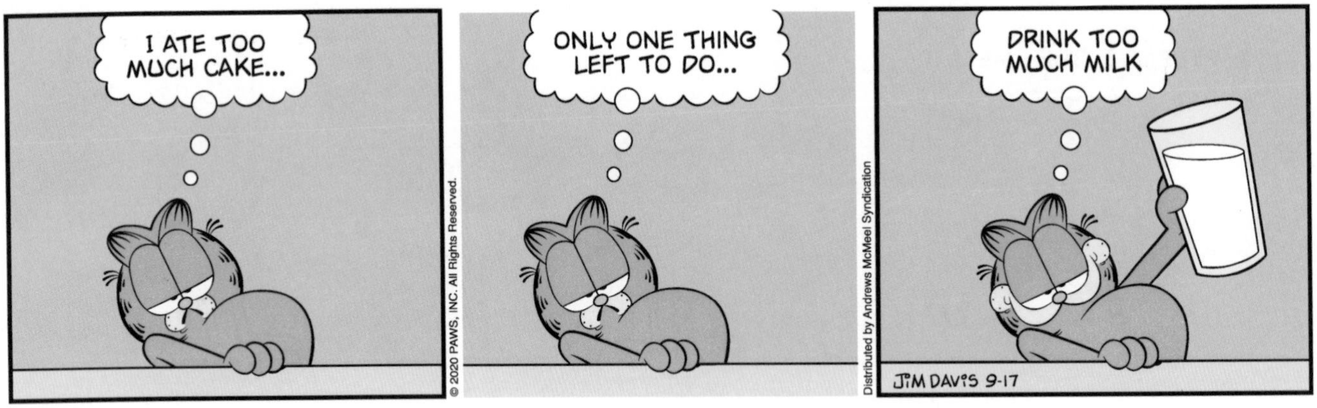
I ATE TOO MUCH CAKE...
ONLY ONE THING LEFT TO DO...
DRINK TOO MUCH MILK
© 2020 PAWS, INC. All Rights Reserved.
Distributed by Andrews McMeel Syndication
JIM DAVIS 9-17

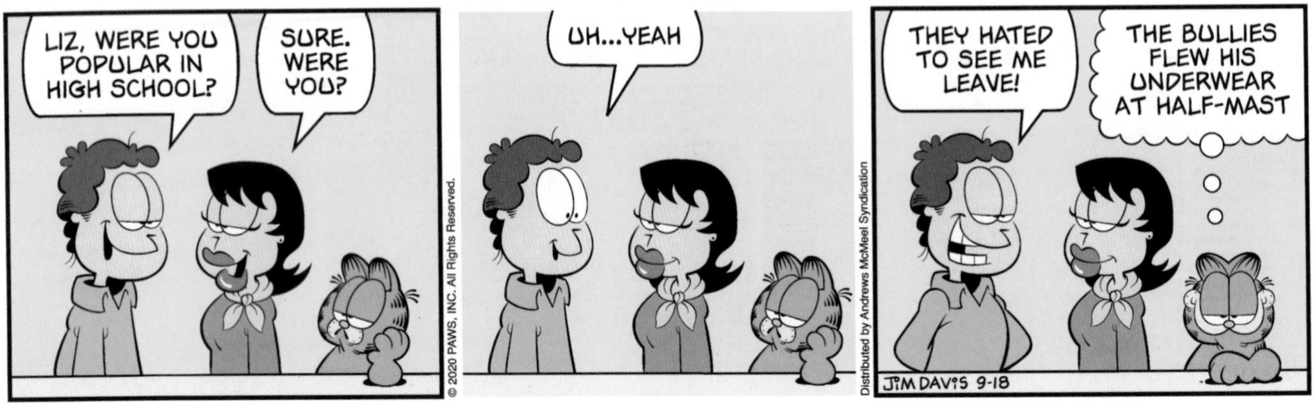
LIZ, WERE YOU POPULAR IN HIGH SCHOOL?
SURE. WERE YOU?
UH...YEAH
THEY HATED TO SEE ME LEAVE!
THE BULLIES FLEW HIS UNDERWEAR AT HALF-MAST
© 2020 PAWS, INC. All Rights Reserved.
Distributed by Andrews McMeel Syndication
JIM DAVIS 9-18

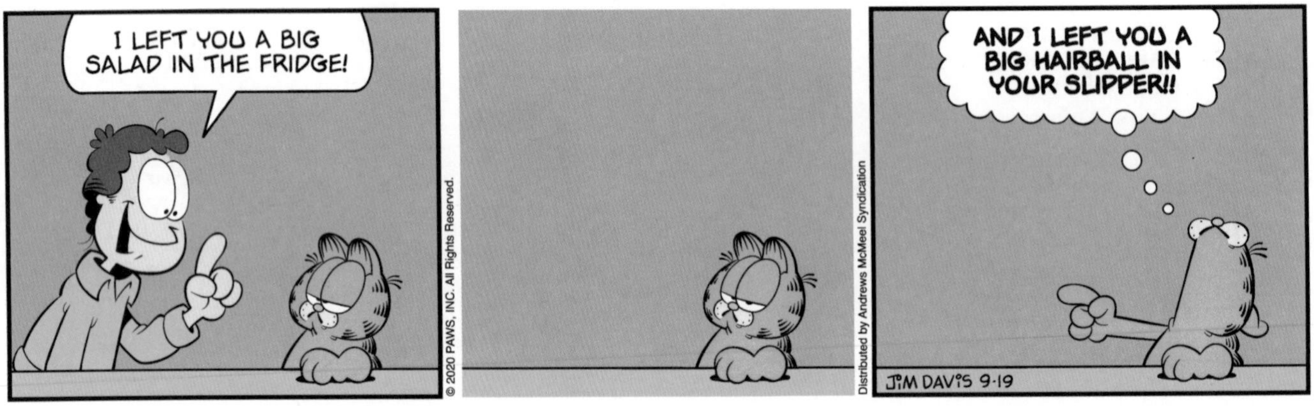
I LEFT YOU A BIG SALAD IN THE FRIDGE!
AND I LEFT YOU A BIG HAIRBALL IN YOUR SLIPPER!!
© 2020 PAWS, INC. All Rights Reserved.
Distributed by Andrews McMeel Syndication
JIM DAVIS 9-19

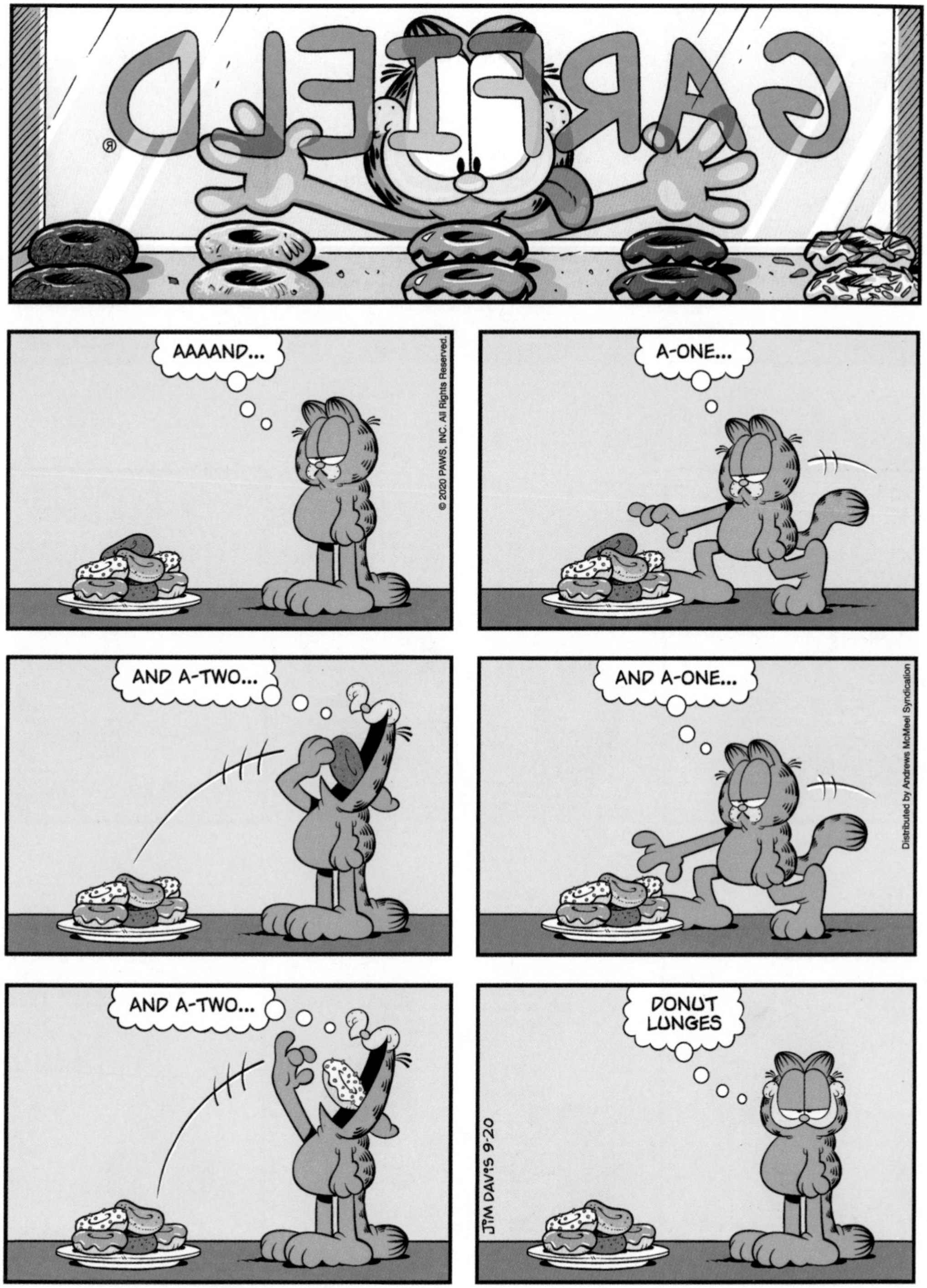
GARFIELD
AAAAND...
© 2020 PAWS, INC. All Rights Reserved.
A-ONE...
AND A-TWO...
AND A-ONE...
Distributed by Andrews McMeel Syndication
AND A-TWO...
JIM DAVIS 9-20
DONUT LUNGES

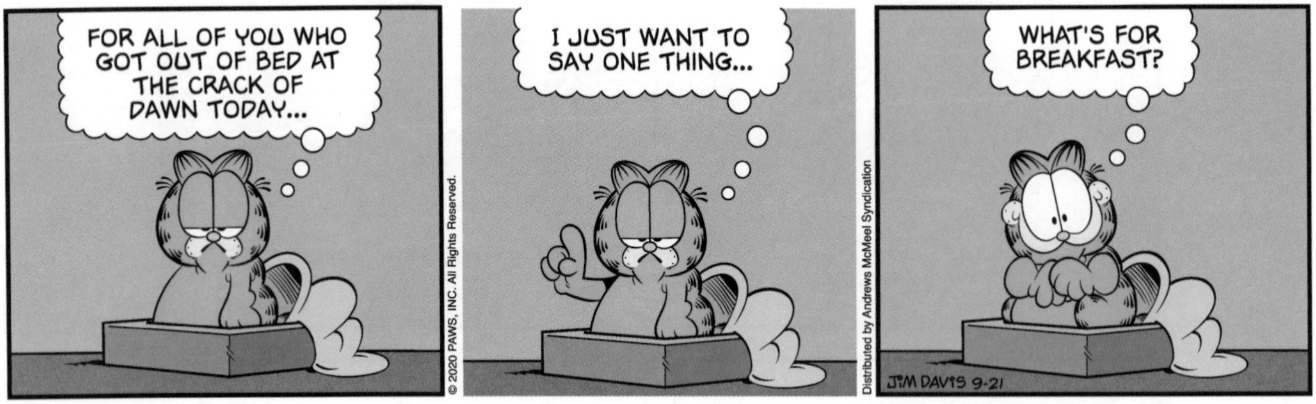
FOR ALL OF YOU WHO GOT OUT OF BED AT THE CRACK OF DAWN TODAY...
I JUST WANT TO SAY ONE THING...
WHAT'S FOR BREAKFAST?
© 2020 PAWS, INC. All Rights Reserved.
Distributed by Andrews McMeel Syndication
JIM DAVIS 9-21

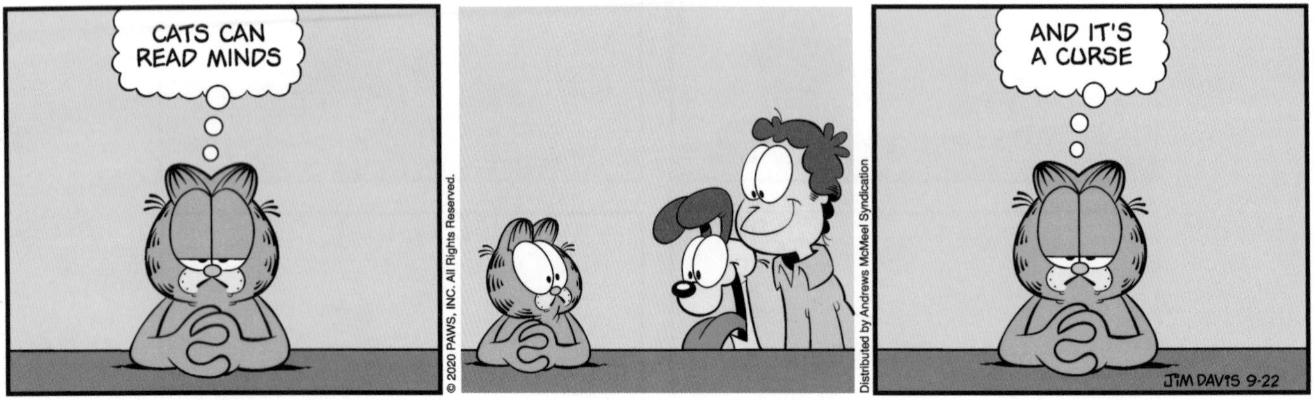
CATS CAN READ MINDS
AND IT'S A CURSE
© 2020 PAWS, INC. All Rights Reserved.
Distributed by Andrews McMeel Syndication
JIM DAVIS 9-22

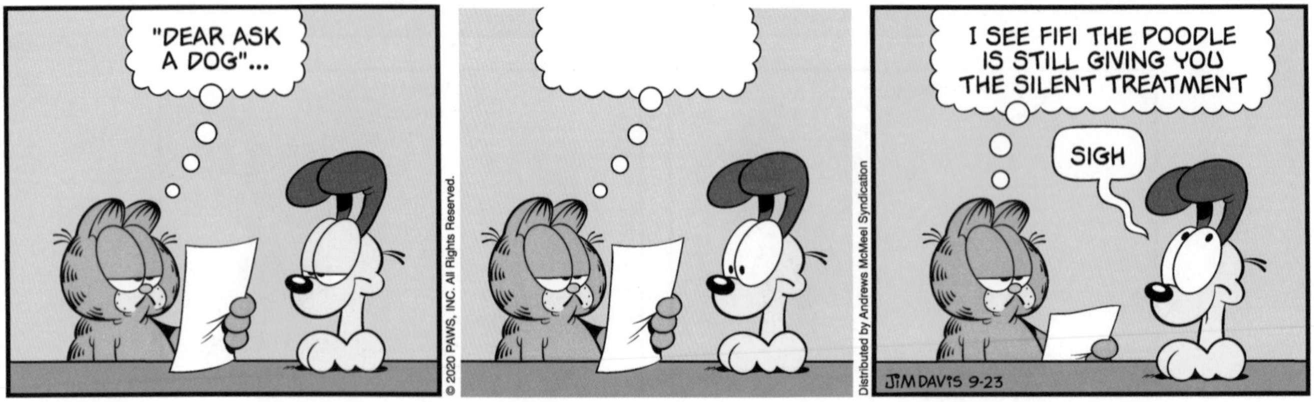
"DEAR ASK A DOG"...
I SEE FIFI THE POODLE IS STILL GIVING YOU THE SILENT TREATMENT
SIGH
© 2020 PAWS, INC. All Rights Reserved.
Distributed by Andrews McMeel Syndication
JIM DAVIS 9-23

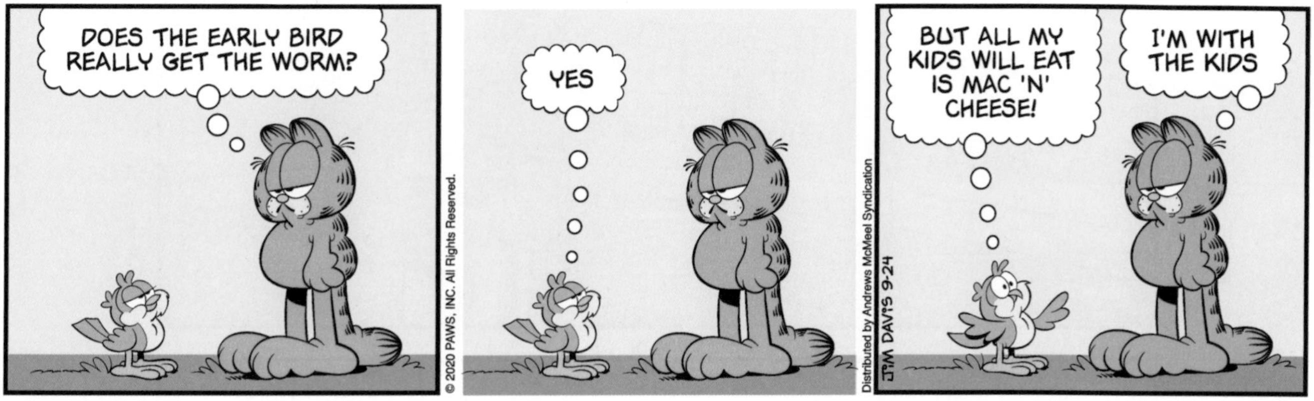
DOES THE EARLY BIRD REALLY GET THE WORM?
YES
BUT ALL MY KIDS WILL EAT IS MAC 'N' CHEESE!
I'M WITH THE KIDS
© 2020 PAWS, INC. All Rights Reserved.
Distributed by Andrews McMeel Syndication
JIM DAVIS 9-24

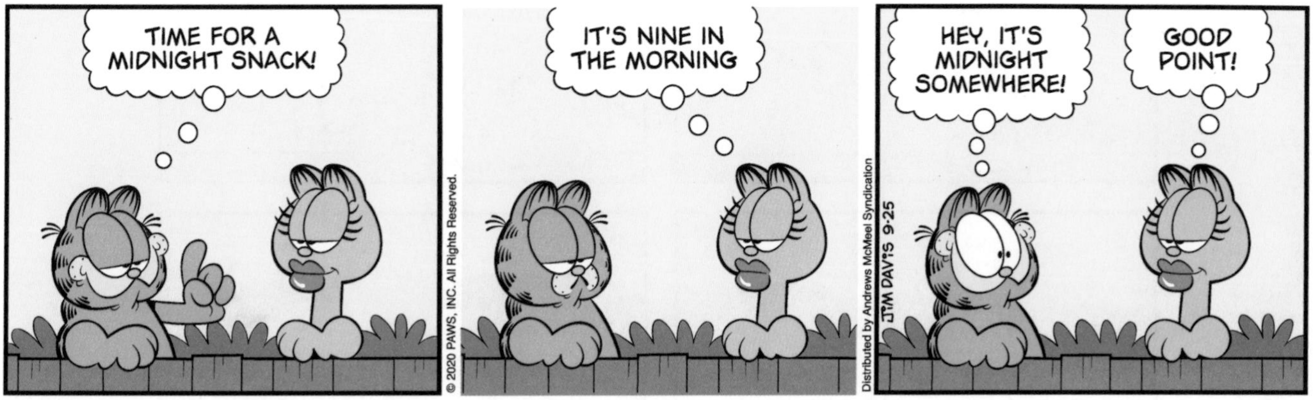
TIME FOR A MIDNIGHT SNACK!
IT'S NINE IN THE MORNING
HEY, IT'S MIDNIGHT SOMEWHERE!
GOOD POINT!
© 2020 PAWS, INC. All Rights Reserved.
Distributed by Andrews McMeel Syndication
JIM DAVIS 9-25

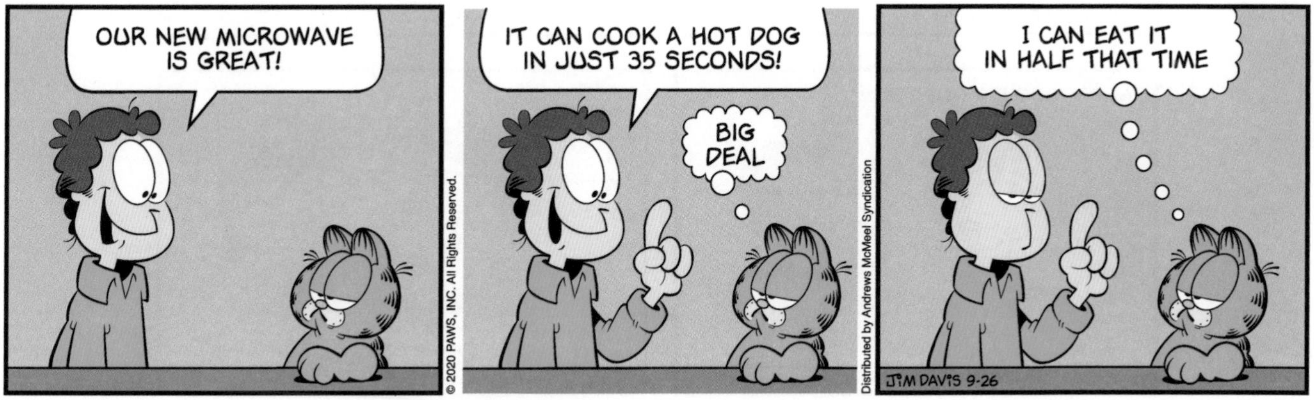
OUR NEW MICROWAVE IS GREAT!
IT CAN COOK A HOT DOG IN JUST 35 SECONDS!
BIG DEAL
I CAN EAT IT IN HALF THAT TIME
© 2020 PAWS, INC. All Rights Reserved.
Distributed by Andrews McMeel Syndication
JIM DAVIS 9-26

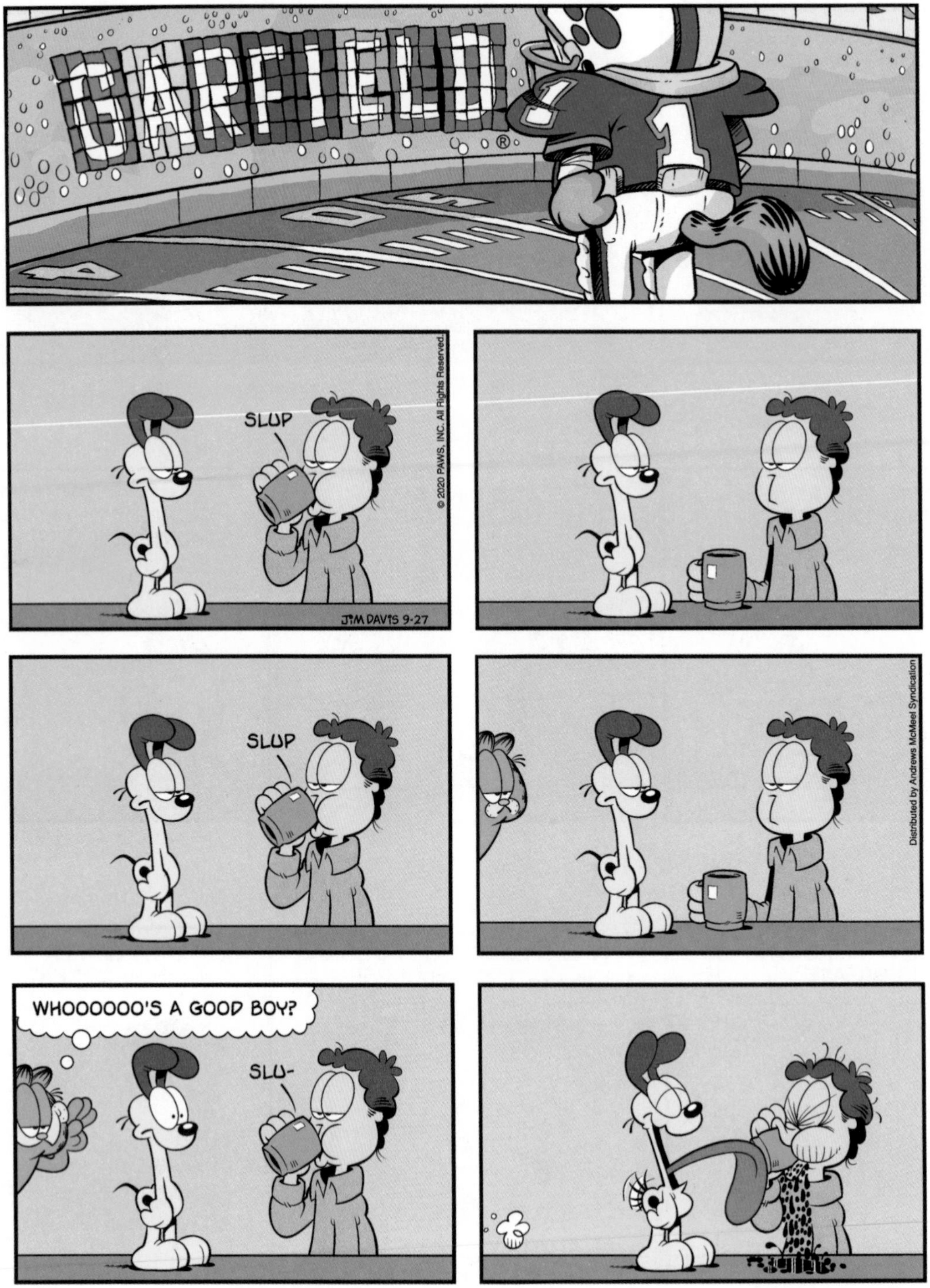
GARFIELD®
SLUP
© 2020 PAWS, INC. All Rights Reserved.
JIM DAVIS 9-27
SLUP
Distributed by Andrews McMeel Syndication
WHOOOOOO'S A GOOD BOY?
SLU-

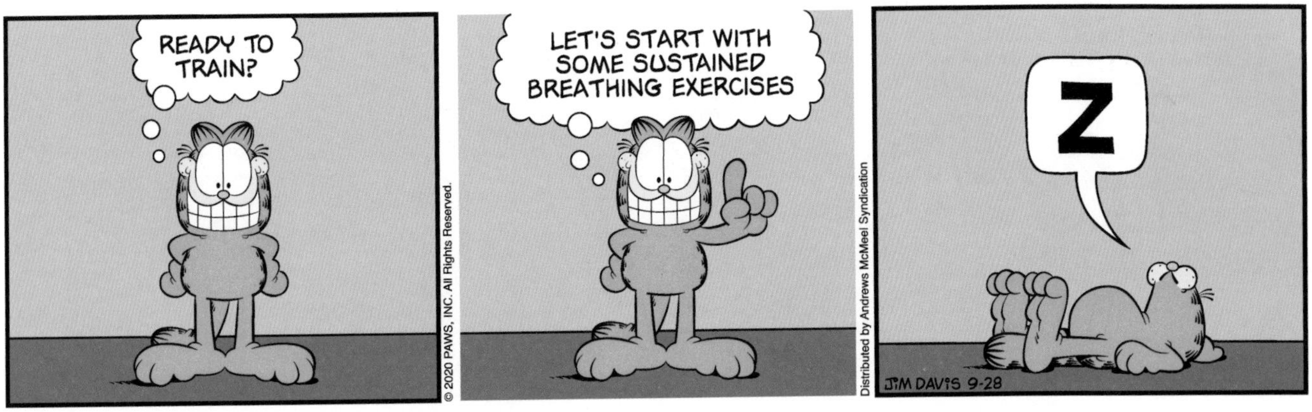
READY TO TRAIN?
LET'S START WITH SOME SUSTAINED BREATHING EXERCISES
Z
JIM DAVIS 9-28
© 2020 PAWS, INC. All Rights Reserved.
Distributed by Andrews McMeel Syndication

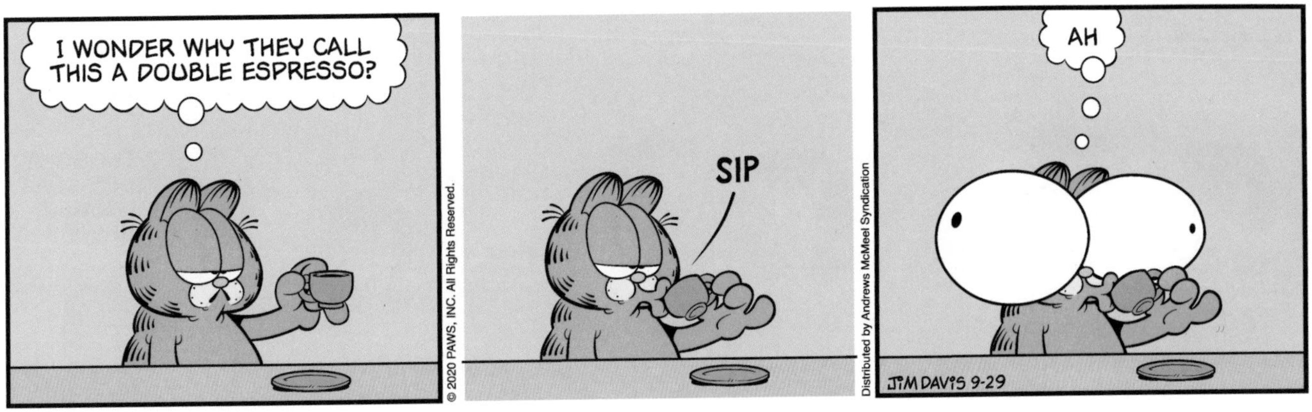
I WONDER WHY THEY CALL THIS A DOUBLE ESPRESSO?
SIP
AH
JIM DAVIS 9-29
© 2020 PAWS, INC. All Rights Reserved.
Distributed by Andrews McMeel Syndication

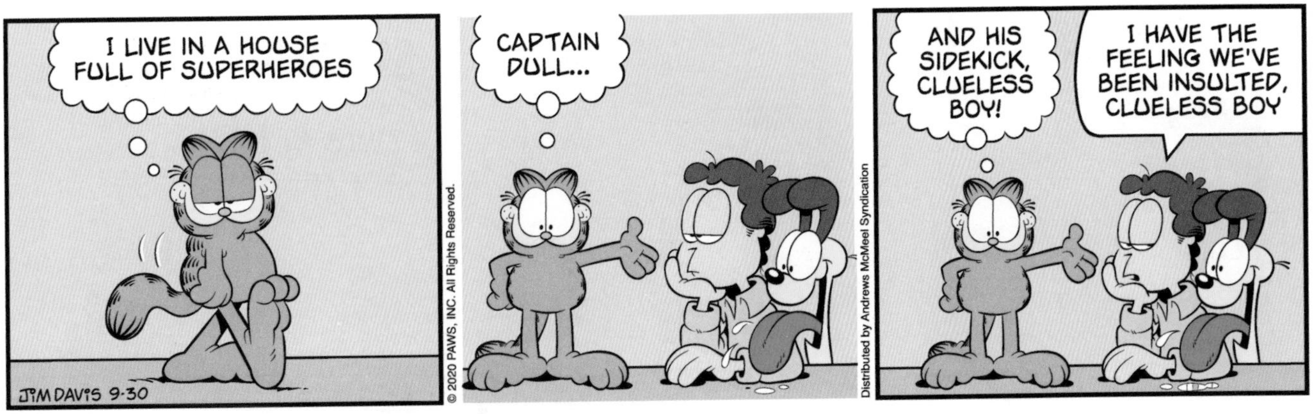
I LIVE IN A HOUSE FULL OF SUPERHEROES
CAPTAIN DULL...
AND HIS SIDEKICK, CLUELESS BOY!
I HAVE THE FEELING WE'VE BEEN INSULTED, CLUELESS BOY
JIM DAVIS 9-30
© 2020 PAWS, INC. All Rights Reserved.
Distributed by Andrews McMeel Syndication

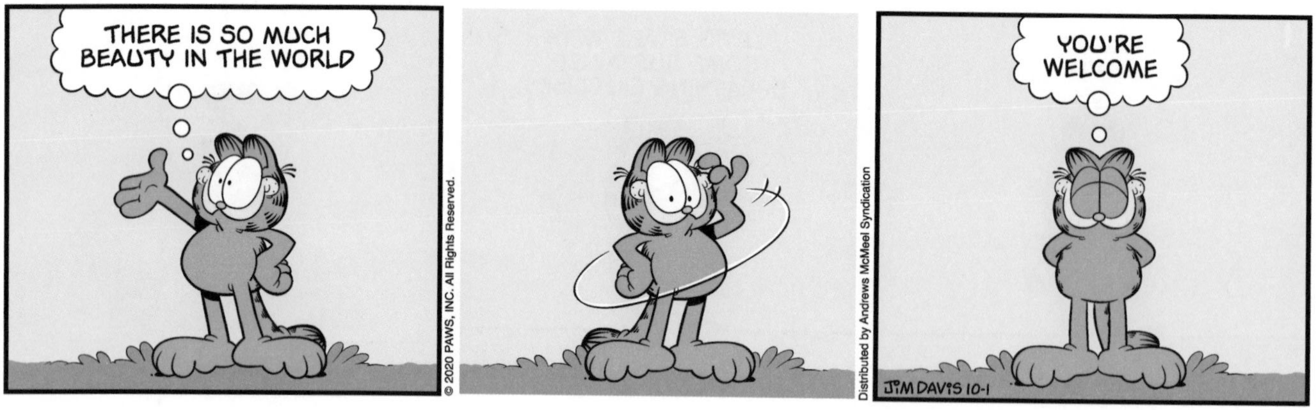
THERE IS SO MUCH BEAUTY IN THE WORLD
YOU'RE WELCOME
JIM DAVIS 10-1
© 2020 PAWS, INC. All Rights Reserved.
Distributed by Andrews McMeel Syndication

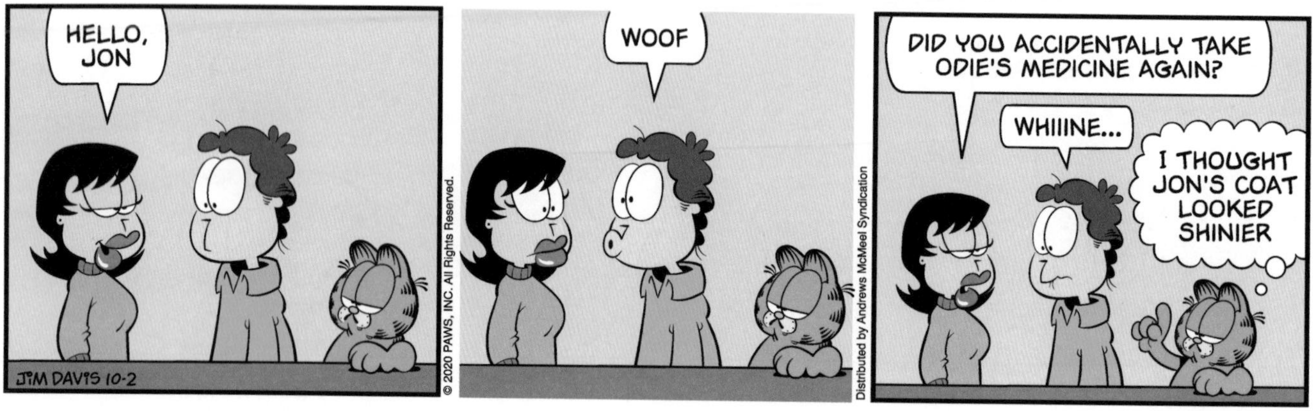
HELLO, JON
WOOF
DID YOU ACCIDENTALLY TAKE ODIE'S MEDICINE AGAIN?
WHIIINE...
I THOUGHT JON'S COAT LOOKED SHINIER
JIM DAVIS 10-2
© 2020 PAWS, INC. All Rights Reserved.
Distributed by Andrews McMeel Syndication

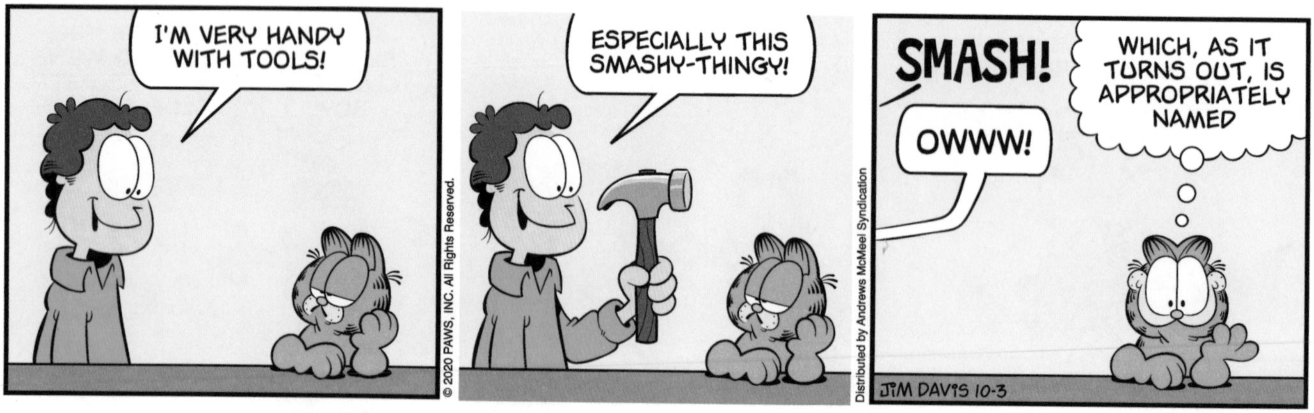
I'M VERY HANDY WITH TOOLS!
ESPECIALLY THIS SMASHY-THINGY!
SMASH!
OWWW!
WHICH, AS IT TURNS OUT, IS APPROPRIATELY NAMED
JIM DAVIS 10-3
© 2020 PAWS, INC. All Rights Reserved.
Distributed by Andrews McMeel Syndication

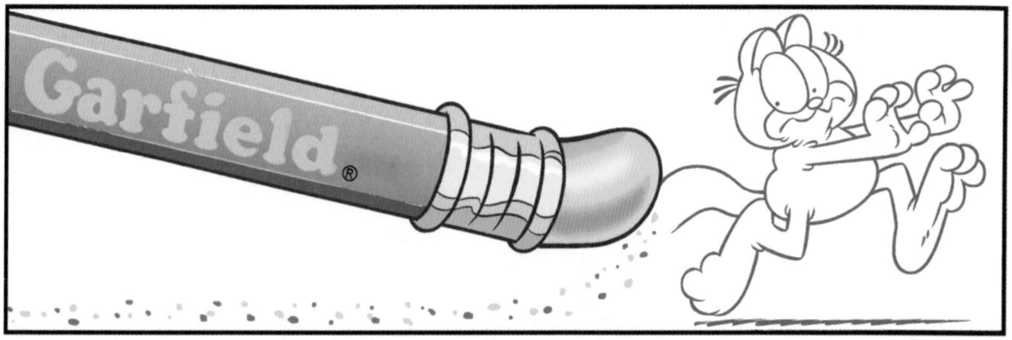
Garfield®

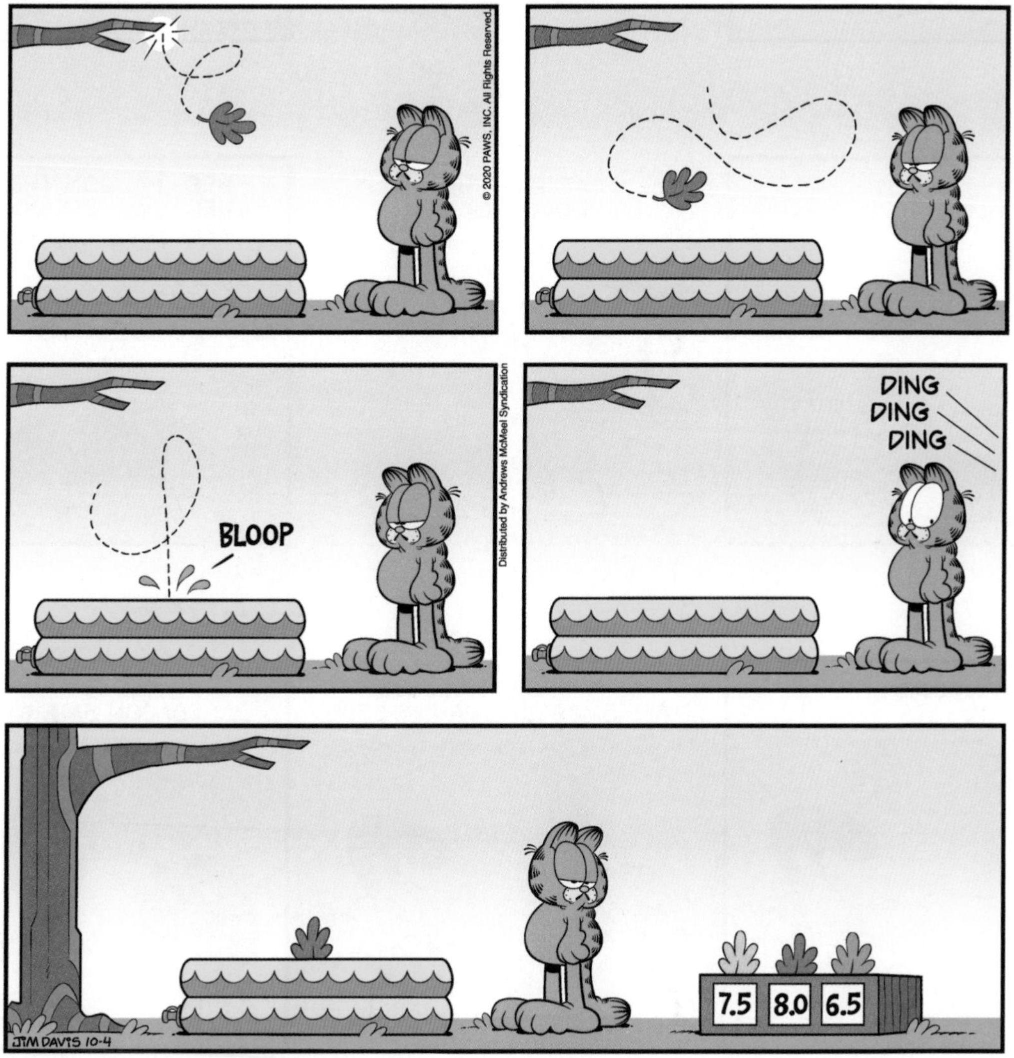
© 2020 PAWS, INC. All Rights Reserved.
Distributed by Andrews McMeel Syndication
BLOOP
DING
DING
DING
JIM DAVIS 10-4
7.5
8.0
6.5

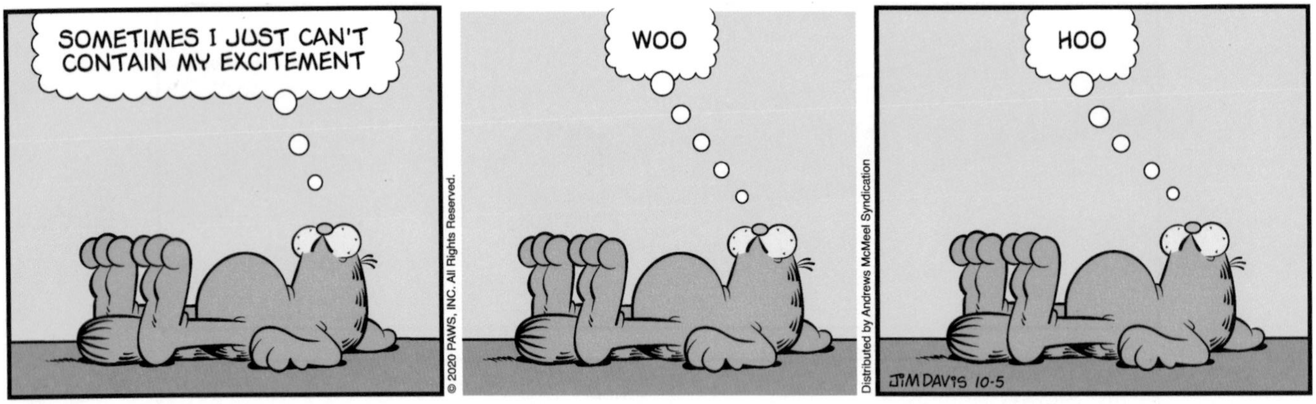
SOMETIMES I JUST CAN'T CONTAIN MY EXCITEMENT
WOO
HOO
© 2020 PAWS, INC. All Rights Reserved.
Distributed by Andrews McMeel Syndication
JIM DAVIS 10-5

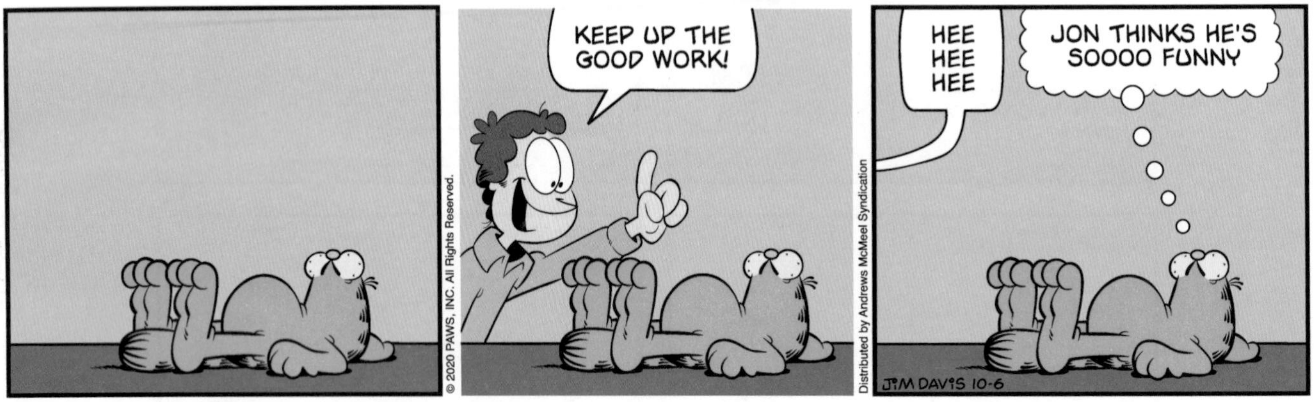
KEEP UP THE GOOD WORK!
HEE HEE HEE
JON THINKS HE'S SOOOO FUNNY
© 2020 PAWS, INC. All Rights Reserved.
Distributed by Andrews McMeel Syndication
JIM DAVIS 10-6

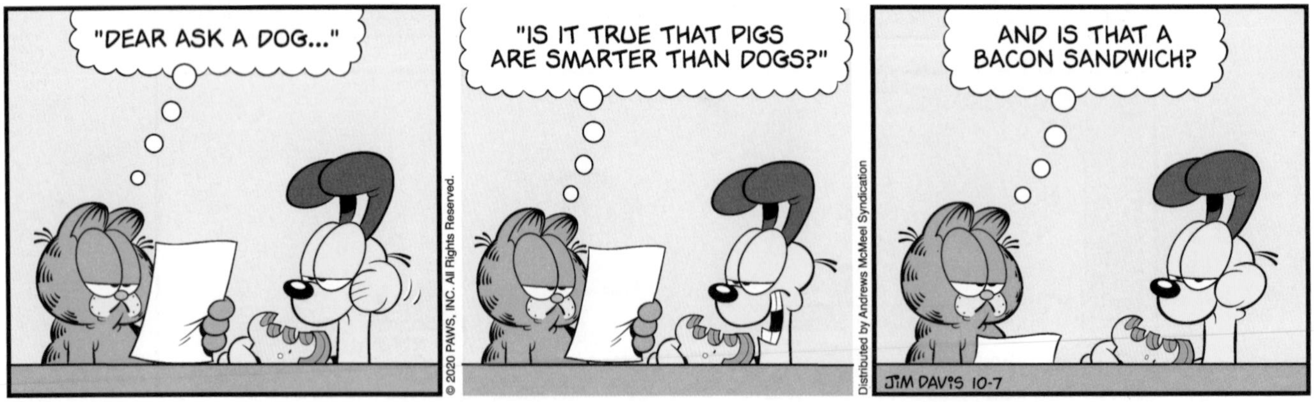
"DEAR ASK A DOG..."
"IS IT TRUE THAT PIGS ARE SMARTER THAN DOGS?"
AND IS THAT A BACON SANDWICH?
© 2020 PAWS, INC. All Rights Reserved.
Distributed by Andrews McMeel Syndication
JIM DAVIS 10-7

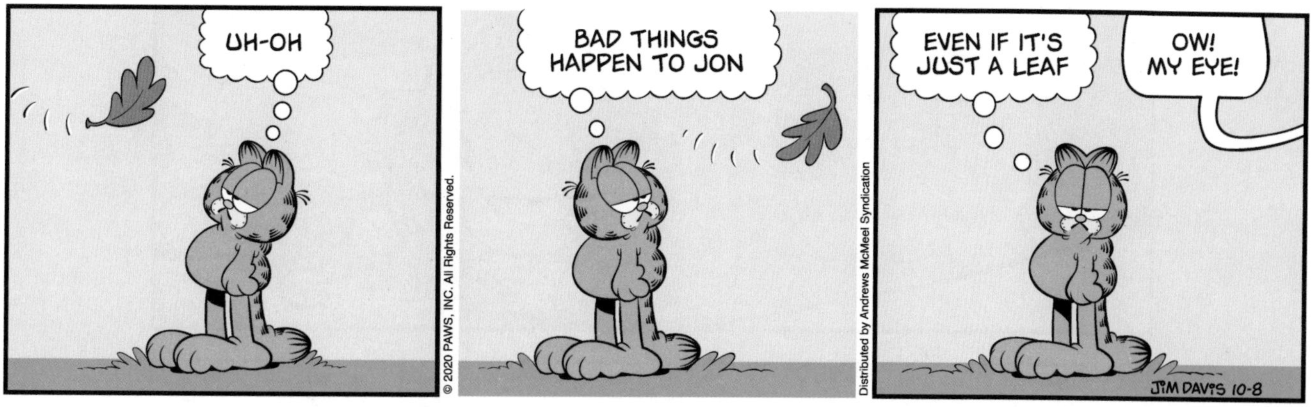
UH-OH
BAD THINGS HAPPEN TO JON
EVEN IF IT'S JUST A LEAF
OW! MY EYE!
© 2020 PAWS, INC. All Rights Reserved.
Distributed by Andrews McMeel Syndication
JIM DAVIS 10-8

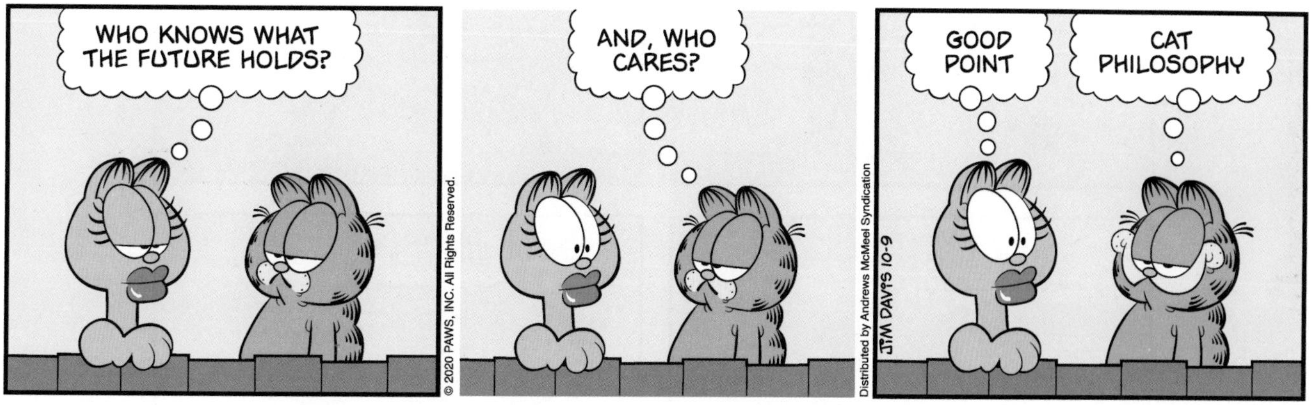
WHO KNOWS WHAT THE FUTURE HOLDS?
AND, WHO CARES?
GOOD POINT
CAT PHILOSOPHY
© 2020 PAWS, INC. All Rights Reserved.
Distributed by Andrews McMeel Syndication
JIM DAVIS 10-9

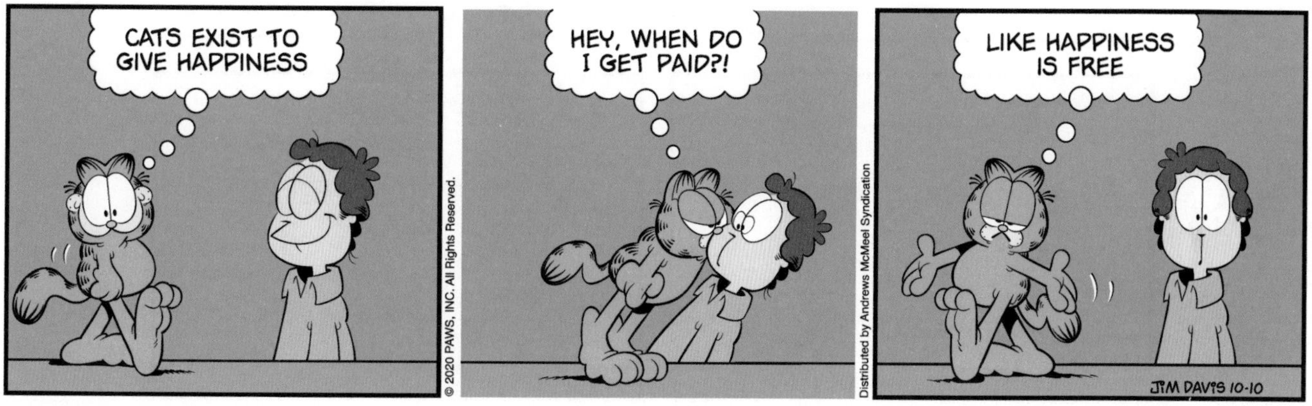
CATS EXIST TO GIVE HAPPINESS
HEY, WHEN DO I GET PAID?!
LIKE HAPPINESS IS FREE
© 2020 PAWS, INC. All Rights Reserved.
Distributed by Andrews McMeel Syndication
JIM DAVIS 10-10

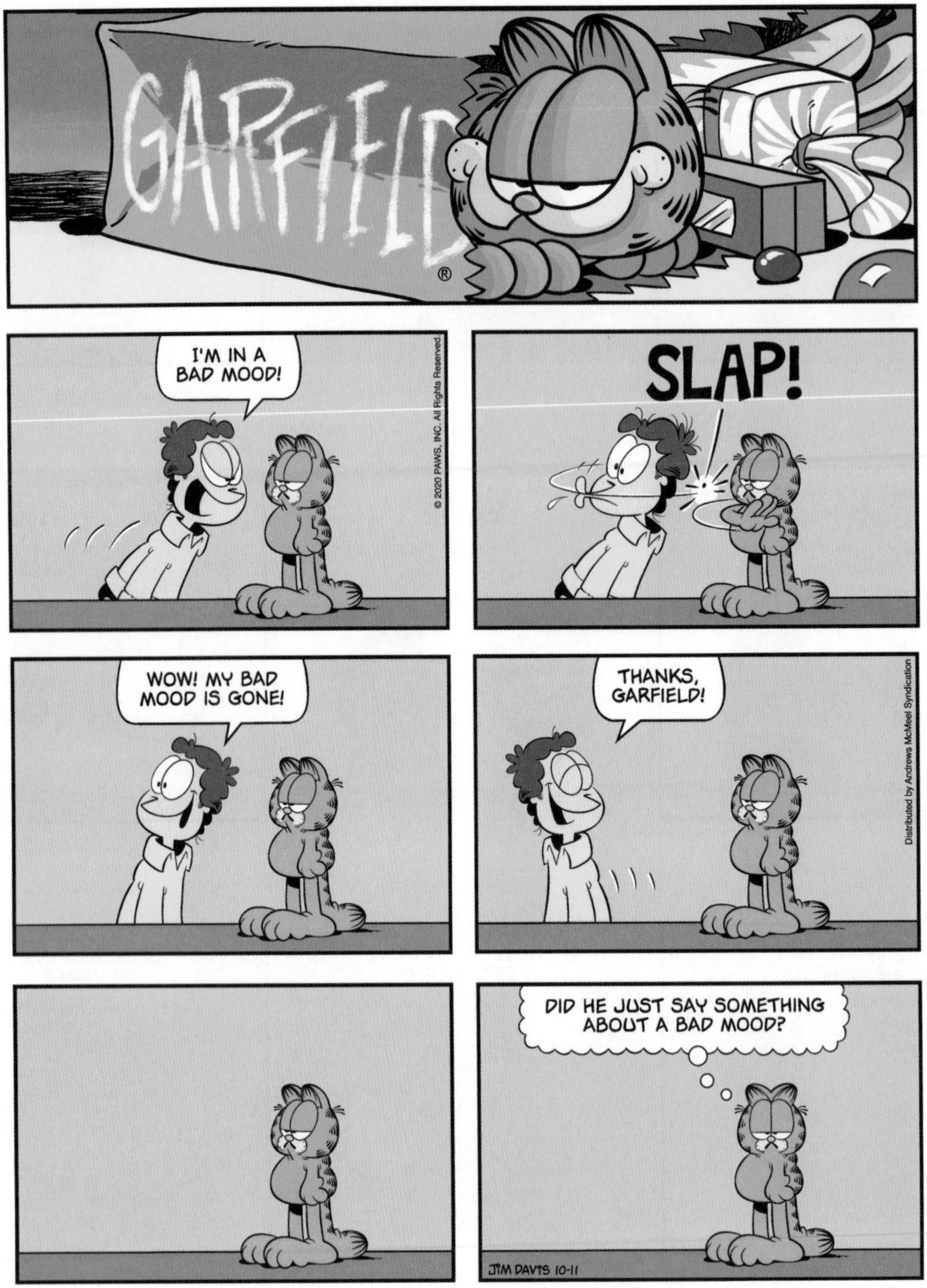
GARFIELD®
I'M IN A BAD MOOD!
© 2020 PAWS, INC. All Rights Reserved.
SLAP!
WOW! MY BAD MOOD IS GONE!
THANKS, GARFIELD!
Distributed by Andrews McMeel Syndication
DID HE JUST SAY SOMETHING ABOUT A BAD MOOD?
JIM DAVIS 10-11

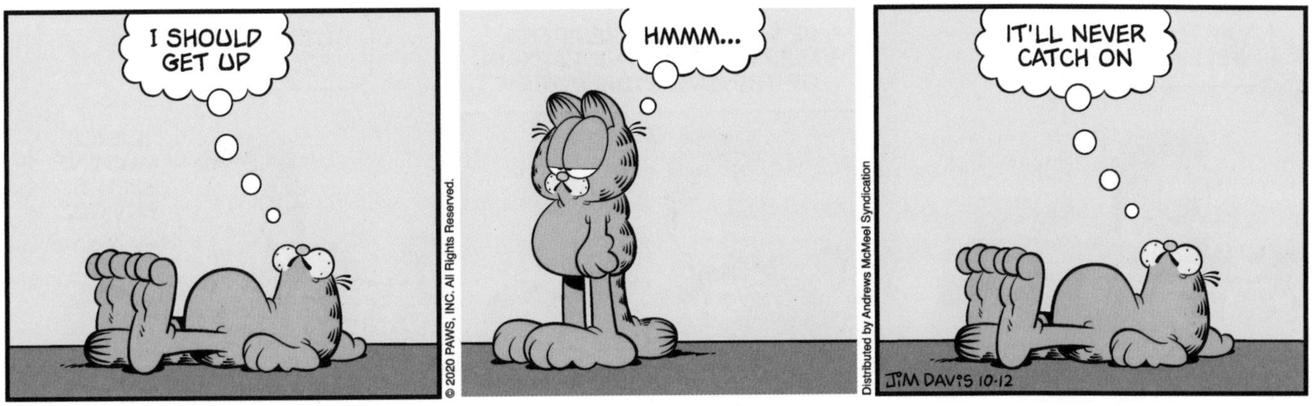
I SHOULD GET UP
HMMM...
IT'LL NEVER CATCH ON
© 2020 PAWS, INC. All Rights Reserved.
Distributed by Andrews McMeel Syndication
JIM DAVIS 10-12

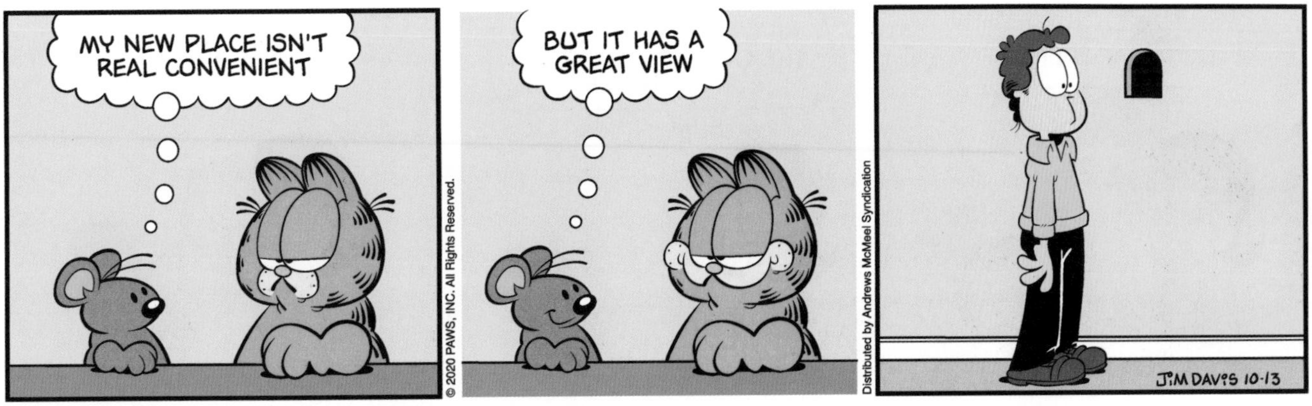
MY NEW PLACE ISN'T REAL CONVENIENT
BUT IT HAS A GREAT VIEW
© 2020 PAWS, INC. All Rights Reserved.
Distributed by Andrews McMeel Syndication
JIM DAVIS 10-13

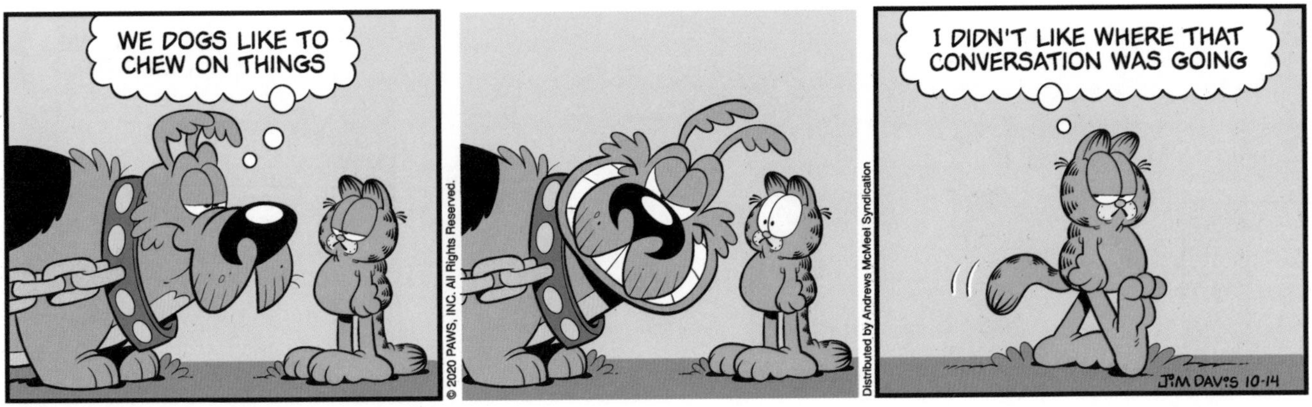
WE DOGS LIKE TO CHEW ON THINGS
I DIDN'T LIKE WHERE THAT CONVERSATION WAS GOING
© 2020 PAWS, INC. All Rights Reserved.
Distributed by Andrews McMeel Syndication
JIM DAVIS 10-14

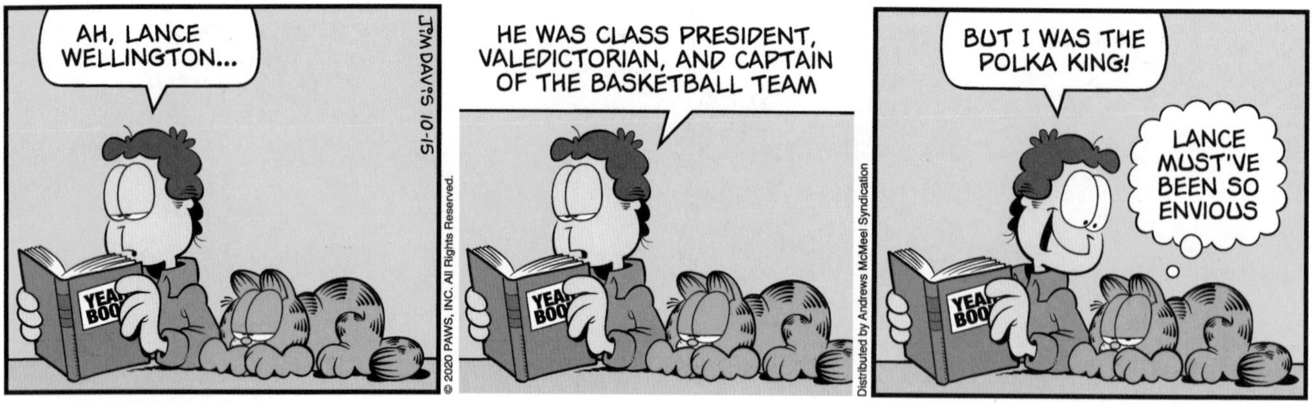
AH, LANCE WELLINGTON...
JIM DAVIS 10-15
HE WAS CLASS PRESIDENT, VALEDICTORIAN, AND CAPTAIN OF THE BASKETBALL TEAM
BUT I WAS THE POLKA KING!
LANCE MUST'VE BEEN SO ENVIOUS
© 2020 PAWS, INC. All Rights Reserved.
Distributed by Andrews McMeel Syndication

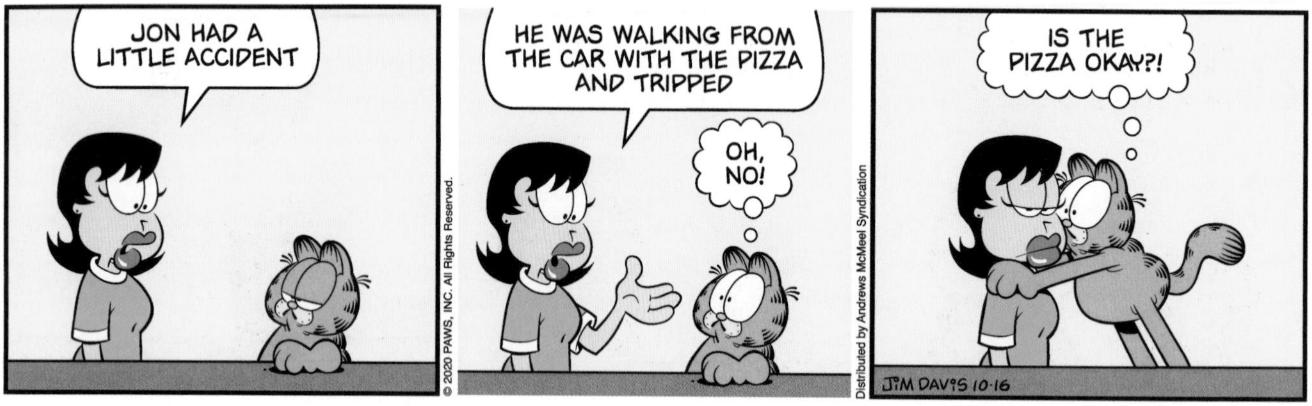
JON HAD A LITTLE ACCIDENT
HE WAS WALKING FROM THE CAR WITH THE PIZZA AND TRIPPED
OH, NO!
IS THE PIZZA OKAY?!
JIM DAVIS 10-16
© 2020 PAWS, INC. All Rights Reserved.
Distributed by Andrews McMeel Syndication

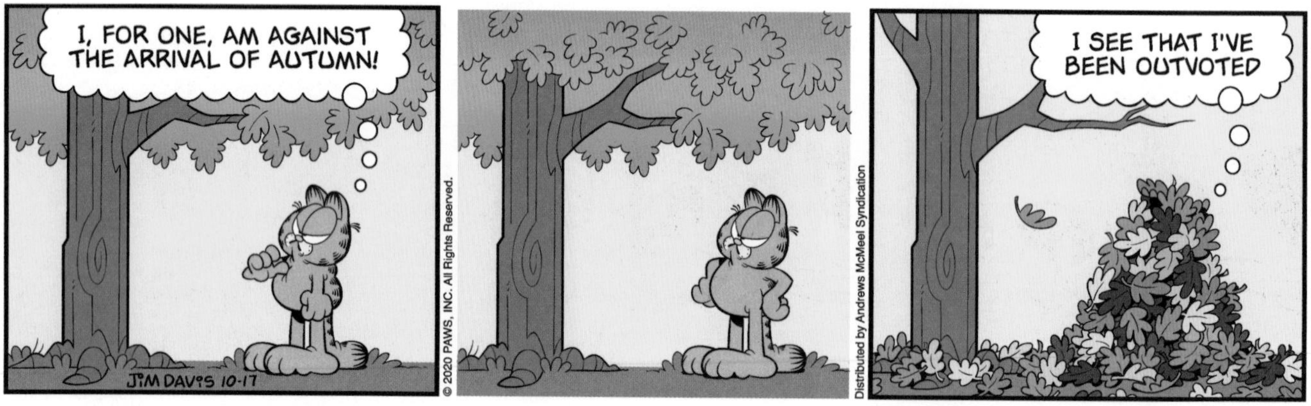
I, FOR ONE, AM AGAINST THE ARRIVAL OF AUTUMN!
JIM DAVIS 10-17
I SEE THAT I'VE BEEN OUTVOTED
© 2020 PAWS, INC. All Rights Reserved.
Distributed by Andrews McMeel Syndication

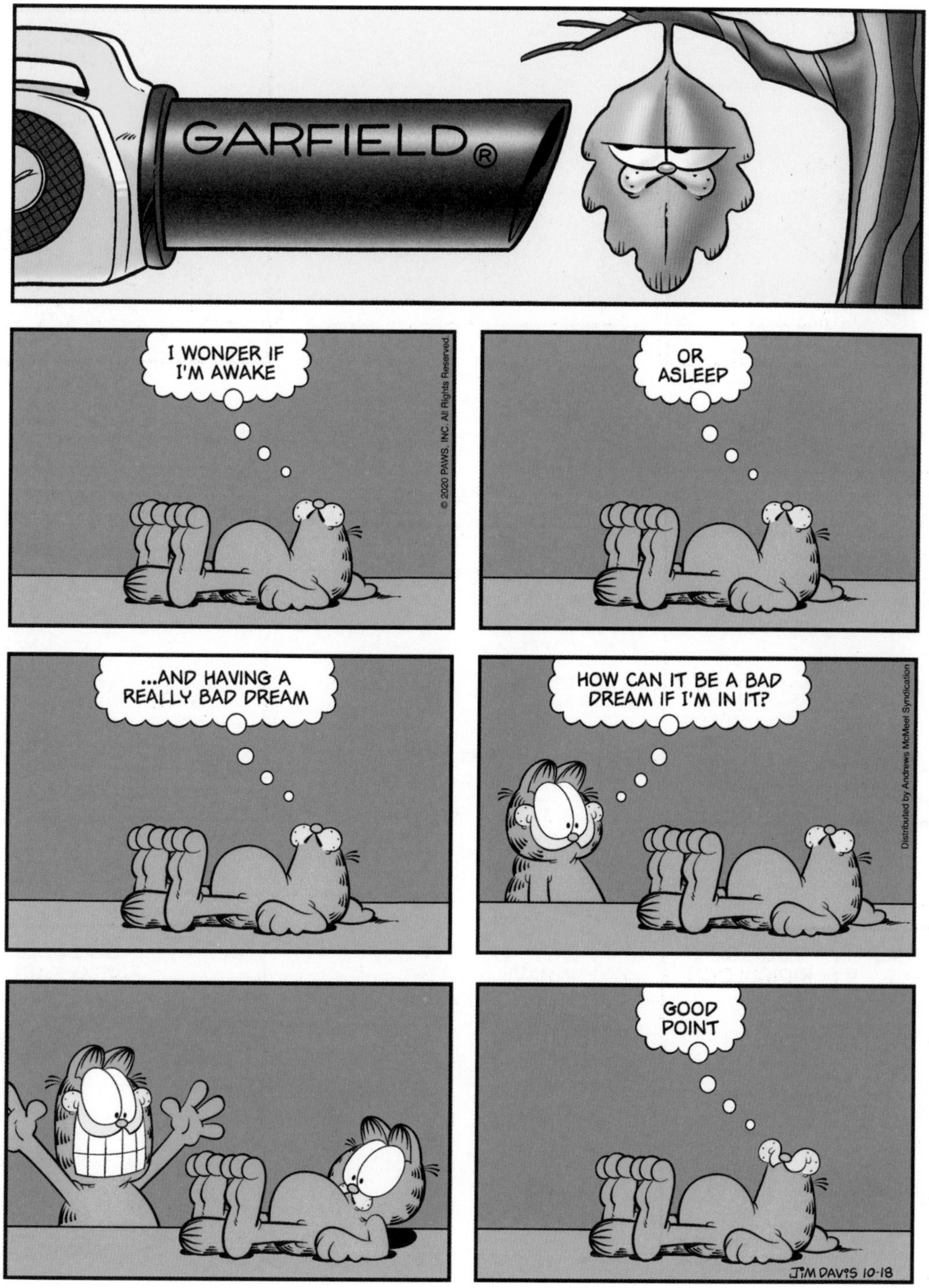
GARFIELD®
I WONDER IF I'M AWAKE
© 2020 PAWS, INC. All Rights Reserved.
OR ASLEEP
...AND HAVING A REALLY BAD DREAM
HOW CAN IT BE A BAD DREAM IF I'M IN IT?
Distributed by Andrews McMeel Syndication
GOOD POINT
JIM DAVIS 10-18

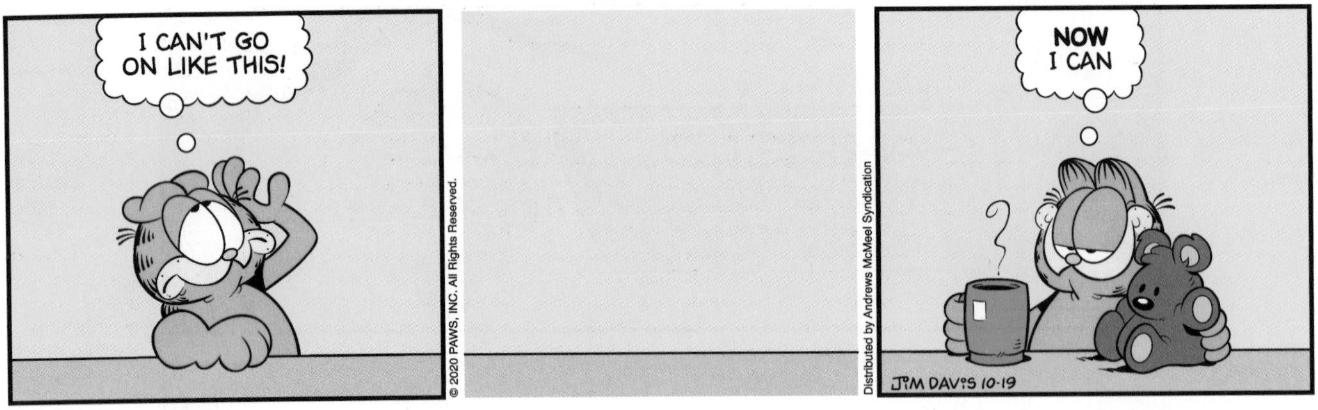
I CAN'T GO ON LIKE THIS!
© 2020 PAWS, INC. All Rights Reserved.
Distributed by Andrews McMeel Syndication
NOW I CAN
JIM DAVIS 10-19

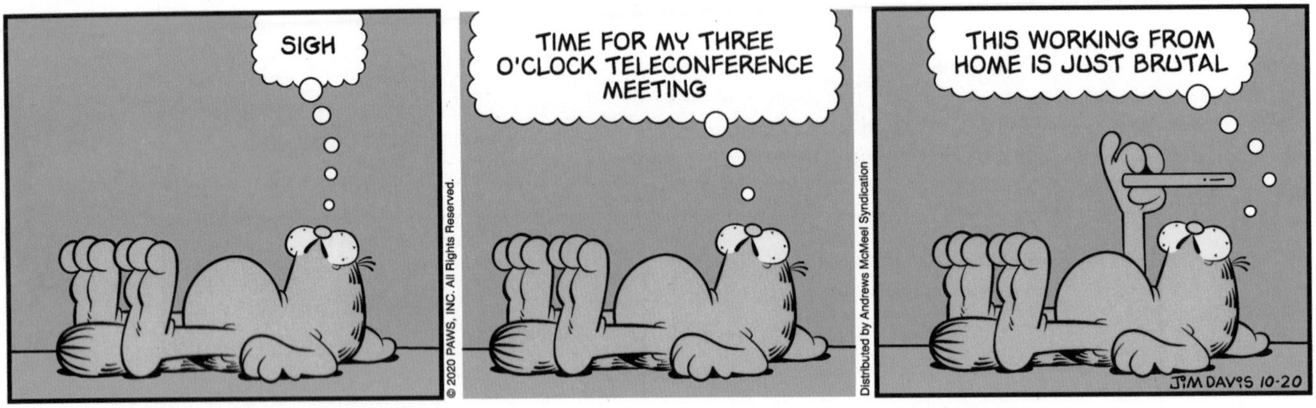
SIGH
© 2020 PAWS, INC. All Rights Reserved.
TIME FOR MY THREE O'CLOCK TELECONFERENCE MEETING
Distributed by Andrews McMeel Syndication
THIS WORKING FROM HOME IS JUST BRUTAL
JIM DAVIS 10-20

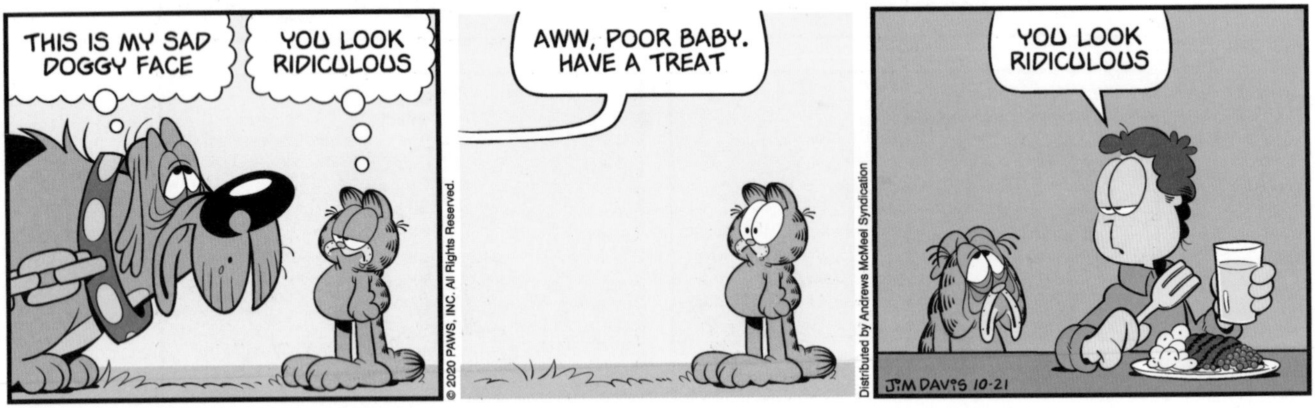
THIS IS MY SAD DOGGY FACE
YOU LOOK RIDICULOUS
© 2020 PAWS, INC. All Rights Reserved.
AWW, POOR BABY. HAVE A TREAT
Distributed by Andrews McMeel Syndication
YOU LOOK RIDICULOUS
JIM DAVIS 10-21

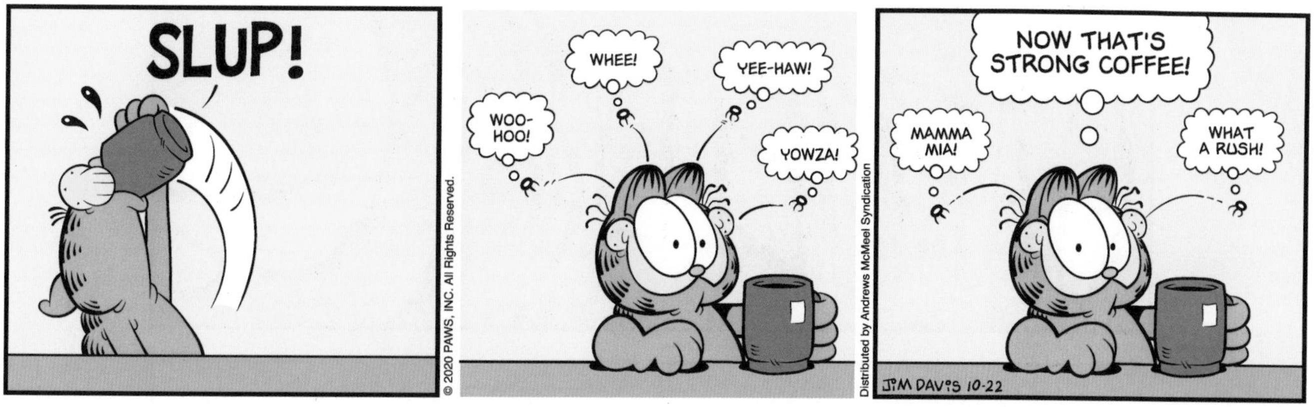
SLUP!
WOO-HOO!
WHEE!
YEE-HAW!
YOWZA!
© 2020 PAWS, INC. All Rights Reserved.
MAMMA MIA!
NOW THAT'S STRONG COFFEE!
WHAT A RUSH!
Distributed by Andrews McMeel Syndication
JIM DAVIS 10-22

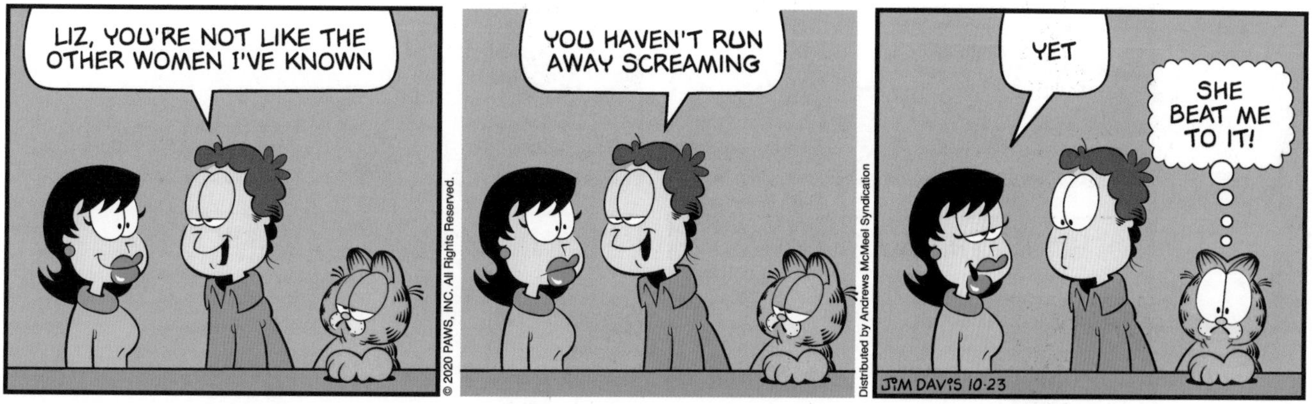
LIZ, YOU'RE NOT LIKE THE OTHER WOMEN I'VE KNOWN
© 2020 PAWS, INC. All Rights Reserved.
YOU HAVEN'T RUN AWAY SCREAMING
Distributed by Andrews McMeel Syndication
YET
SHE BEAT ME TO IT!
JIM DAVIS 10-23

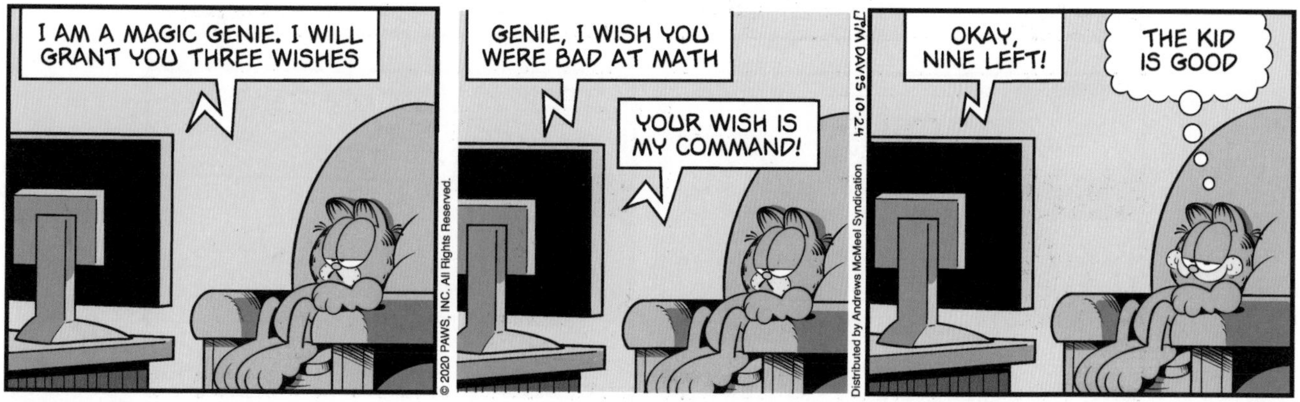
I AM A MAGIC GENIE. I WILL GRANT YOU THREE WISHES
© 2020 PAWS, INC. All Rights Reserved.
GENIE, I WISH YOU WERE BAD AT MATH
YOUR WISH IS MY COMMAND!
JIM DAVIS 10-24
Distributed by Andrews McMeel Syndication
OKAY, NINE LEFT!
THE KID IS GOOD

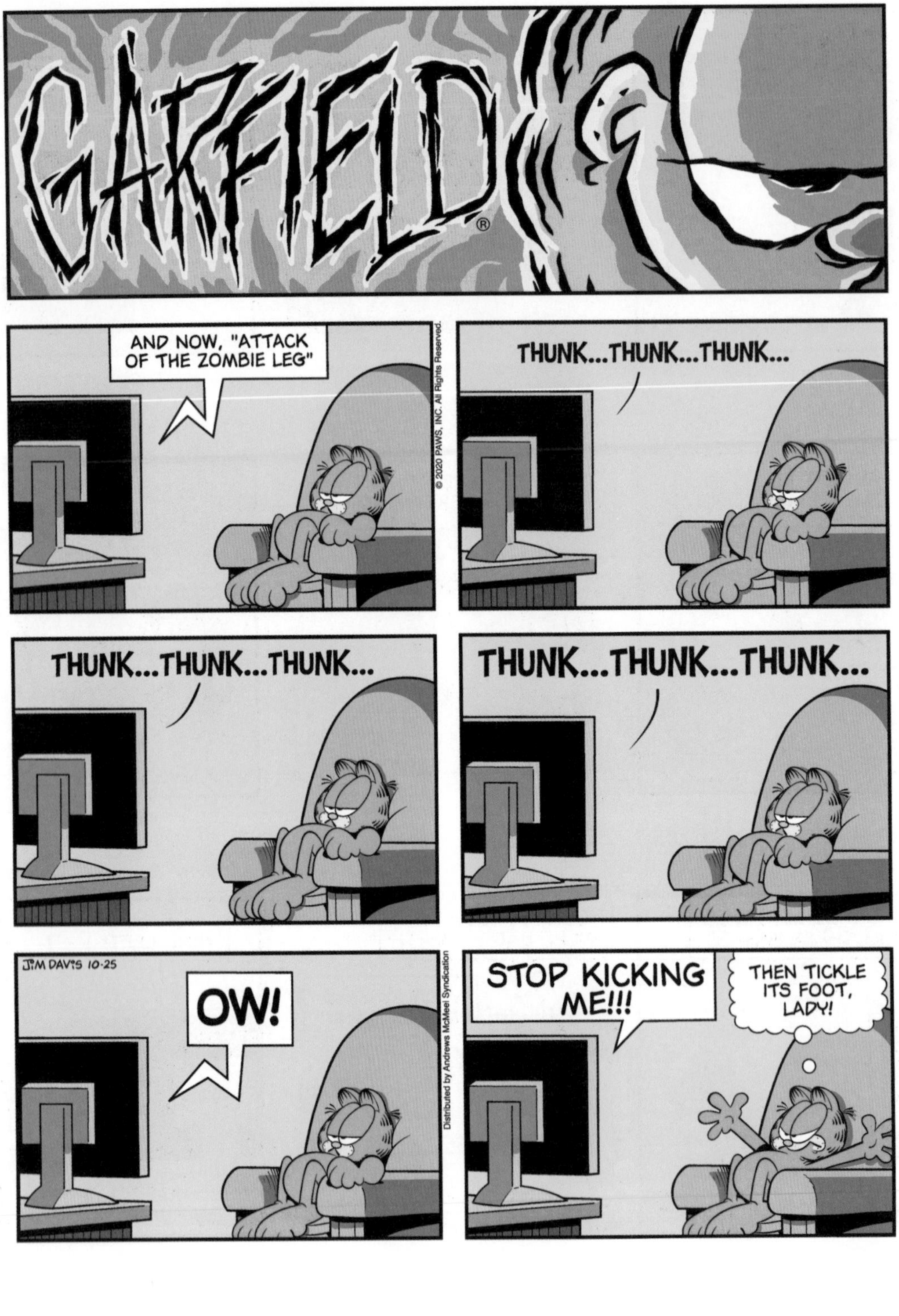
GARFIELD®
AND NOW, "ATTACK OF THE ZOMBIE LEG"
THUNK...THUNK...THUNK...
THUNK...THUNK...THUNK...
THUNK...THUNK...THUNK...
JIM DAVIS 10-25
OW!
STOP KICKING ME!!!
THEN TICKLE ITS FOOT, LADY!

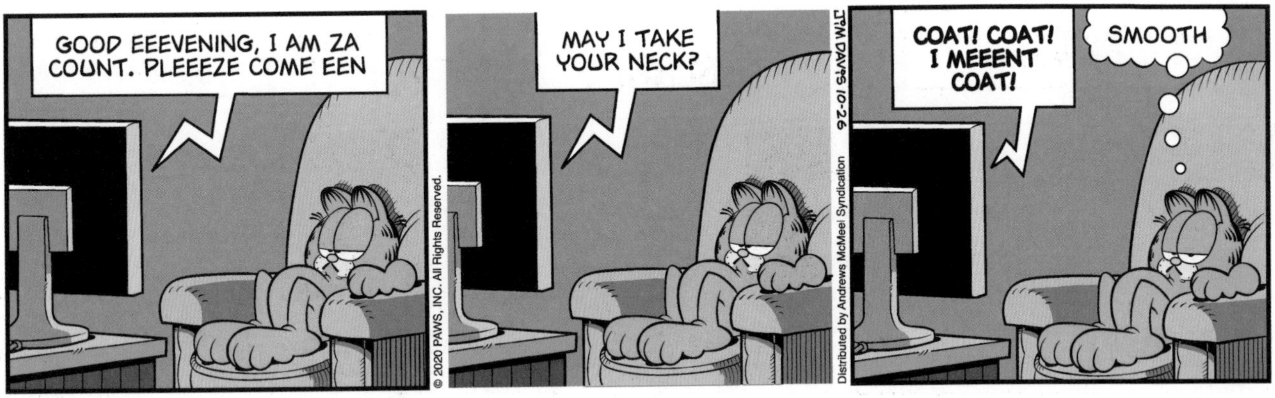
GOOD EEEVENING, I AM ZA COUNT. PLEEEZE COME EEN
MAY I TAKE YOUR NECK?
JIM DAVIS 10-26
COAT! COAT! I MEEENT COAT!
SMOOTH
© 2020 PAWS, INC. All Rights Reserved.
Distributed by Andrews McMeel Syndication

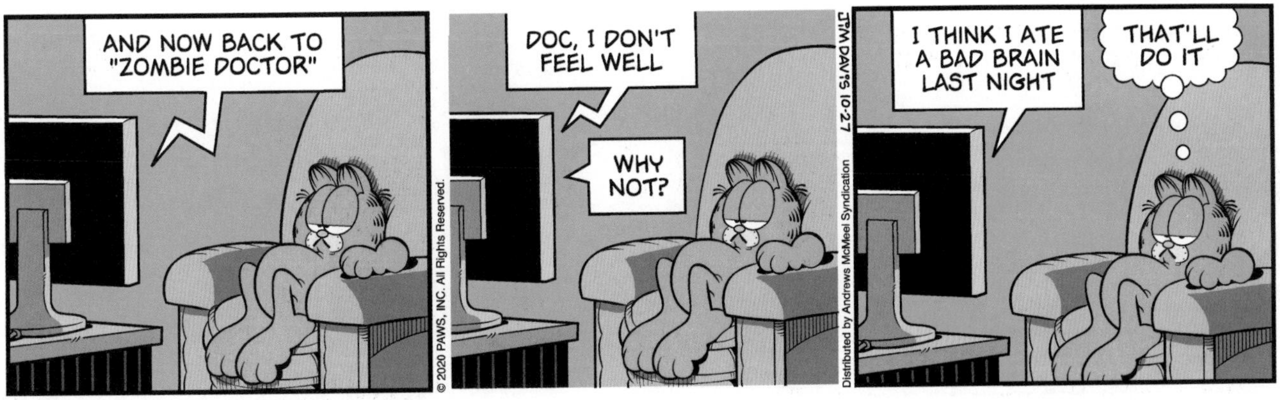
AND NOW BACK TO "ZOMBIE DOCTOR"
DOC, I DON'T FEEL WELL
WHY NOT?
JIM DAVIS 10-27
I THINK I ATE A BAD BRAIN LAST NIGHT
THAT'LL DO IT
© 2020 PAWS, INC. All Rights Reserved.
Distributed by Andrews McMeel Syndication

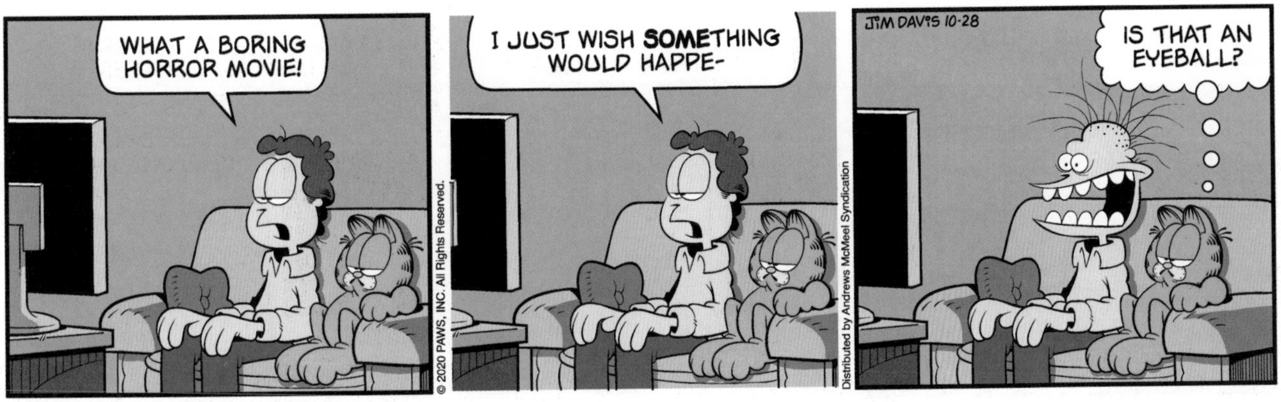
WHAT A BORING HORROR MOVIE!
I JUST WISH **SOME**THING WOULD HAPPE-
JIM DAVIS 10-28
IS THAT AN EYEBALL?
© 2020 PAWS, INC. All Rights Reserved.
Distributed by Andrews McMeel Syndication

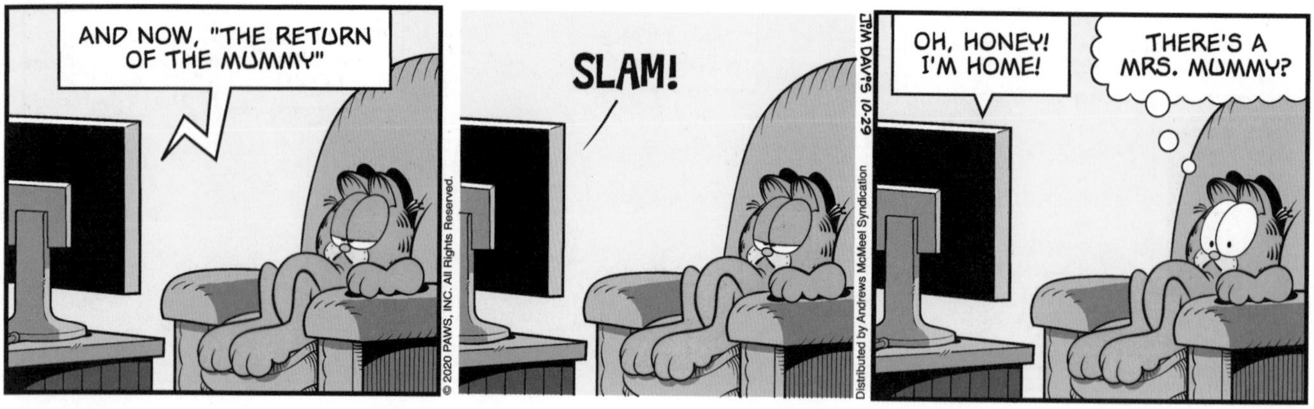
AND NOW, "THE RETURN OF THE MUMMY"
SLAM!
© 2020 PAWS, INC. All Rights Reserved.
JIM DAVIS 10-29
Distributed by Andrews McMeel Syndication
OH, HONEY! I'M HOME!
THERE'S A MRS. MUMMY?

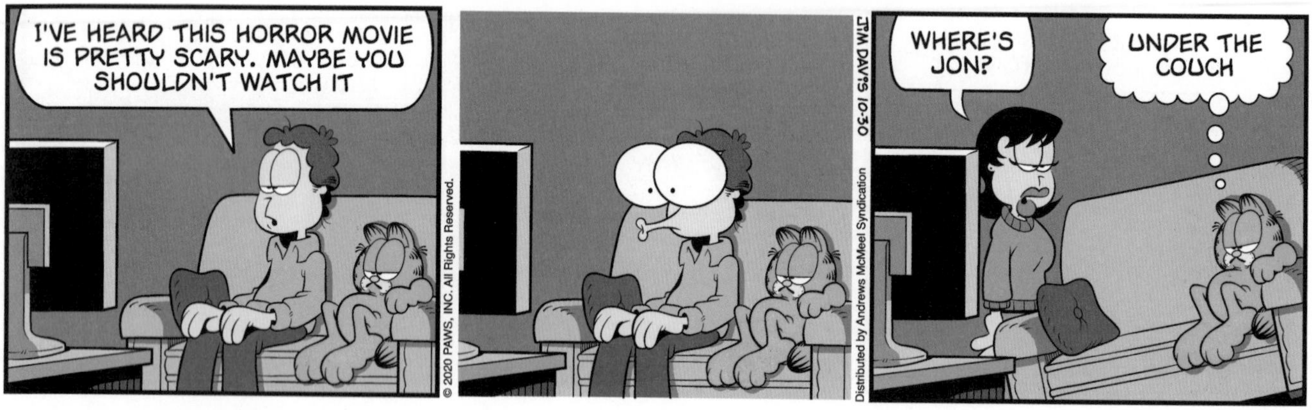
I'VE HEARD THIS HORROR MOVIE IS PRETTY SCARY. MAYBE YOU SHOULDN'T WATCH IT
© 2020 PAWS, INC. All Rights Reserved.
JIM DAVIS 10-30
Distributed by Andrews McMeel Syndication
WHERE'S JON?
UNDER THE COUCH

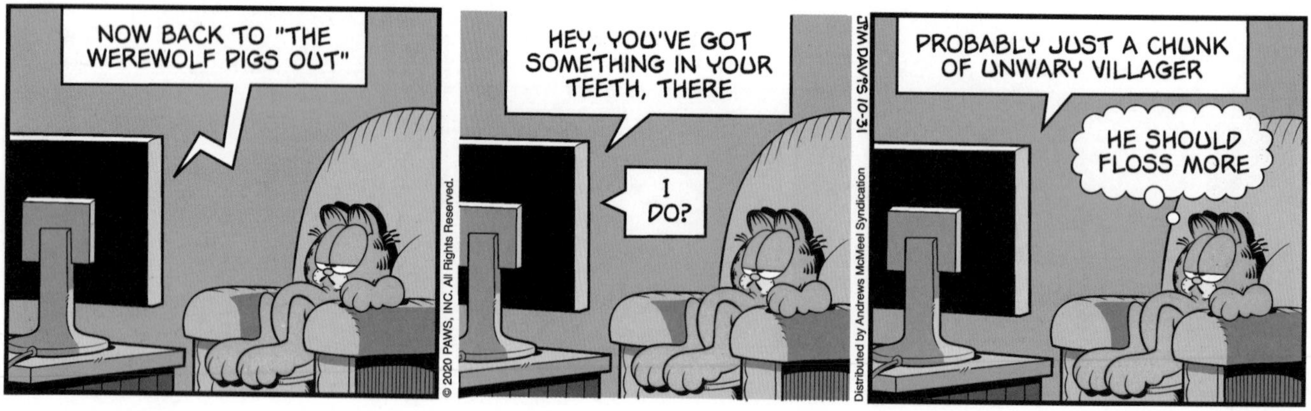
NOW BACK TO "THE WEREWOLF PIGS OUT"
HEY, YOU'VE GOT SOMETHING IN YOUR TEETH, THERE
I DO?
© 2020 PAWS, INC. All Rights Reserved.
JIM DAVIS 10-31
Distributed by Andrews McMeel Syndication
PROBABLY JUST A CHUNK OF UNWARY VILLAGER
HE SHOULD FLOSS MORE

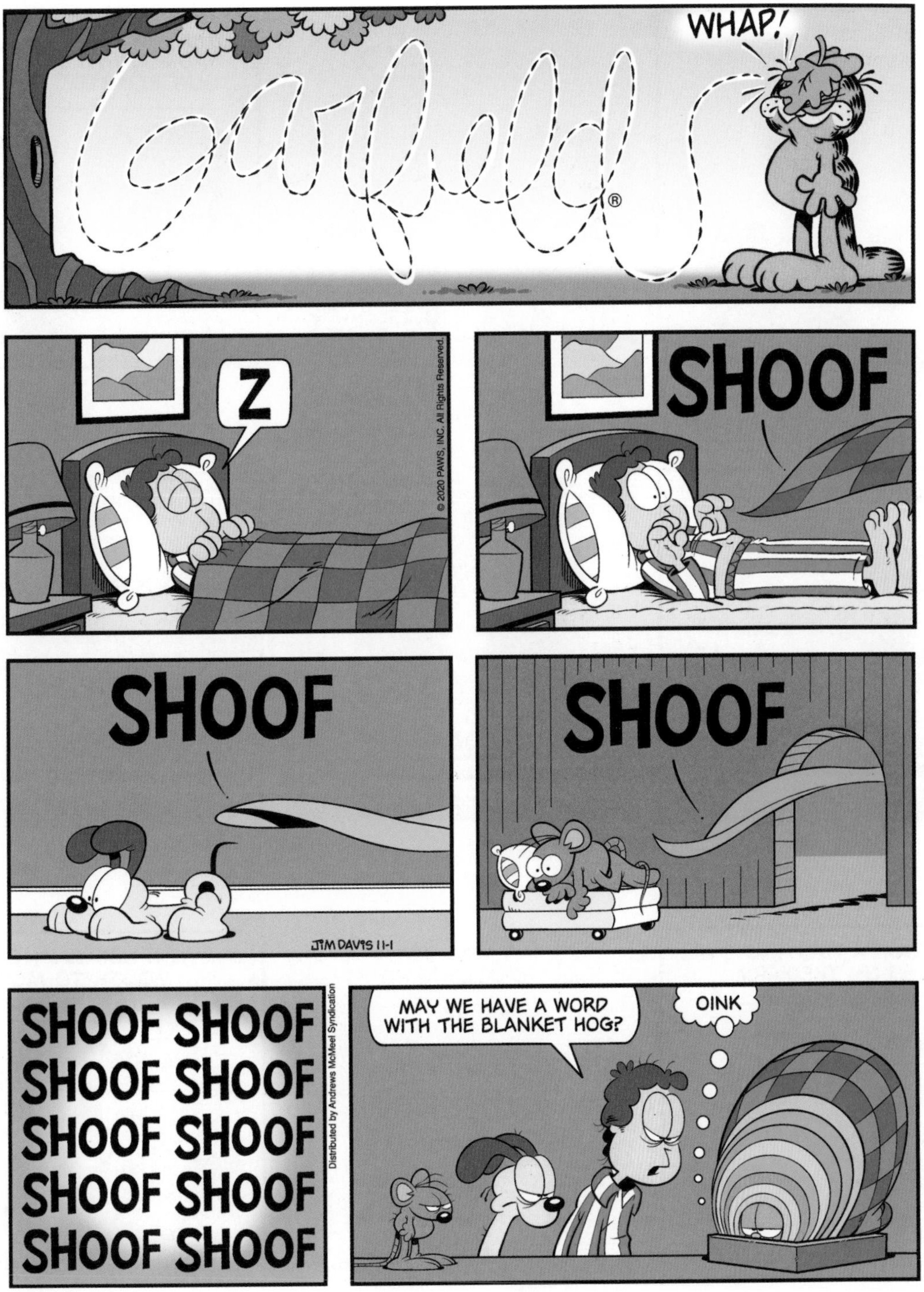
WHAP!
garfield®
Z
© 2020 PAWS, INC. All Rights Reserved.
SHOOF
SHOOF
SHOOF
JIM DAVIS 11-1
SHOOF SHOOF
SHOOF SHOOF
SHOOF SHOOF
SHOOF SHOOF
SHOOF SHOOF
Distributed by Andrews McMeel Syndication
MAY WE HAVE A WORD WITH THE BLANKET HOG?
OINK

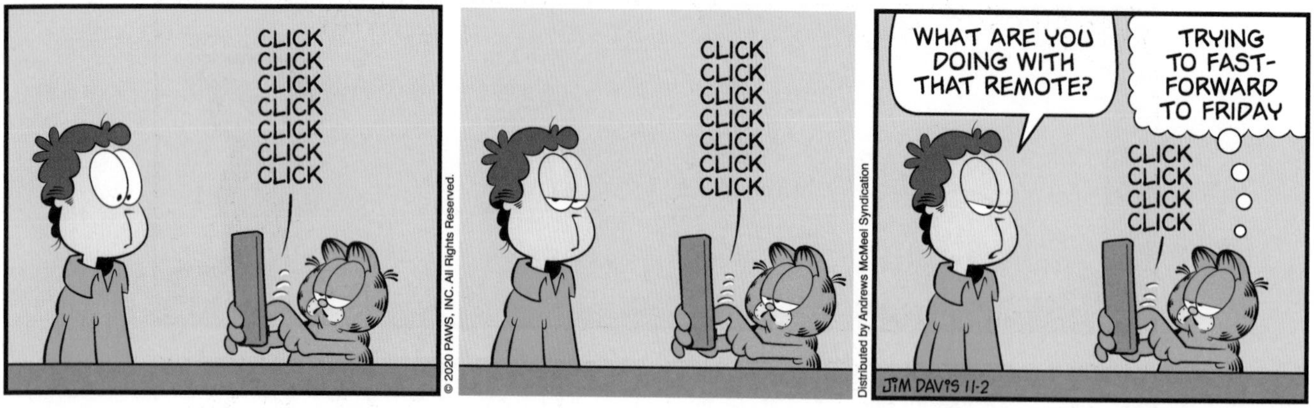
CLICK CLICK CLICK CLICK CLICK CLICK CLICK
CLICK CLICK CLICK CLICK CLICK CLICK CLICK
© 2020 PAWS, INC. All Rights Reserved.
Distributed by Andrews McMeel Syndication
WHAT ARE YOU DOING WITH THAT REMOTE?
TRYING TO FAST-FORWARD TO FRIDAY
CLICK CLICK CLICK CLICK
JIM DAVIS 11-2

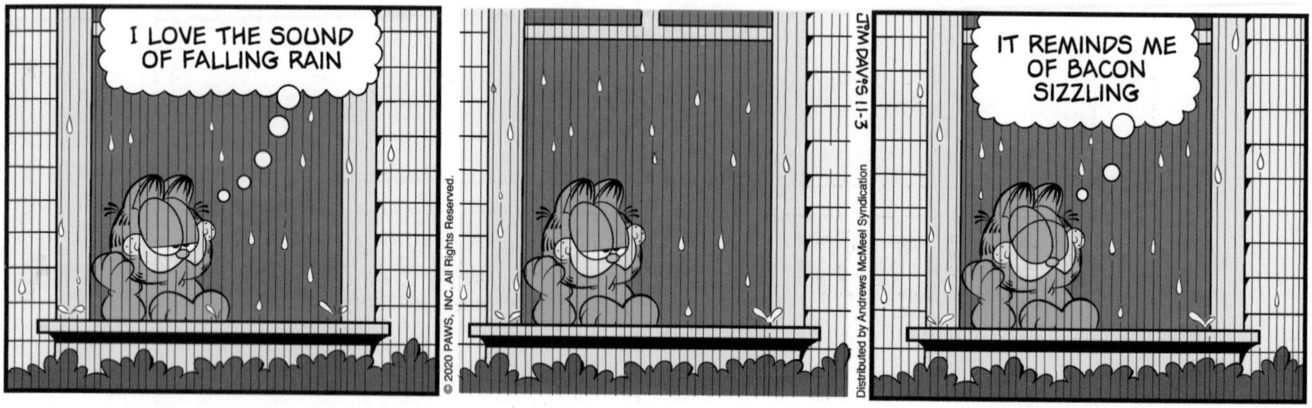
I LOVE THE SOUND OF FALLING RAIN
© 2020 PAWS, INC. All Rights Reserved.
JIM DAVIS 11-3
Distributed by Andrews McMeel Syndication
IT REMINDS ME OF BACON SIZZLING

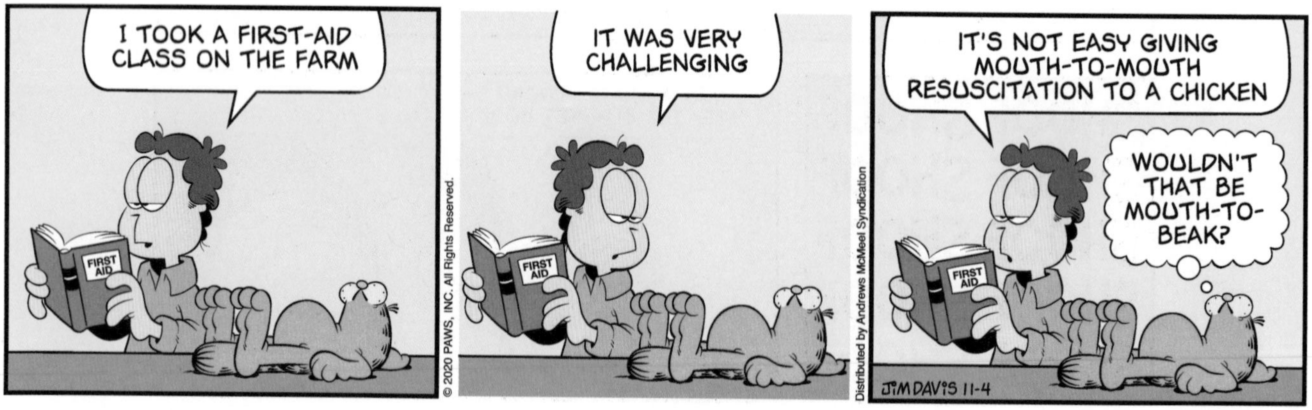
I TOOK A FIRST-AID CLASS ON THE FARM
FIRST AID
© 2020 PAWS, INC. All Rights Reserved.
IT WAS VERY CHALLENGING
FIRST AID
Distributed by Andrews McMeel Syndication
IT'S NOT EASY GIVING MOUTH-TO-MOUTH RESUSCITATION TO A CHICKEN
WOULDN'T THAT BE MOUTH-TO-BEAK?
FIRST AID
JIM DAVIS 11-4

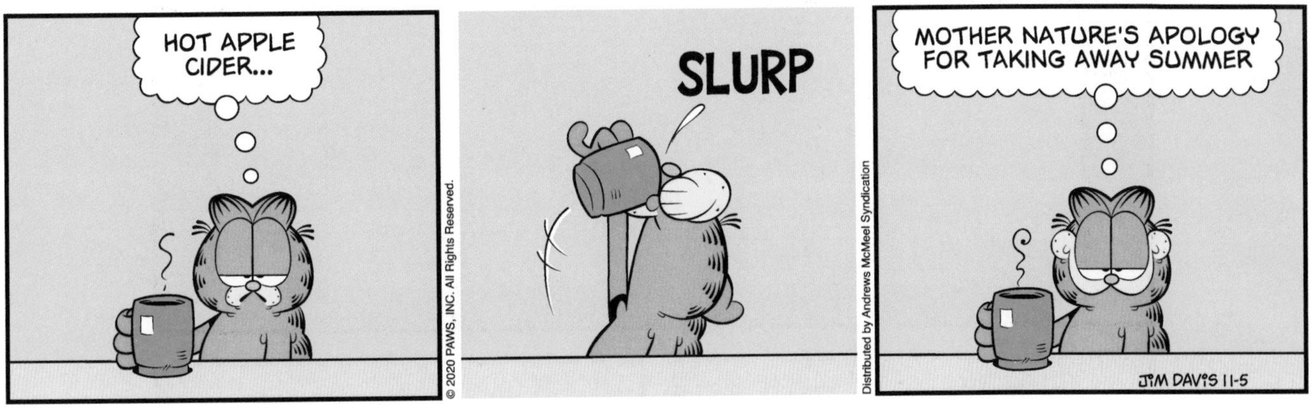
HOT APPLE CIDER...
SLURP
MOTHER NATURE'S APOLOGY FOR TAKING AWAY SUMMER
© 2020 PAWS, INC. All Rights Reserved.
Distributed by Andrews McMeel Syndication
JIM DAVIS 11-5

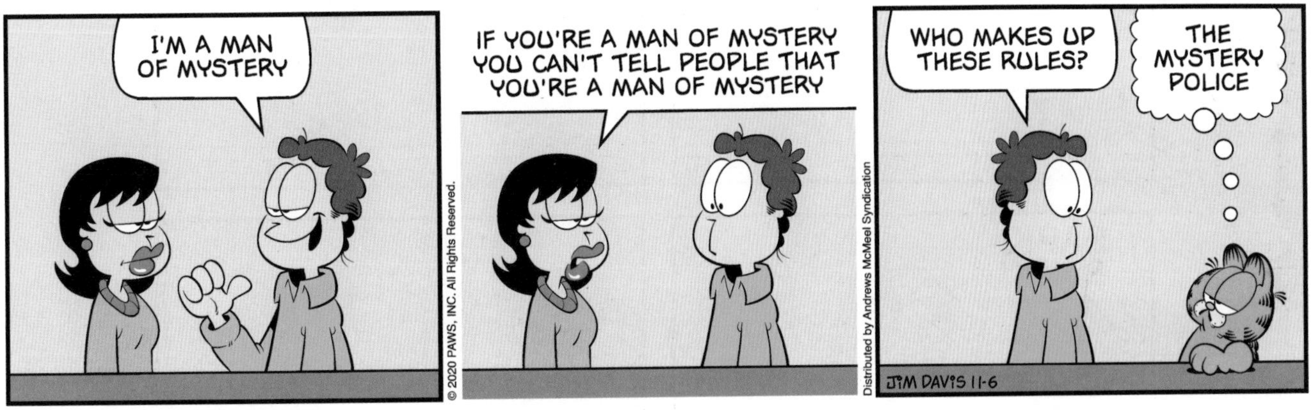
I'M A MAN OF MYSTERY
IF YOU'RE A MAN OF MYSTERY YOU CAN'T TELL PEOPLE THAT YOU'RE A MAN OF MYSTERY
WHO MAKES UP THESE RULES?
THE MYSTERY POLICE
© 2020 PAWS, INC. All Rights Reserved.
Distributed by Andrews McMeel Syndication
JIM DAVIS 11-6

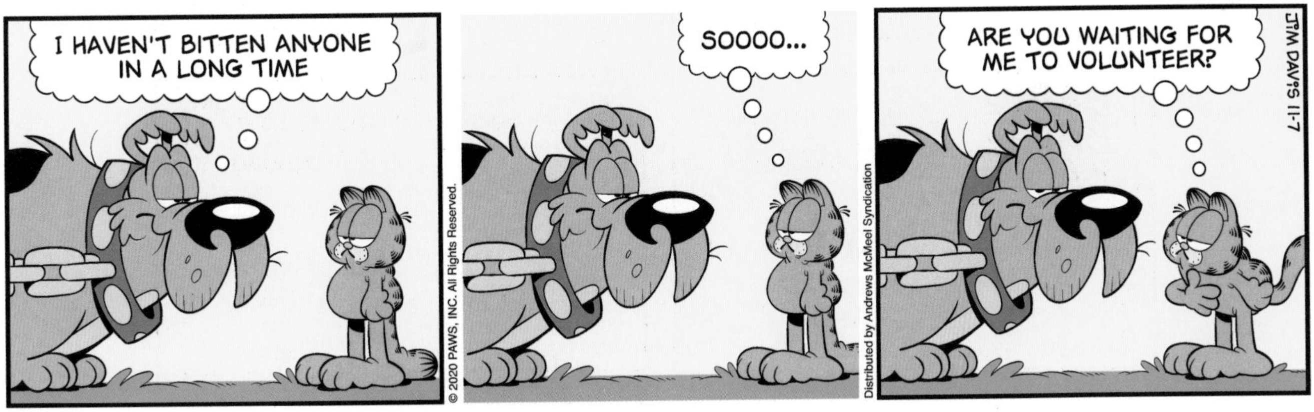
I HAVEN'T BITTEN ANYONE IN A LONG TIME
SOOOO...
ARE YOU WAITING FOR ME TO VOLUNTEER?
© 2020 PAWS, INC. All Rights Reserved.
Distributed by Andrews McMeel Syndication
JIM DAVIS 11-7

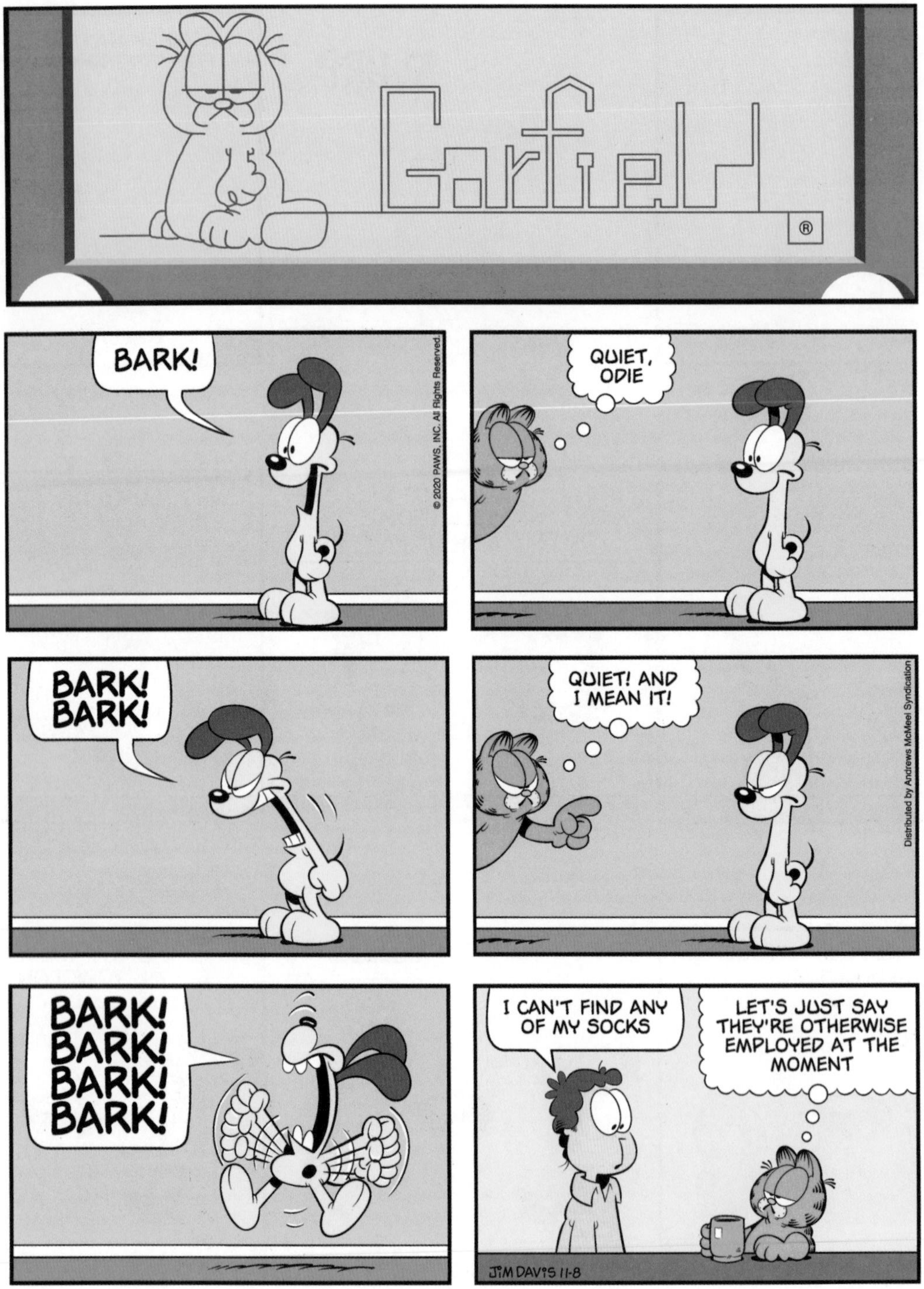
Garfield®
BARK!
© 2020 PAWS, INC. All Rights Reserved.
QUIET, ODIE
BARK! BARK!
QUIET! AND I MEAN IT!
Distributed by Andrews McMeel Syndication
BARK! BARK! BARK! BARK!
I CAN'T FIND ANY OF MY SOCKS
LET'S JUST SAY THEY'RE OTHERWISE EMPLOYED AT THE MOMENT
JIM DAVIS 11-8

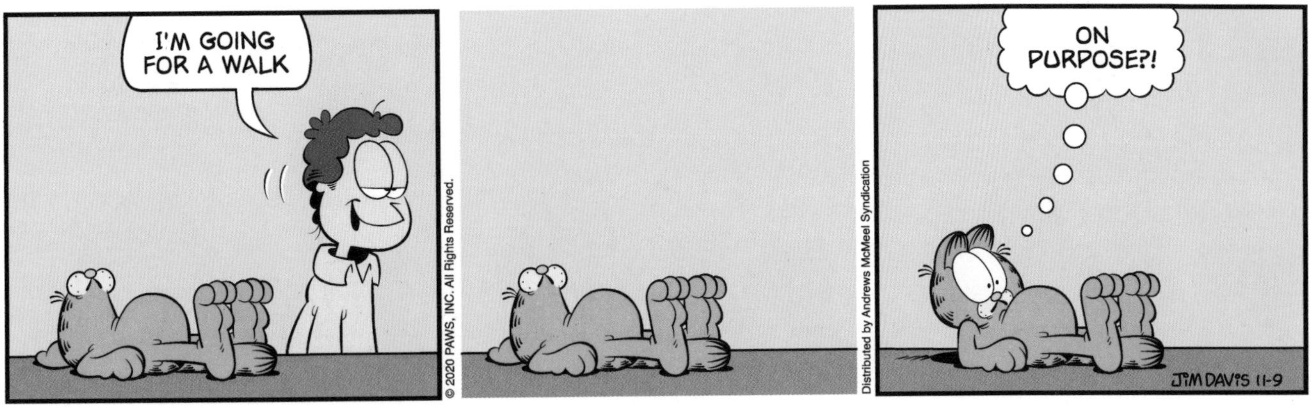
I'M GOING FOR A WALK
ON PURPOSE?!
© 2020 PAWS, INC. All Rights Reserved.
Distributed by Andrews McMeel Syndication
JIM DAVIS 11-9

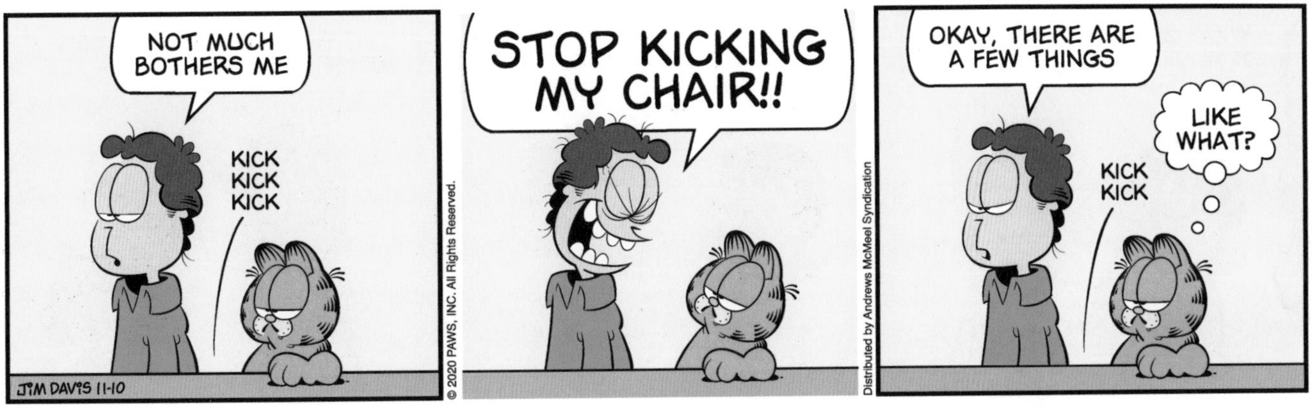
NOT MUCH BOTHERS ME
KICK KICK KICK
JIM DAVIS 11-10
STOP KICKING MY CHAIR!!
© 2020 PAWS, INC. All Rights Reserved.
OKAY, THERE ARE A FEW THINGS
KICK KICK
LIKE WHAT?
Distributed by Andrews McMeel Syndication

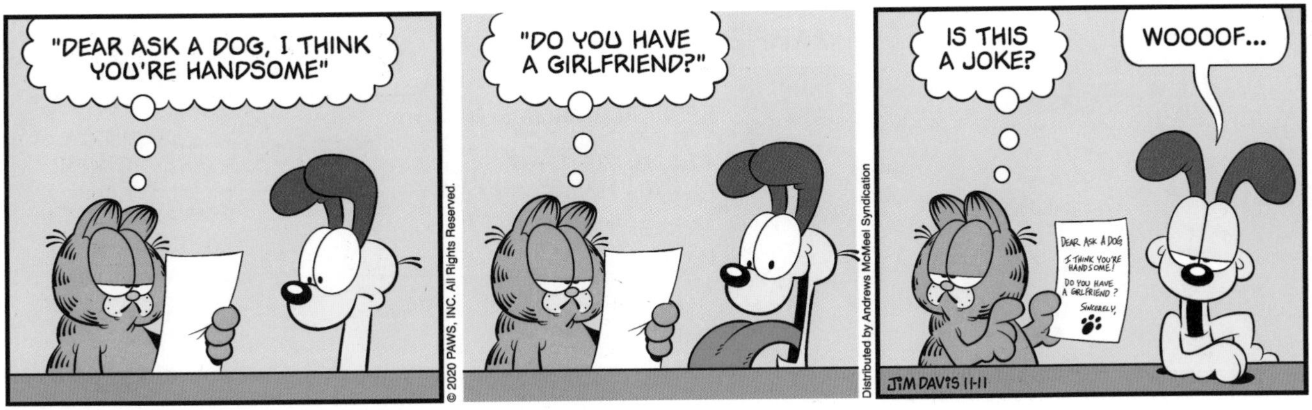
"DEAR ASK A DOG, I THINK YOU'RE HANDSOME"
"DO YOU HAVE A GIRLFRIEND?"
© 2020 PAWS, INC. All Rights Reserved.
IS THIS A JOKE?
WOOOOF...
DEAR ASK A DOG
I THINK YOU'RE HANDSOME!
DO YOU HAVE A GIRLFRIEND ?
SINCERELY,
Distributed by Andrews McMeel Syndication
JIM DAVIS 11-11

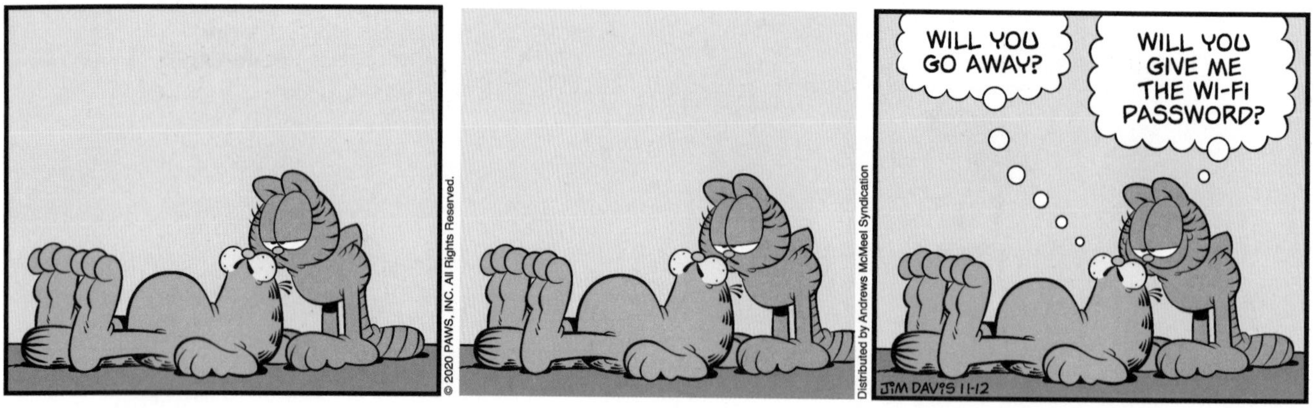
© 2020 PAWS, INC. All Rights Reserved.
Distributed by Andrews McMeel Syndication
WILL YOU GO AWAY?
WILL YOU GIVE ME THE WI-FI PASSWORD?
JIM DAVIS 11-12

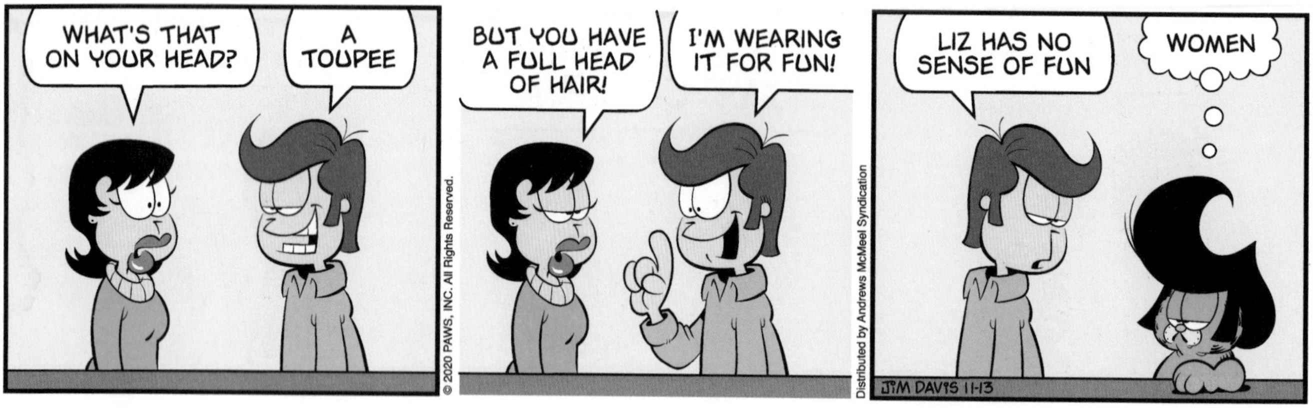
WHAT'S THAT ON YOUR HEAD?
A TOUPEE
© 2020 PAWS, INC. All Rights Reserved.
BUT YOU HAVE A FULL HEAD OF HAIR!
I'M WEARING IT FOR FUN!
Distributed by Andrews McMeel Syndication
LIZ HAS NO SENSE OF FUN
WOMEN
JIM DAVIS 11-13

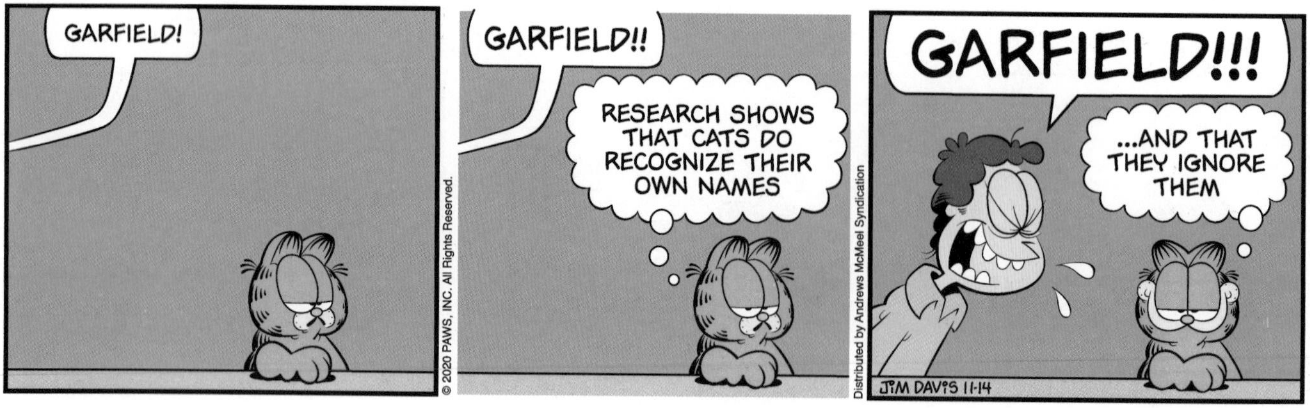
GARFIELD!
© 2020 PAWS, INC. All Rights Reserved.
GARFIELD!!
RESEARCH SHOWS THAT CATS DO RECOGNIZE THEIR OWN NAMES
Distributed by Andrews McMeel Syndication
GARFIELD!!!
...AND THAT THEY IGNORE THEM
JIM DAVIS 11-14

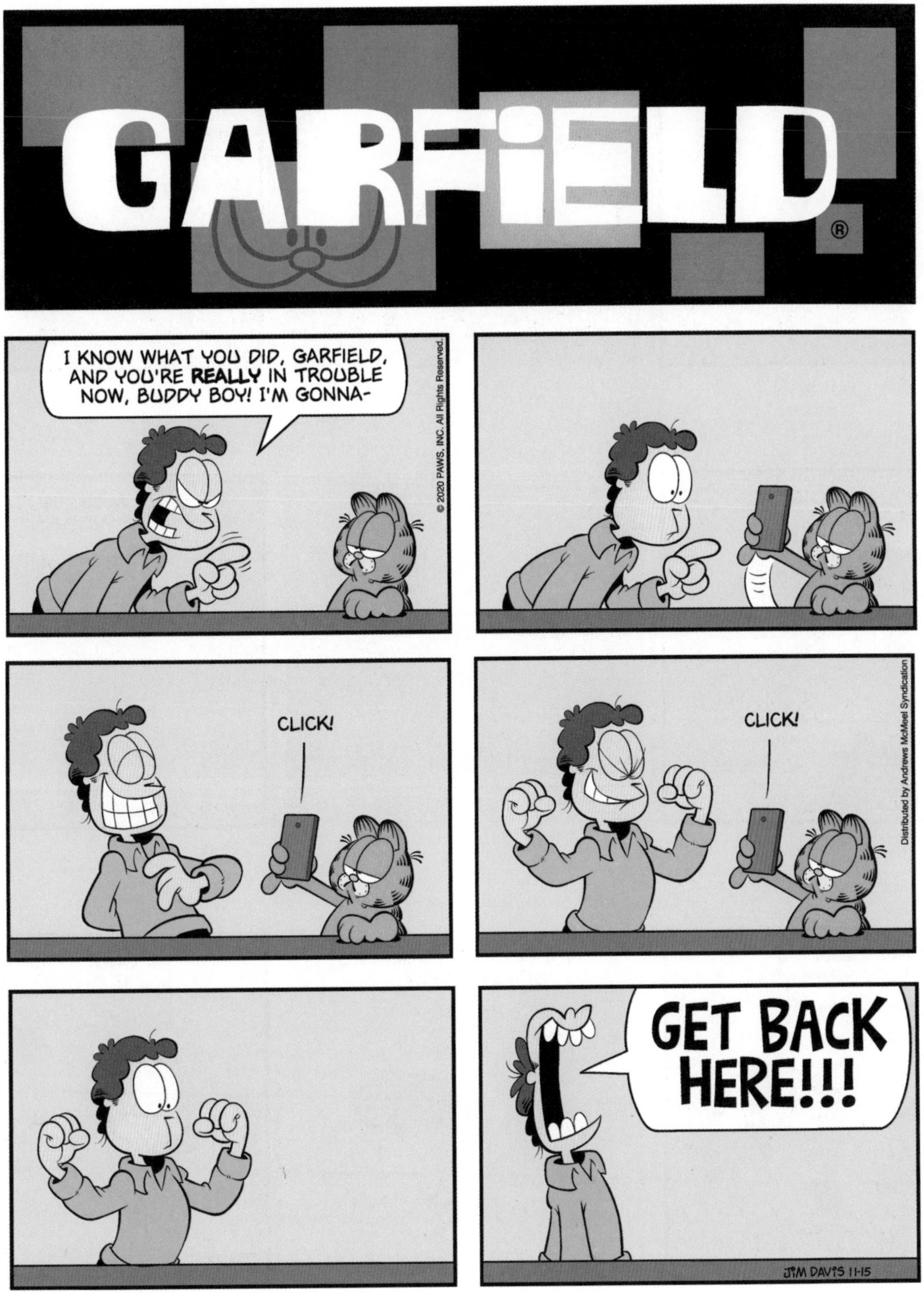

GARFIELD®
I KNOW WHAT YOU DID, GARFIELD, AND YOU'RE REALLY IN TROUBLE NOW, BUDDY BOY! I'M GONNA-
© 2020 PAWS, INC. All Rights Reserved.
CLICK!
CLICK!
Distributed by Andrews McMeel Syndication
GET BACK HERE!!!
JIM DAVIS 11-15

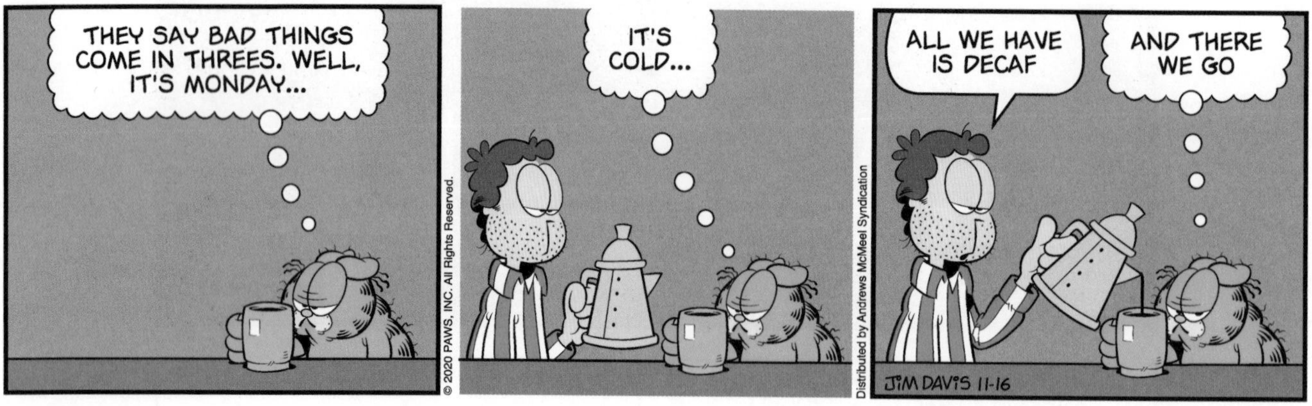
THEY SAY BAD THINGS COME IN THREES. WELL, IT'S MONDAY...
IT'S COLD...
© 2020 PAWS, INC. All Rights Reserved.
ALL WE HAVE IS DECAF
AND THERE WE GO
Distributed by Andrews McMeel Syndication
JIM DAVIS 11-16

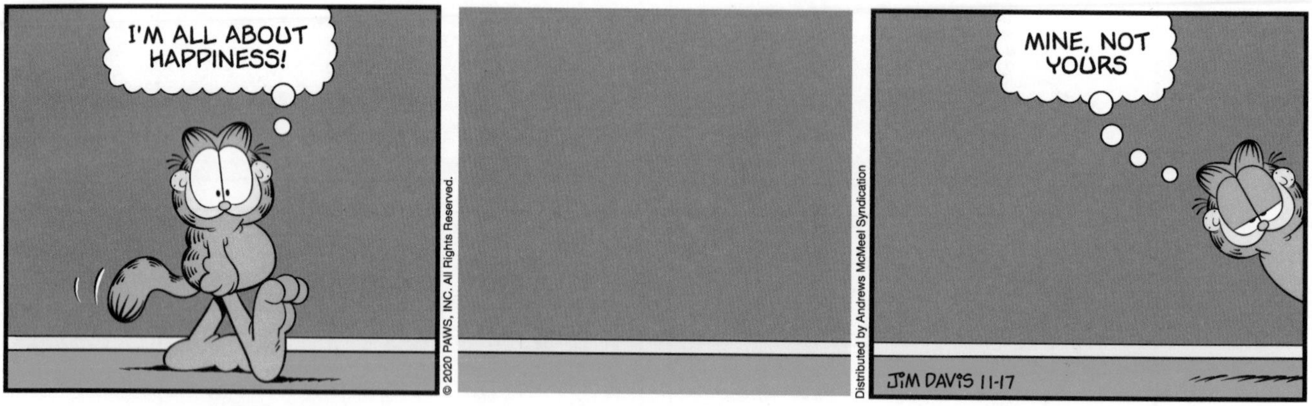
I'M ALL ABOUT HAPPINESS!
© 2020 PAWS, INC. All Rights Reserved.
MINE, NOT YOURS
Distributed by Andrews McMeel Syndication
JIM DAVIS 11-17

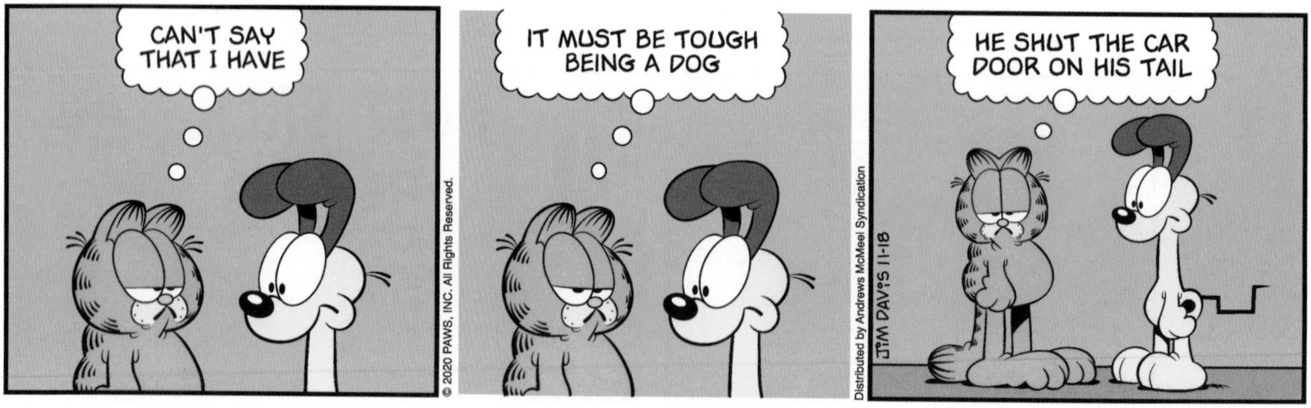
CAN'T SAY THAT I HAVE
© 2020 PAWS, INC. All Rights Reserved.
IT MUST BE TOUGH BEING A DOG
Distributed by Andrews McMeel Syndication
JIM DAVIS 11-18
HE SHUT THE CAR DOOR ON HIS TAIL

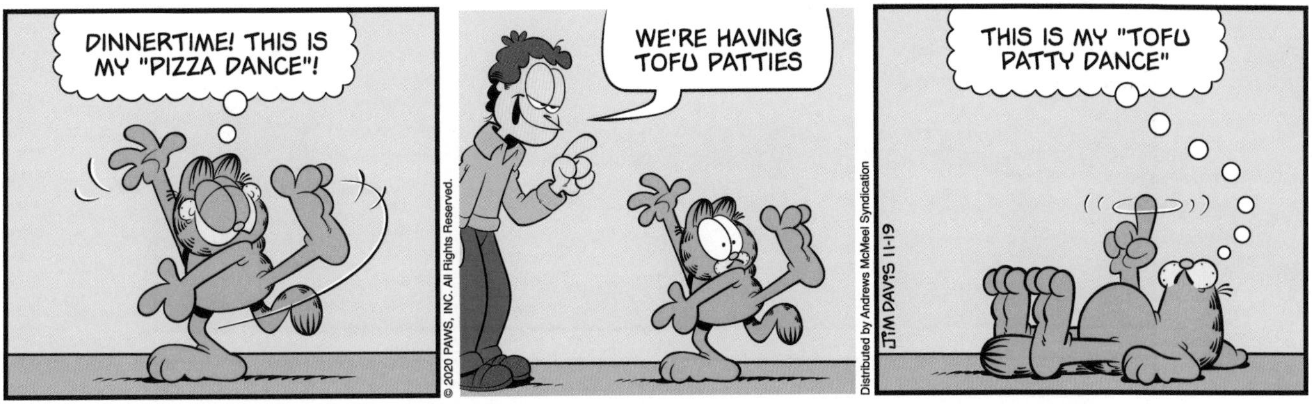
DINNERTIME! THIS IS MY "PIZZA DANCE"!
WE'RE HAVING TOFU PATTIES
THIS IS MY "TOFU PATTY DANCE"
JIM DAVIS 11-19
© 2020 PAWS, INC. All Rights Reserved.
Distributed by Andrews McMeel Syndication

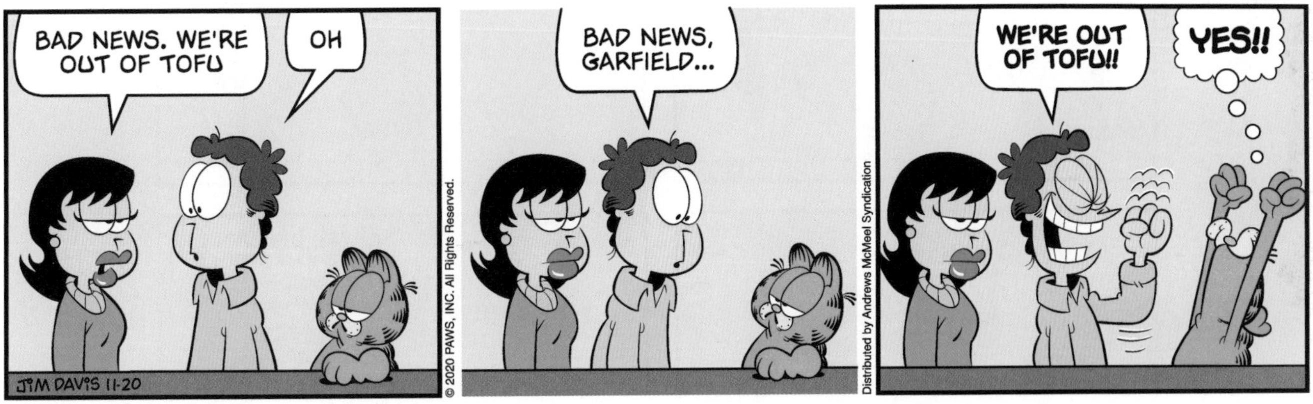
BAD NEWS. WE'RE OUT OF TOFU
OH
BAD NEWS, GARFIELD...
WE'RE OUT OF TOFU!!
YES!!
JIM DAVIS 11-20
© 2020 PAWS, INC. All Rights Reserved.
Distributed by Andrews McMeel Syndication

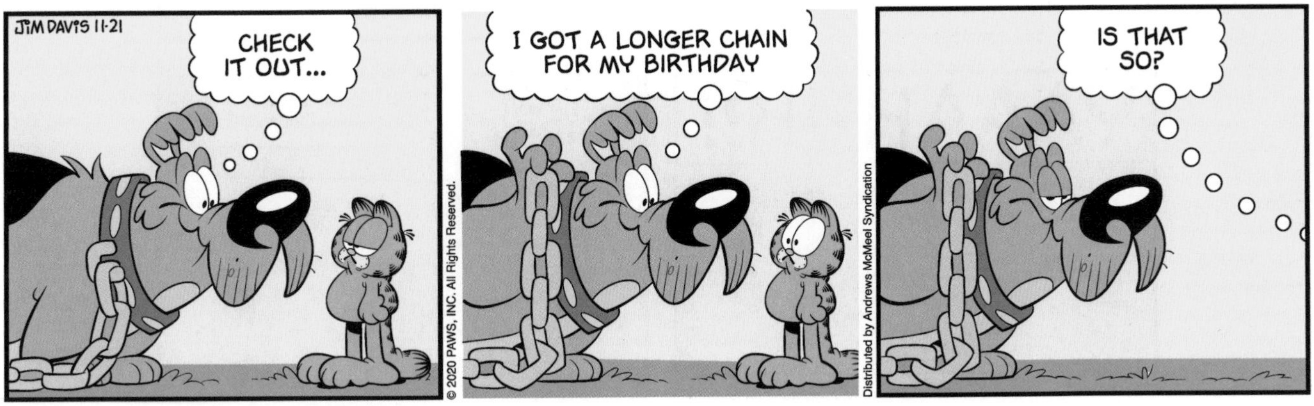
CHECK IT OUT...
I GOT A LONGER CHAIN FOR MY BIRTHDAY
IS THAT SO?
JIM DAVIS 11-21
© 2020 PAWS, INC. All Rights Reserved.
Distributed by Andrews McMeel Syndication

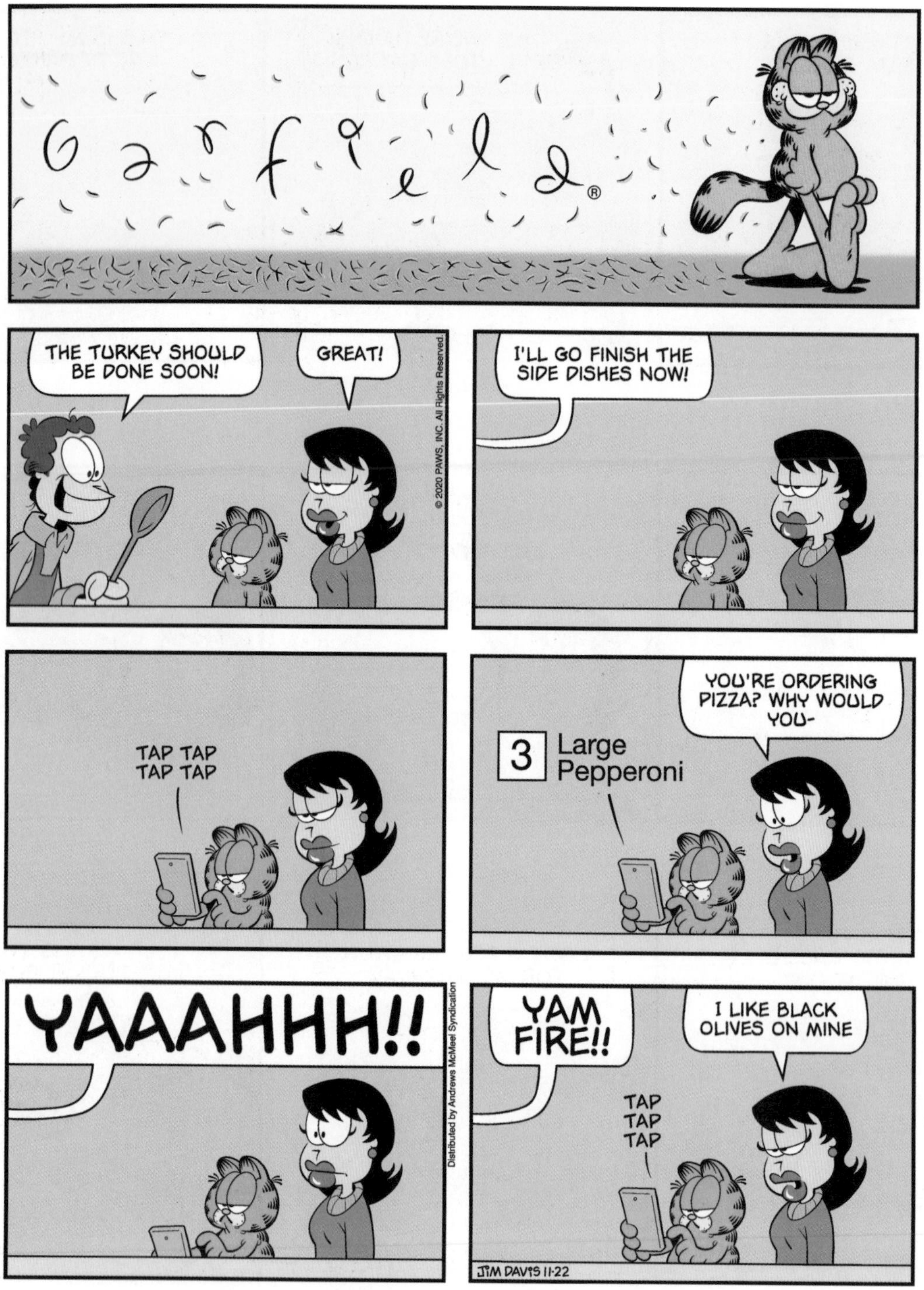
garfield®
THE TURKEY SHOULD BE DONE SOON!
GREAT!
© 2020 PAWS, INC. All Rights Reserved.
I'LL GO FINISH THE SIDE DISHES NOW!
TAP TAP TAP TAP
3 Large Pepperoni
YOU'RE ORDERING PIZZA? WHY WOULD YOU-
YAAAHHH!!
Distributed by Andrews McMeel Syndication
YAM FIRE!!
TAP TAP TAP
I LIKE BLACK OLIVES ON MINE
JIM DAVIS 11-22

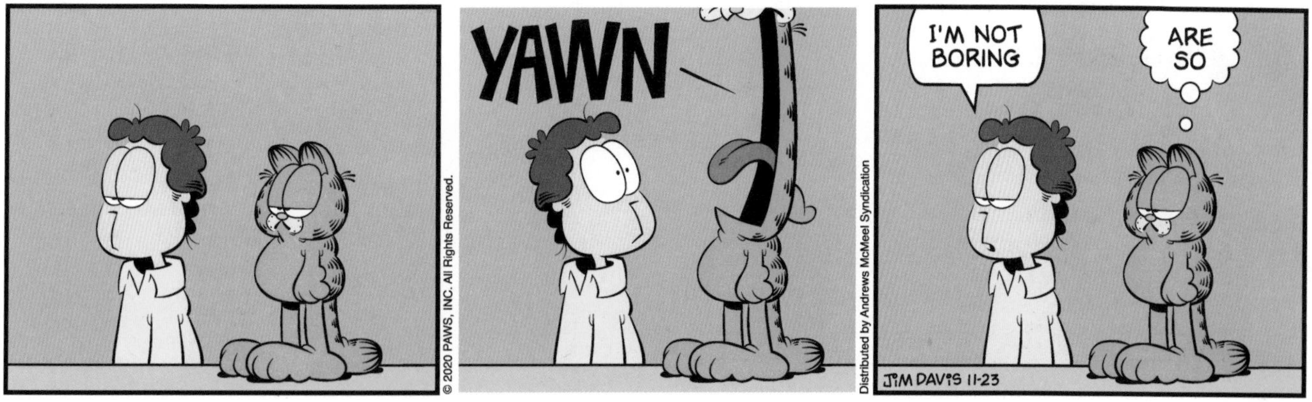
© 2020 PAWS, INC. All Rights Reserved.
YAWN
Distributed by Andrews McMeel Syndication
I'M NOT BORING
ARE SO
JIM DAVIS 11-23

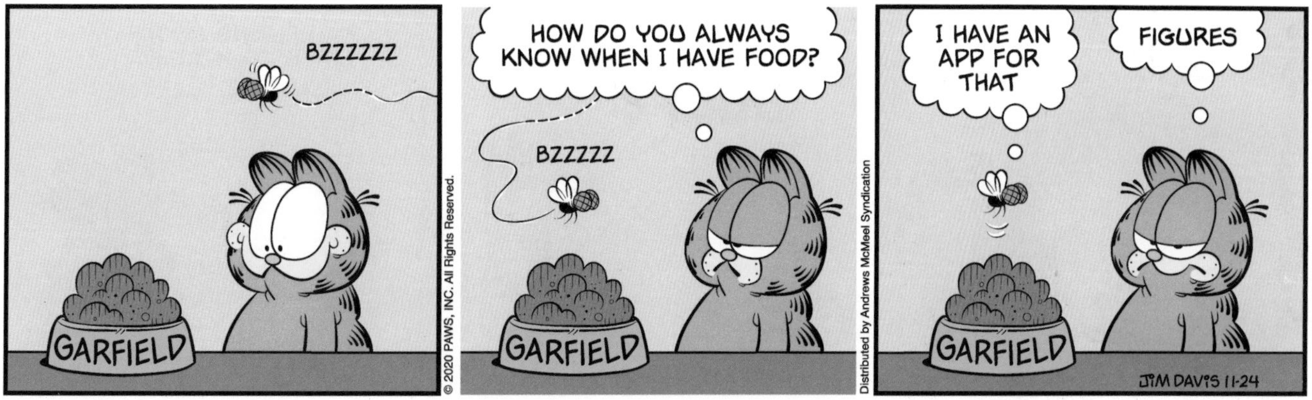
BZZZZZZ
© 2020 PAWS, INC. All Rights Reserved.
GARFIELD
HOW DO YOU ALWAYS KNOW WHEN I HAVE FOOD?
BZZZZZ
GARFIELD
Distributed by Andrews McMeel Syndication
I HAVE AN APP FOR THAT
FIGURES
GARFIELD
JIM DAVIS 11-24

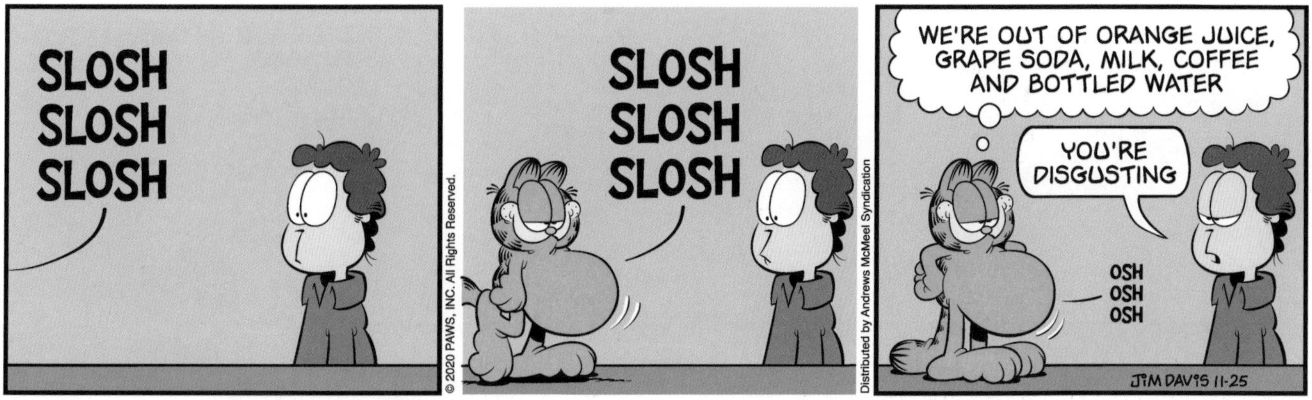
SLOSH
SLOSH
SLOSH
© 2020 PAWS, INC. All Rights Reserved.
SLOSH
SLOSH
SLOSH
Distributed by Andrews McMeel Syndication
WE'RE OUT OF ORANGE JUICE, GRAPE SODA, MILK, COFFEE AND BOTTLED WATER
YOU'RE DISGUSTING
OSH
OSH
OSH
JIM DAVIS 11-25

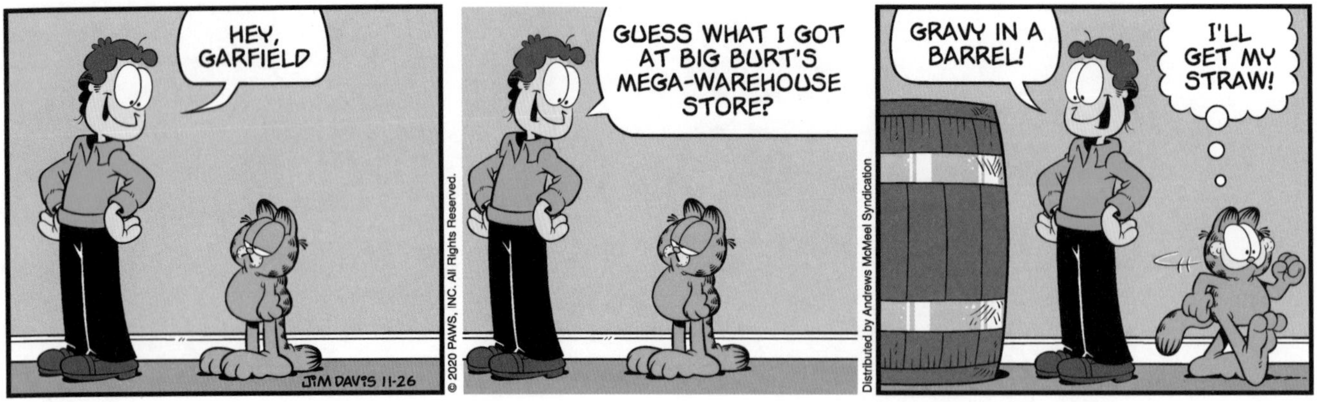
HEY, GARFIELD
JIM DAVIS 11-26
© 2020 PAWS, INC. All Rights Reserved.
GUESS WHAT I GOT AT BIG BURT'S MEGA-WAREHOUSE STORE?
Distributed by Andrews McMeel Syndication
GRAVY IN A BARREL!
I'LL GET MY STRAW!

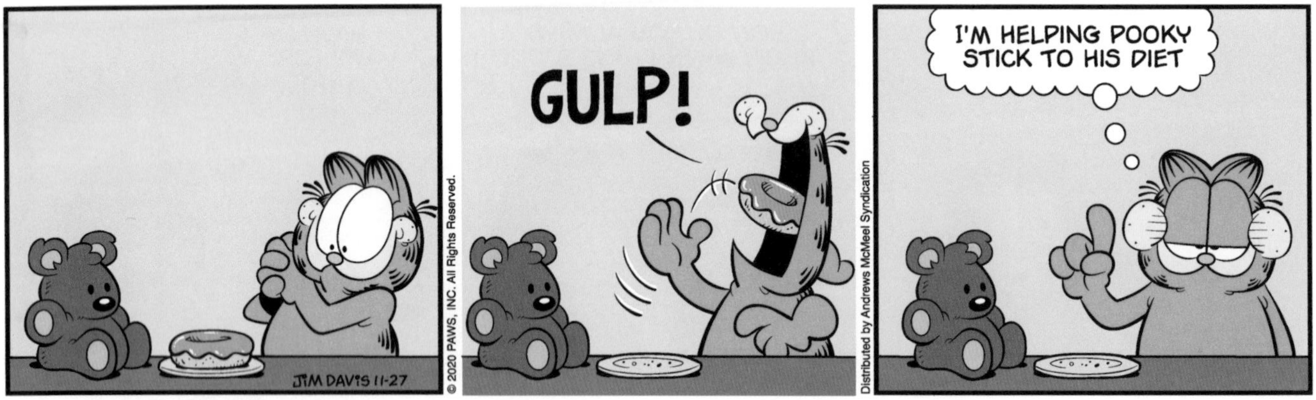
JIM DAVIS 11-27
© 2020 PAWS, INC. All Rights Reserved.
GULP!
Distributed by Andrews McMeel Syndication
I'M HELPING POOKY STICK TO HIS DIET

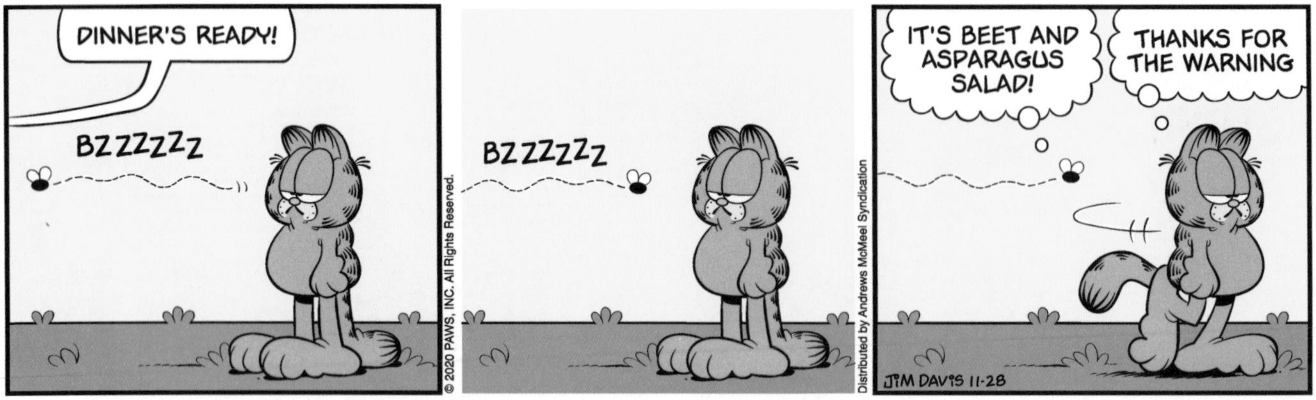
DINNER'S READY!
BZZZZZZ
© 2020 PAWS, INC. All Rights Reserved.
BZZZZZZ
Distributed by Andrews McMeel Syndication
IT'S BEET AND ASPARAGUS SALAD!
THANKS FOR THE WARNING
JIM DAVIS 11-28

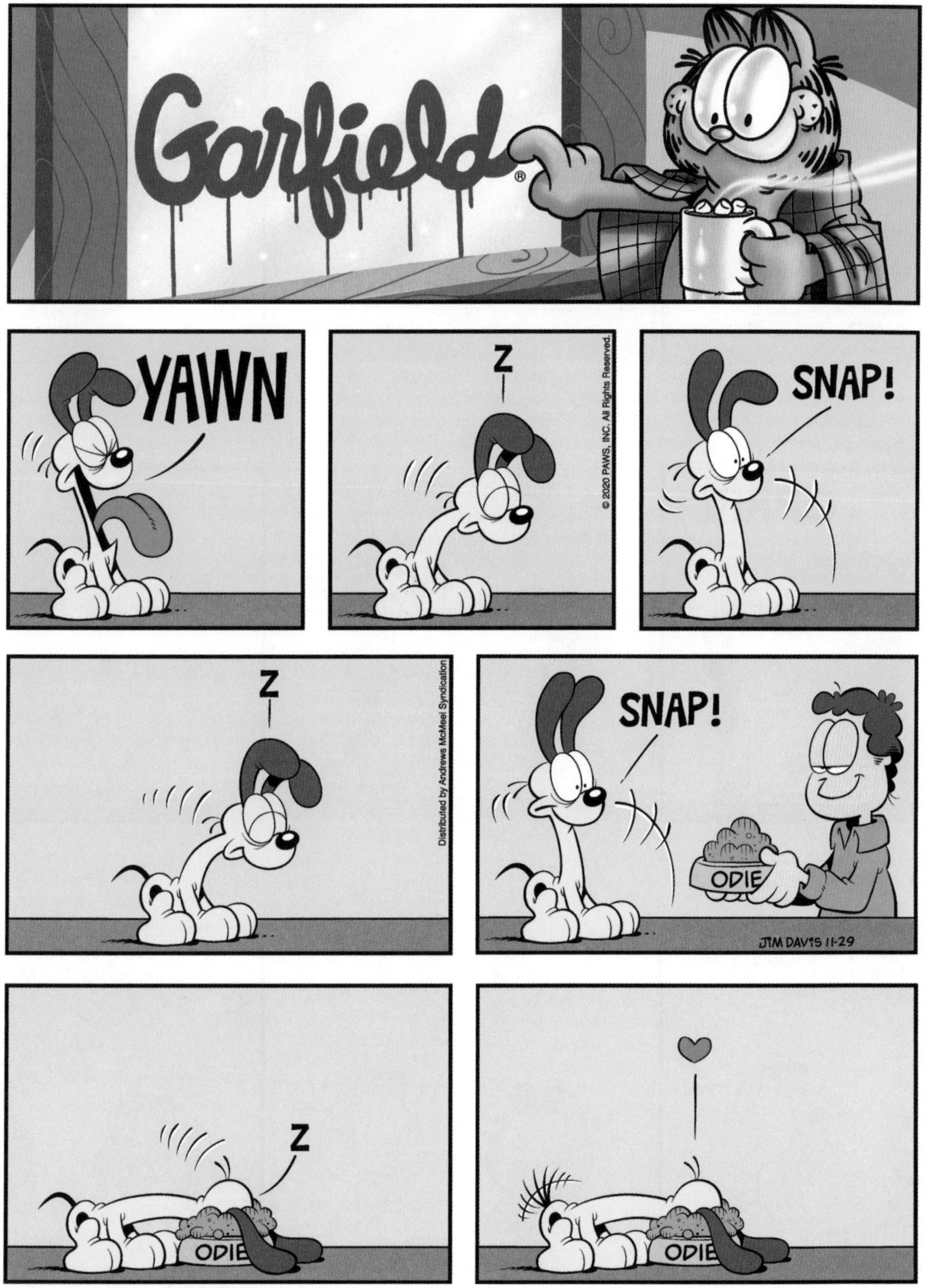
Garfield®
YAWN
Z
SNAP!
© 2020 PAWS, INC. All Rights Reserved.
Z
Distributed by Andrews McMeel Syndication
SNAP!
ODIE
JIM DAVIS 11-29
Z
ODIE
ODIE

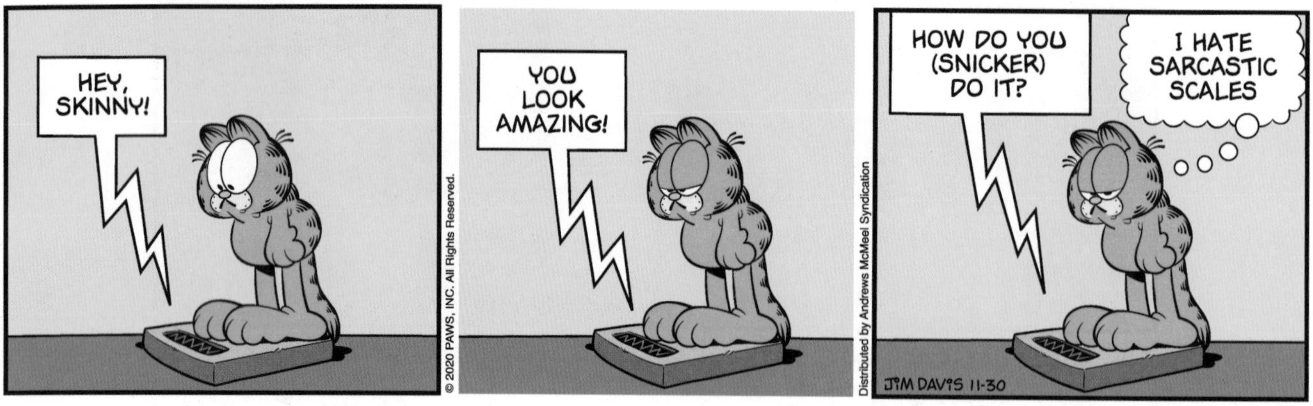
HEY, SKINNY!
YOU LOOK AMAZING!
HOW DO YOU (SNICKER) DO IT?
I HATE SARCASTIC SCALES
JIM DAVIS 11-30
© 2020 PAWS, INC. All Rights Reserved.
Distributed by Andrews McMeel Syndication

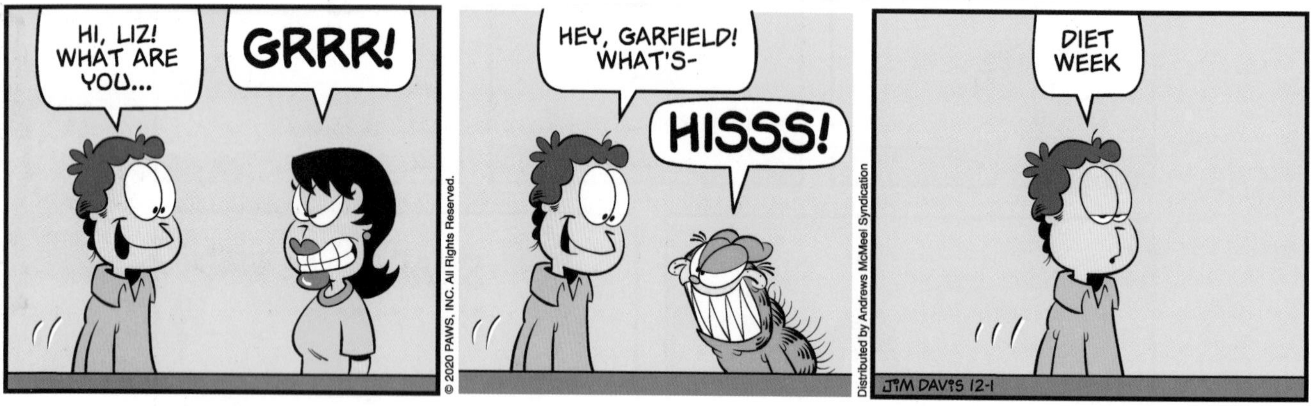
HI, LIZ! WHAT ARE YOU...
GRRR!
HEY, GARFIELD! WHAT'S-
HISSS!
DIET WEEK
JIM DAVIS 12-1
© 2020 PAWS, INC. All Rights Reserved.
Distributed by Andrews McMeel Syndication

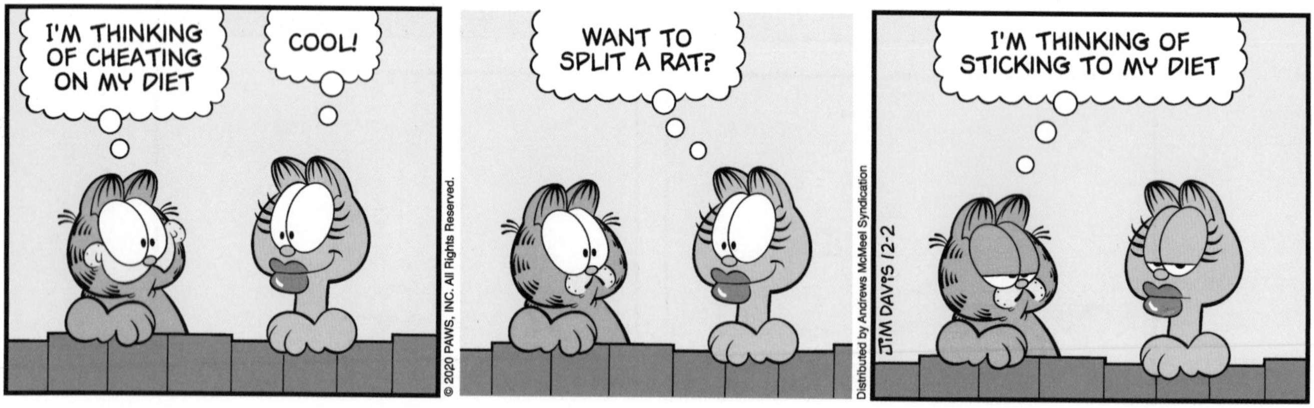
I'M THINKING OF CHEATING ON MY DIET
COOL!
WANT TO SPLIT A RAT?
I'M THINKING OF STICKING TO MY DIET
JIM DAVIS 12-2
© 2020 PAWS, INC. All Rights Reserved.
Distributed by Andrews McMeel Syndication

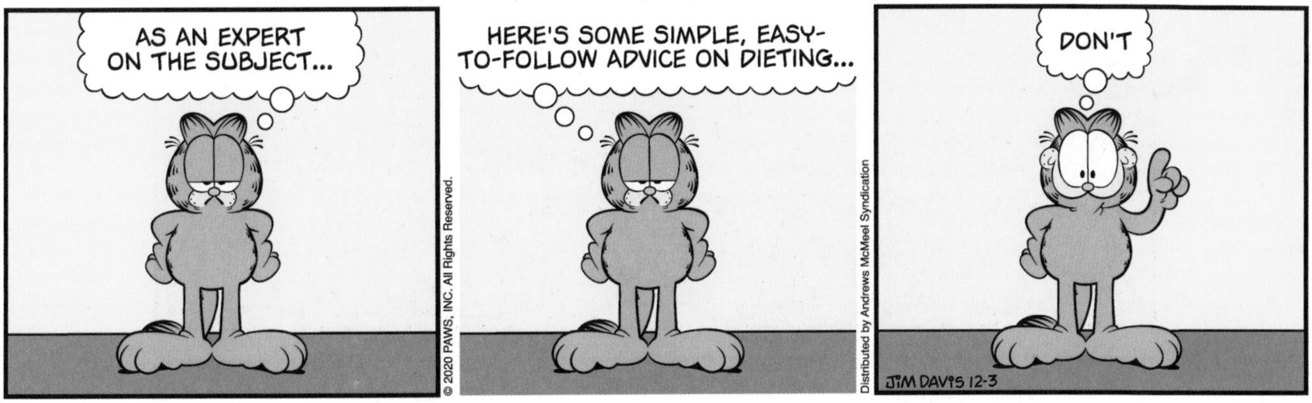
AS AN EXPERT ON THE SUBJECT...
HERE'S SOME SIMPLE, EASY-TO-FOLLOW ADVICE ON DIETING...
DON'T
© 2020 PAWS, INC. All Rights Reserved.
Distributed by Andrews McMeel Syndication
JIM DAVIS 12-3

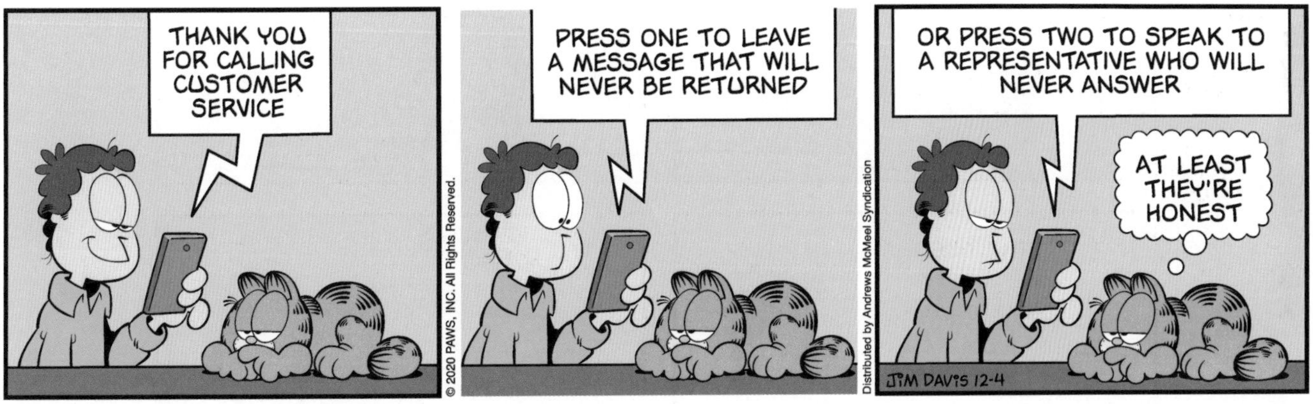
THANK YOU FOR CALLING CUSTOMER SERVICE
PRESS ONE TO LEAVE A MESSAGE THAT WILL NEVER BE RETURNED
OR PRESS TWO TO SPEAK TO A REPRESENTATIVE WHO WILL NEVER ANSWER
AT LEAST THEY'RE HONEST
© 2020 PAWS, INC. All Rights Reserved.
Distributed by Andrews McMeel Syndication
JIM DAVIS 12-4

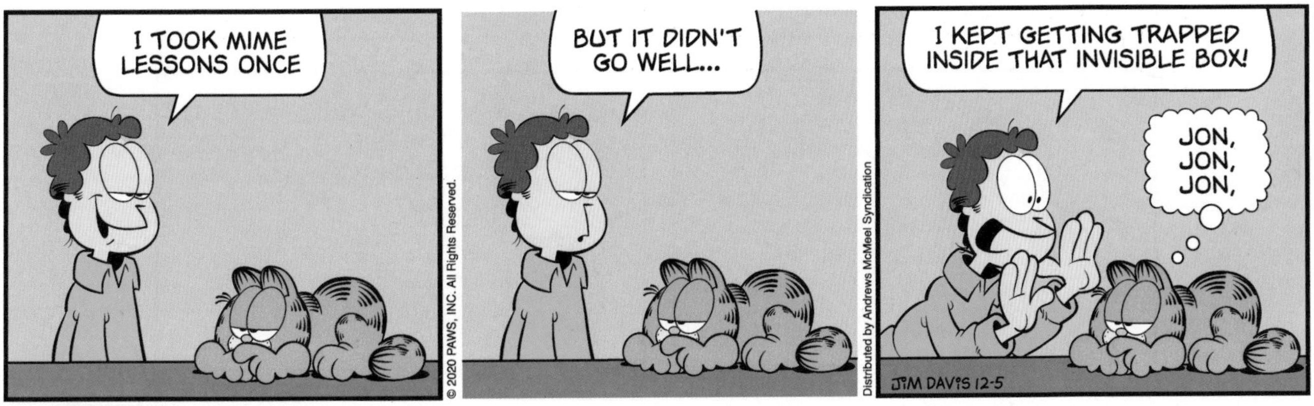
I TOOK MIME LESSONS ONCE
BUT IT DIDN'T GO WELL...
I KEPT GETTING TRAPPED INSIDE THAT INVISIBLE BOX!
JON, JON, JON,
© 2020 PAWS, INC. All Rights Reserved.
Distributed by Andrews McMeel Syndication
JIM DAVIS 12-5

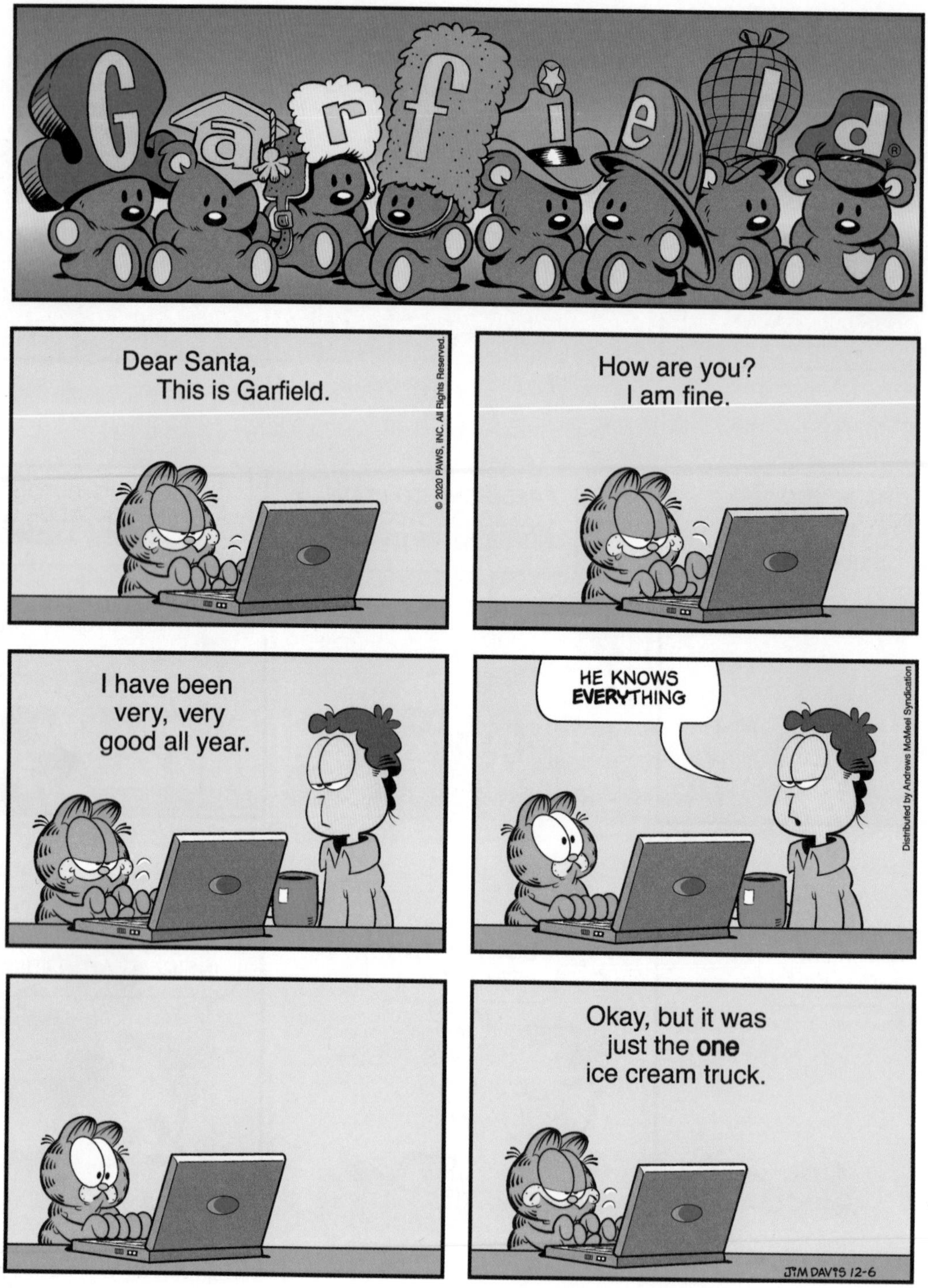

Garfield®
Dear Santa,
This is Garfield.
© 2020 PAWS, INC. All Rights Reserved.
How are you?
I am fine.
I have been
very, very
good all year.
HE KNOWS
EVERYTHING
Distributed by Andrews McMeel Syndication
Okay, but it was
just the **one**
ice cream truck.
JIM DAVIS 12-6

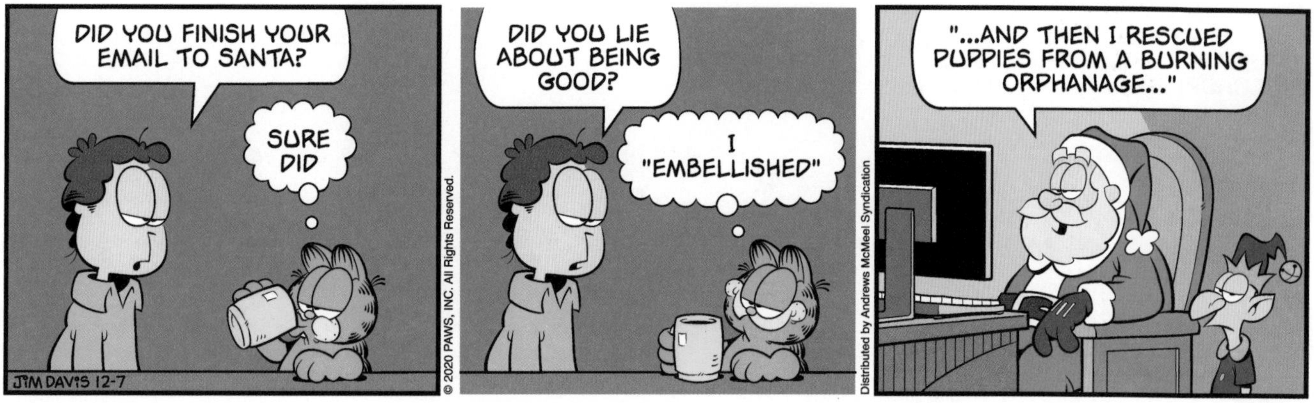
DID YOU FINISH YOUR EMAIL TO SANTA?
SURE DID
JIM DAVIS 12-7
© 2020 PAWS, INC. All Rights Reserved.
DID YOU LIE ABOUT BEING GOOD?
I "EMBELLISHED"
Distributed by Andrews McMeel Syndication
"...AND THEN I RESCUED PUPPIES FROM A BURNING ORPHANAGE..."

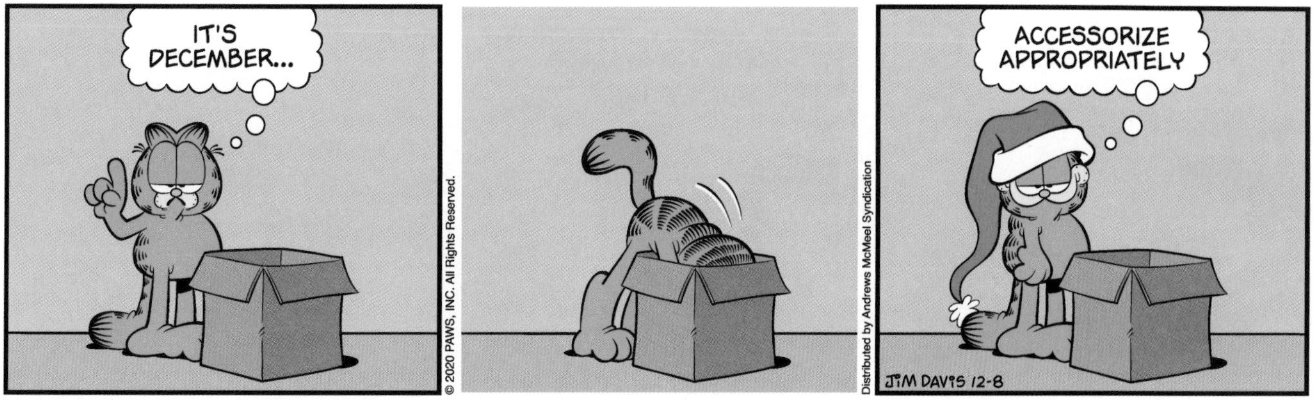
IT'S DECEMBER...
© 2020 PAWS, INC. All Rights Reserved.
Distributed by Andrews McMeel Syndication
ACCESSORIZE APPROPRIATELY
JIM DAVIS 12-8

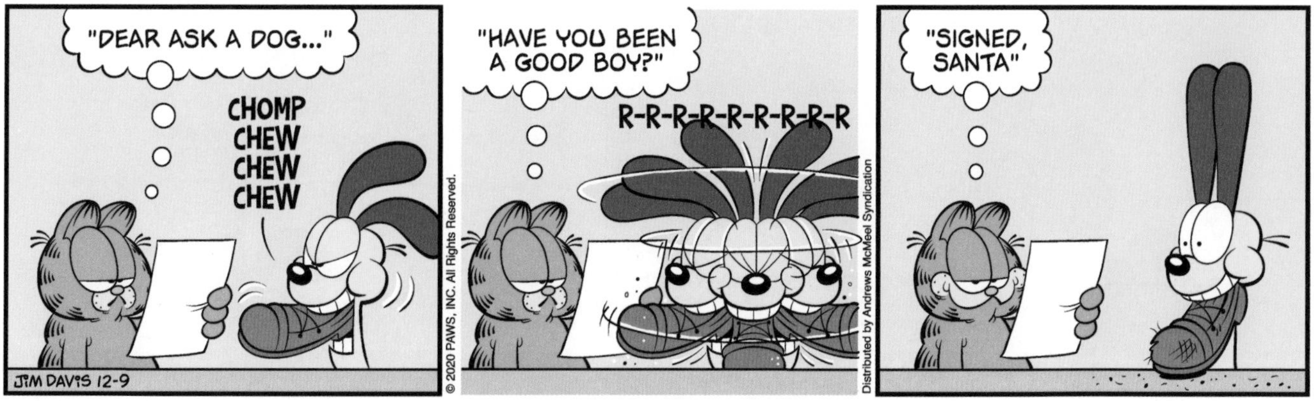
"DEAR ASK A DOG..."
CHOMP CHEW CHEW CHEW
JIM DAVIS 12-9
© 2020 PAWS, INC. All Rights Reserved.
"HAVE YOU BEEN A GOOD BOY?"
R-R-R-R-R-R-R-R-R
Distributed by Andrews McMeel Syndication
"SIGNED, SANTA"

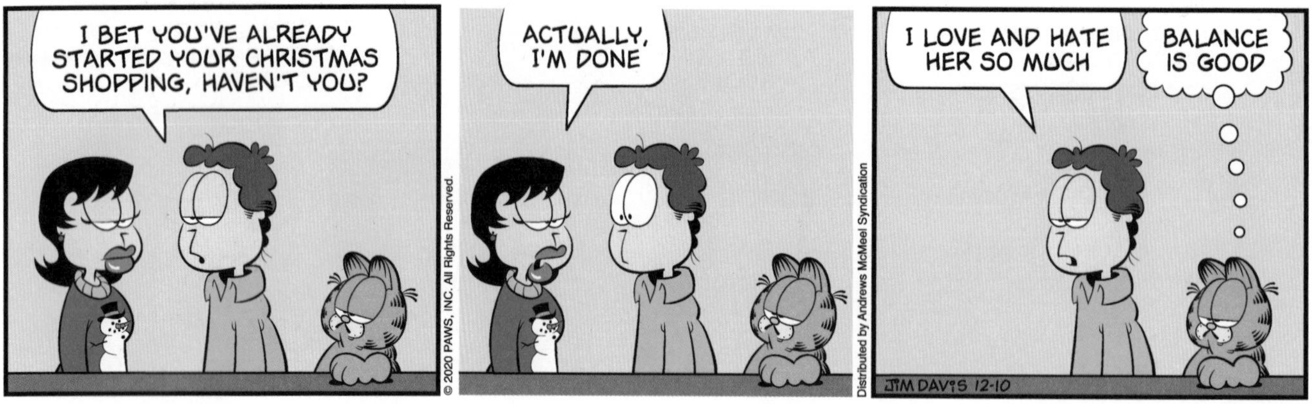
I BET YOU'VE ALREADY STARTED YOUR CHRISTMAS SHOPPING, HAVEN'T YOU?
ACTUALLY, I'M DONE
I LOVE AND HATE HER SO MUCH
BALANCE IS GOOD
JIM DAVIS 12-10
© 2020 PAWS, INC. All Rights Reserved.
Distributed by Andrews McMeel Syndication

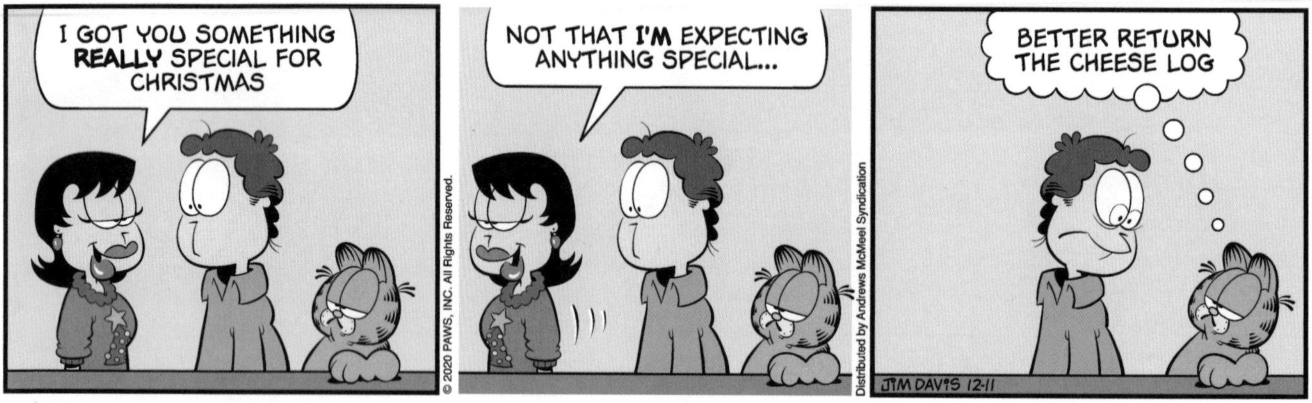
I GOT YOU SOMETHING **REALLY** SPECIAL FOR CHRISTMAS
NOT THAT **I'M** EXPECTING ANYTHING SPECIAL...
BETTER RETURN THE CHEESE LOG
JIM DAVIS 12-11
© 2020 PAWS, INC. All Rights Reserved.
Distributed by Andrews McMeel Syndication

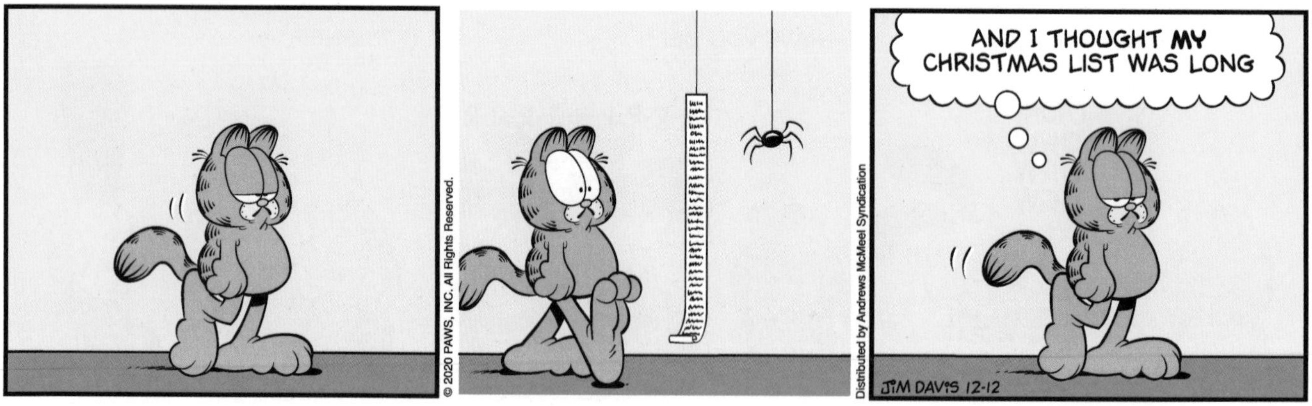
AND I THOUGHT **MY** CHRISTMAS LIST WAS LONG
JIM DAVIS 12-12
© 2020 PAWS, INC. All Rights Reserved.
Distributed by Andrews McMeel Syndication

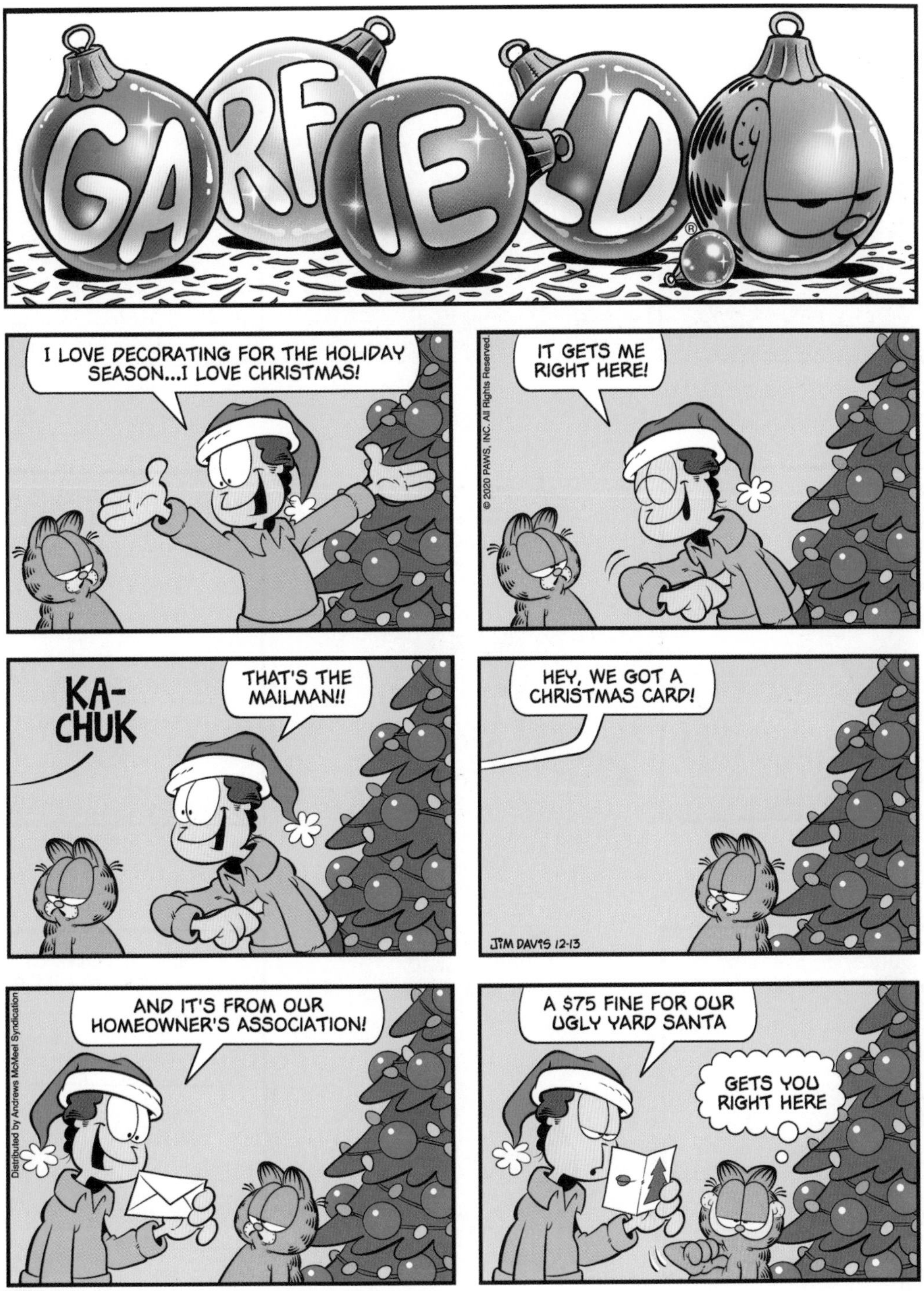
GARFIELD®
I LOVE DECORATING FOR THE HOLIDAY SEASON...I LOVE CHRISTMAS!
© 2020 PAWS, INC. All Rights Reserved.
IT GETS ME RIGHT HERE!
KA-CHUK
THAT'S THE MAILMAN!!
HEY, WE GOT A CHRISTMAS CARD!
JIM DAVIS 12-13
Distributed by Andrews McMeel Syndication
AND IT'S FROM OUR HOMEOWNER'S ASSOCIATION!
A $75 FINE FOR OUR UGLY YARD SANTA
GETS YOU RIGHT HERE

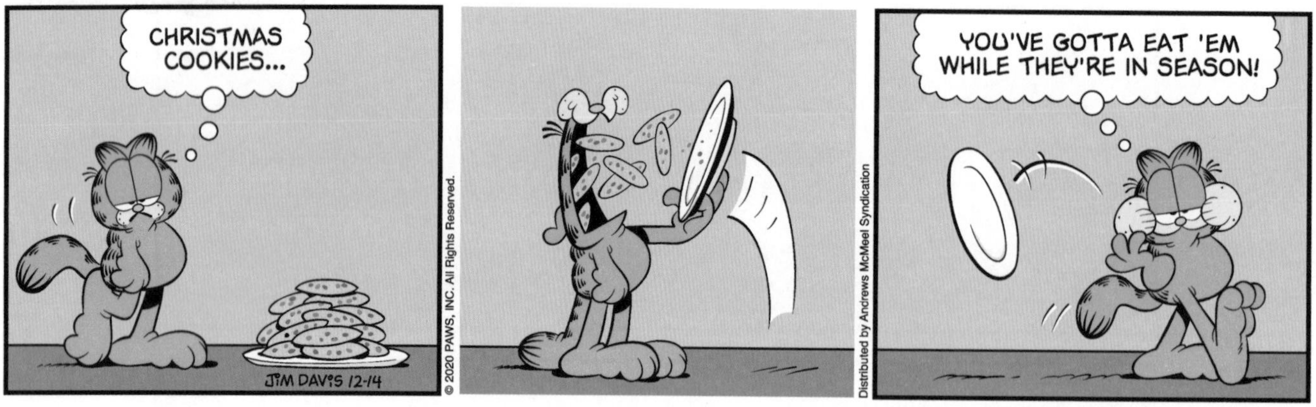
CHRISTMAS COOKIES...
JIM DAVIS 12-14
© 2020 PAWS, INC. All Rights Reserved.
Distributed by Andrews McMeel Syndication
YOU'VE GOTTA EAT 'EM WHILE THEY'RE IN SEASON!

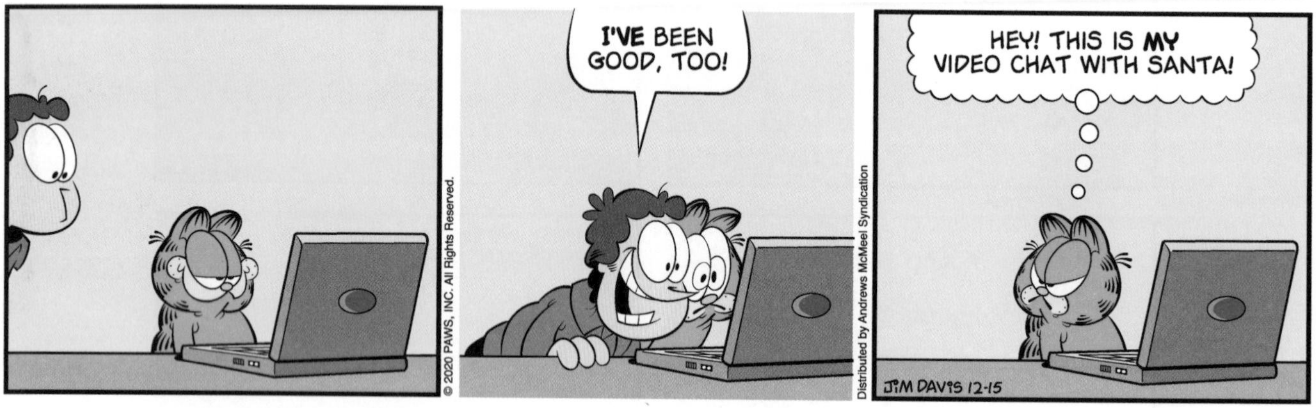
© 2020 PAWS, INC. All Rights Reserved.
I'VE BEEN GOOD, TOO!
Distributed by Andrews McMeel Syndication
HEY! THIS IS **MY** VIDEO CHAT WITH SANTA!
JIM DAVIS 12-15

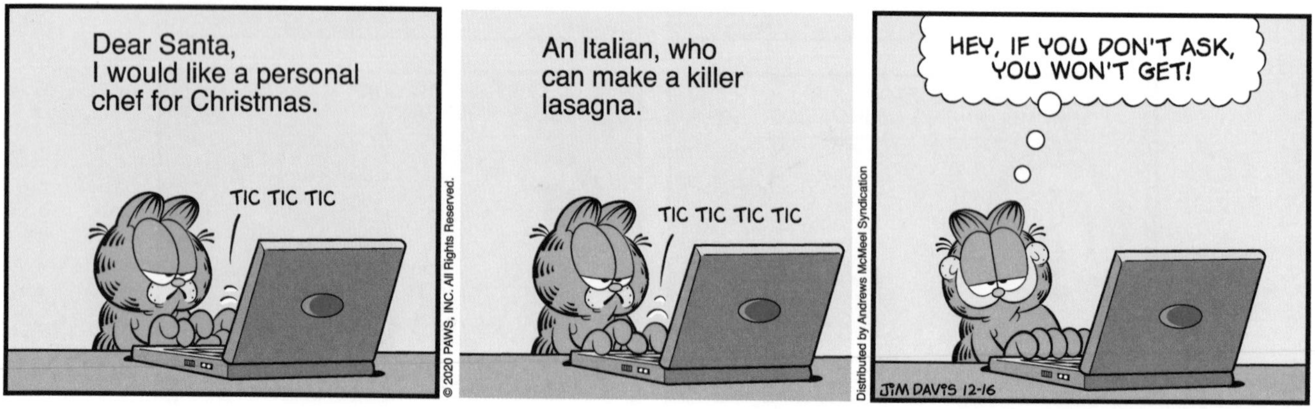
Dear Santa,
I would like a personal chef for Christmas.
TIC TIC TIC
© 2020 PAWS, INC. All Rights Reserved.
An Italian, who can make a killer lasagna.
TIC TIC TIC TIC
Distributed by Andrews McMeel Syndication
HEY, IF YOU DON'T ASK, YOU WON'T GET!
JIM DAVIS 12-16

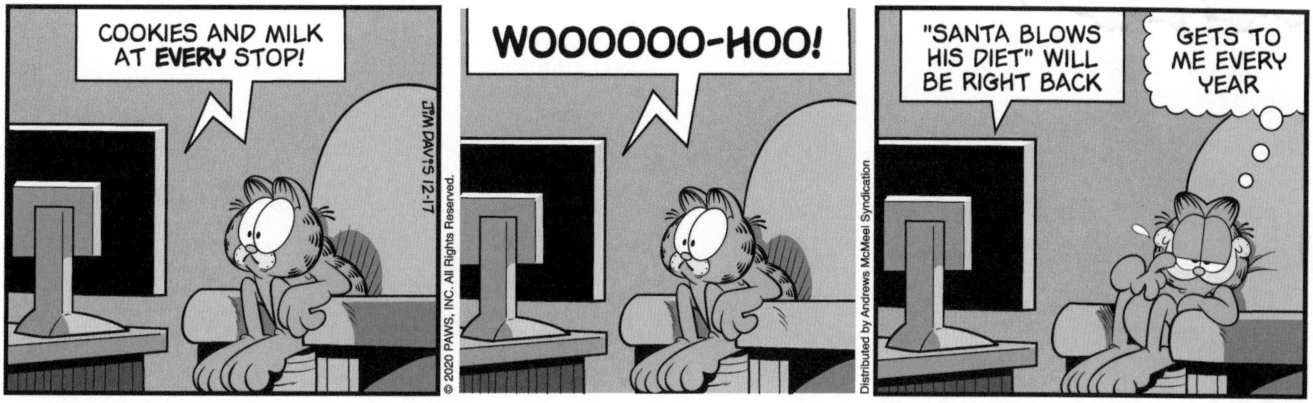
COOKIES AND MILK AT **EVERY** STOP!
JIM DAVIS 12-17
© 2020 PAWS, INC. All Rights Reserved.
WOOOOOO-HOO!
Distributed by Andrews McMeel Syndication
"SANTA BLOWS HIS DIET" WILL BE RIGHT BACK
GETS TO ME EVERY YEAR

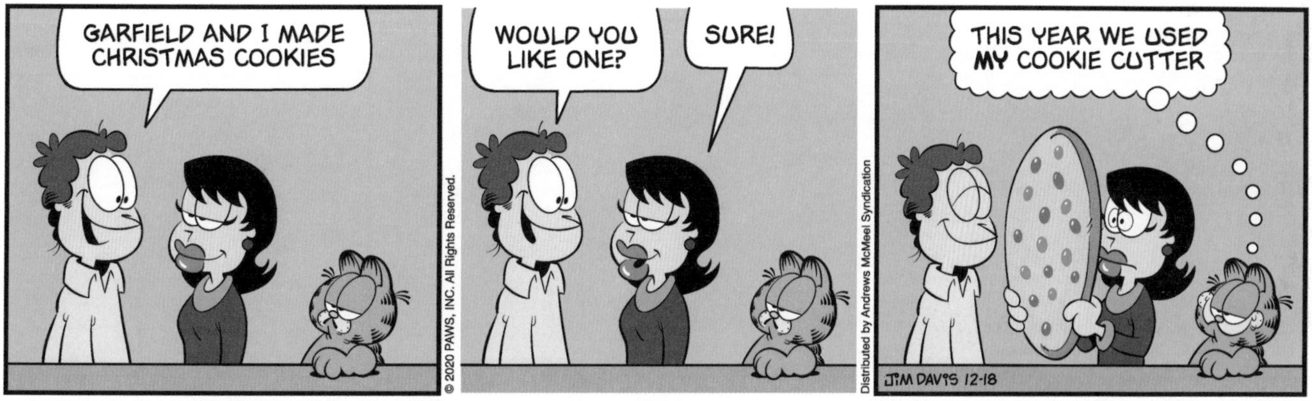
GARFIELD AND I MADE CHRISTMAS COOKIES
© 2020 PAWS, INC. All Rights Reserved.
WOULD YOU LIKE ONE?
SURE!
Distributed by Andrews McMeel Syndication
THIS YEAR WE USED **MY** COOKIE CUTTER
JIM DAVIS 12-18

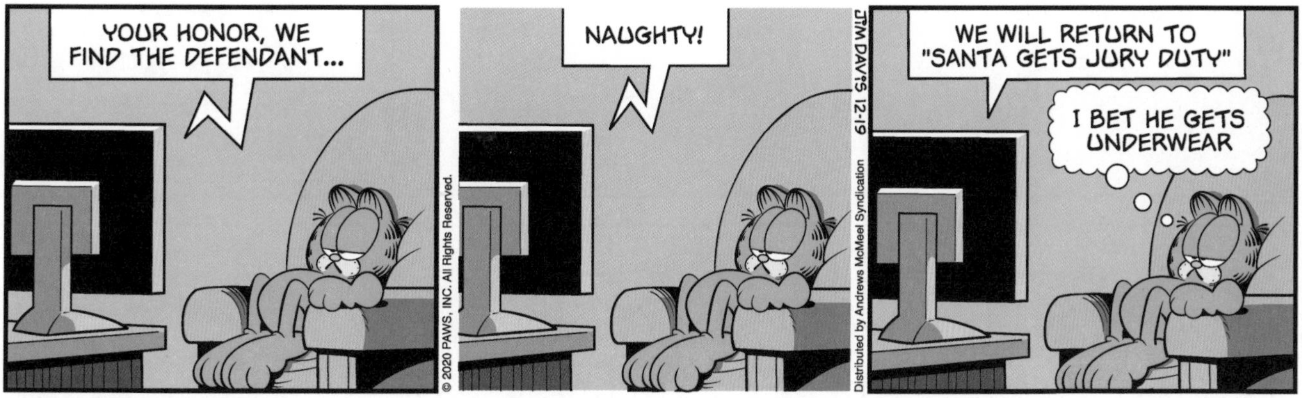
YOUR HONOR, WE FIND THE DEFENDANT...
© 2020 PAWS, INC. All Rights Reserved.
NAUGHTY!
JIM DAVIS 12-19
Distributed by Andrews McMeel Syndication
WE WILL RETURN TO "SANTA GETS JURY DUTY"
I BET HE GETS UNDERWEAR

BEWARE SUNDAY DRIVERS!

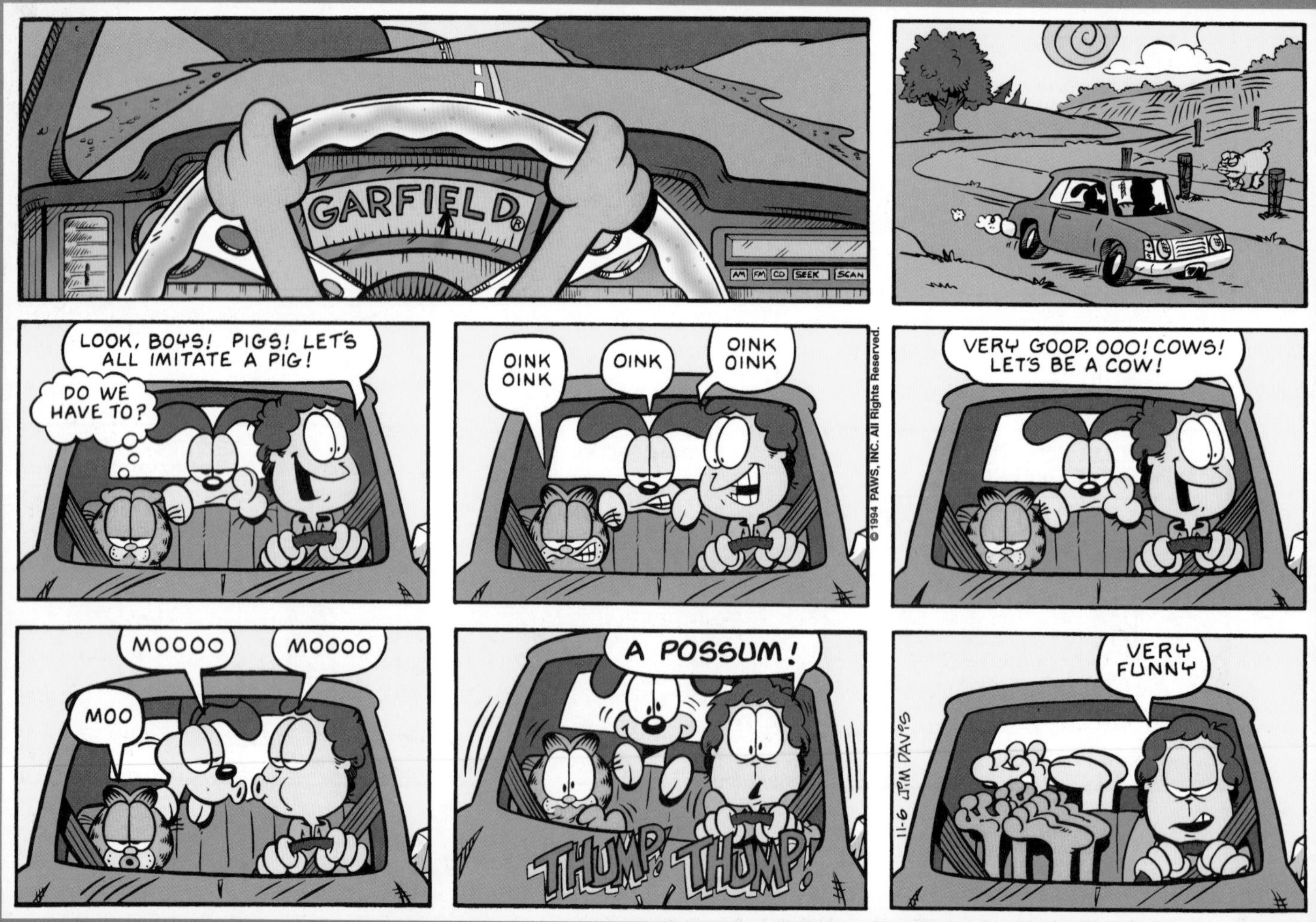
GARFIELD
AM FM CD SEEK SCAN
LOOK, BOYS! PIGS! LET'S ALL IMITATE A PIG!
DO WE HAVE TO?
OINK OINK
OINK
OINK OINK
© 1994 PAWS, INC. All Rights Reserved.
VERY GOOD. OOO! COWS! LET'S BE A COW!
MOO
MOOOO
MOOOO
A POSSUM!
THUMP! THUMP!
VERY FUNNY

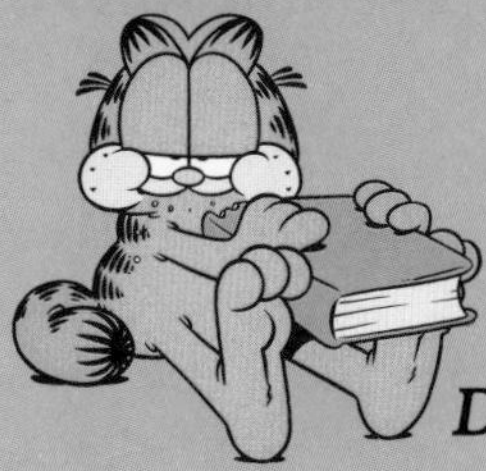

STRIPS, SPECIALS OR BESTSELLING BOOKS...

GARFIELD'S ON EVERYONE'S MENU.

Don't miss even one episode in the Tubby Tabby's hilarious series!

Title	No.	ISBN
✿ GARFIELD AT LARGE	(#1)	978-0-345-44382-3
✿ GARFIELD GAINS WEIGHT	(#2)	978-0-345-44975-7
✿ GARFIELD BIGGER THAN LIFE	(#3)	978-0-345-45027-2
✿ GARFIELD WEIGHS IN	(#4)	978-0-345-45205-4
✿ GARFIELD TAKES THE CAKE	(#5)	978-0-345-44978-8
✿ GARFIELD EATS HIS HEART OUT	(#6)	978-0-345-46459-0
✿ GARFIELD SITS AROUND THE HOUSE	(#7)	978-0-345-46463-7
✿ GARFIELD TIPS THE SCALES	(#8)	978-0-345-46909-0
✿ GARFIELD LOSES HIS FEET	(#9)	978-0-345-46467-5
✿ GARFIELD MAKES IT BIG	(#10)	978-0-345-46468-2
✿ GARFIELD ROLLS ON	(#11)	978-0-345-47561-9
✿ GARFIELD OUT TO LUNCH	(#12)	978-0-345-47562-6
✿ GARFIELD FOOD FOR THOUGHT	(#13)	978-0-345-47563-3
✿ GARFIELD SWALLOWS HIS PRIDE	(#14)	978-0-345-91386-9
✿ GARFIELD WORLDWIDE	(#15)	978-0-345-91754-6
✿ GARFIELD ROUNDS OUT	(#16)	978-0-345-49169-5
✿ GARFIELD CHEWS THE FAT	(#17)	978-0-345-49170-1
✿ GARFIELD GOES TO WAIST	(#18)	978-0-345-49173-2
✿ GARFIELD HANGS OUT	(#19)	978-0-345-49174-9
✿ GARFIELD TAKES UP SPACE	(#20)	978-0-345-49178-7
✿ GARFIELD SAYS A MOUTHFUL	(#21)	978-0-345-49179-4
✿ GARFIELD BY THE POUND	(#22)	978-0-345-52558-1
✿ GARFIELD KEEPS HIS CHINS UP	(#23)	978-0-345-52559-8
✿ GARFIELD TAKES HIS LICKS	(#24)	978-0-345-52587-1
✿ GARFIELD HITS THE BIG TIME	(#25)	978-0-345-52589-5
✿ GARFIELD PULLS HIS WEIGHT	(#26)	978-0-345-52594-9
✿ GARFIELD DISHES IT OUT	(#27)	978-0-345-52595-6
✿ GARFIELD LIFE IN THE FAT LANE	(#28)	978-0-345-52600-7
✿ GARFIELD TONS OF FUN	(#29)	978-0-345-52601-4
✿ GARFIELD BIGGER AND BETTER	(#30)	978-0-345-52605-2
✿ GARFIELD HAMS IT UP	(#31)	978-0-345-52606-9
✿ GARFIELD THINKS BIG	(#32)	978-0-425-28516-9
✿ GARFIELD THROWS HIS WEIGHT AROUND	(#33)	978-0-425-28559-6
✿ GARFIELD LIFE TO THE FULLEST	(#34)	978-0-425-28564-0
✿ GARFIELD FEEDS THE KITTY	(#35)	978-0-425-28569-5
✿ GARFIELD HOGS THE SPOTLIGHT	(#36)	978-0-425-28574-9
GARFIELD BEEFS UP	(#37)	978-0-345-44109-6
GARFIELD GETS COOKIN'	(#38)	978-0-345-44582-7
GARFIELD EATS CROW	(#39)	978-0-345-45201-6
GARFIELD SURVIVAL OF THE FATTEST	(#40)	978-0-345-46458-3
GARFIELD OLDER AND WIDER	(#41)	978-0-345-46462-0
GARFIELD PIGS OUT	(#42)	978-0-345-46466-8
GARFIELD BLOTS OUT THE SUN	(#43)	978-0-345-46615-0
GARFIELD GOES BANANAS	(#44)	978-0-345-91346-3
GARFIELD LARGE & IN CHARGE	(#45)	978-0-345-49172-5
GARFIELD SPILLS THE BEANS	(#46)	978-0-345-49177-0
GARFIELD GETS HIS JUST DESSERTS	(#47)	978-0-345-91387-6
GARFIELD WILL EAT FOR FOOD	(#48)	978-0-345-49176-3
GARFIELD WEIGHS HIS OPTIONS	(#49)	978-0-345-49181-7
GARFIELD POTBELLY OF GOLD	(#50)	978-0-345-52244-3
GARFIELD SHOVELS IT IN	(#51)	978-0-345-52419-5
GARFIELD LARD OF THE JUNGLE	(#52)	978-0-345-52584-0
GARFIELD BRINGS HOME THE BACON	(#53)	978-0-345-52586-4
GARFIELD GETS IN A PICKLE	(#54)	978-0-345-52590-1
GARFIELD SINGS FOR HIS SUPPER	(#55)	978-0-345-52593-2
GARFIELD CAUTION: WIDE LOAD	(#56)	978-0-345-52596-3
GARFIELD SOUPED UP	(#57)	978-0-345-52598-7
GARFIELD GOES TO HIS HAPPY PLACE	(#58)	978-0-345-52602-1
GARFIELD THE BIG CHEESE	(#59)	978-0-345-52604-5
GARFIELD CLEANS HIS PLATE	(#60)	978-0-345-52608-3
GARFIELD CHICKENS OUT	(#61)	978-0-425-28515-2
GARFIELD LISTENS TO HIS GUT	(#62)	978-0-425-28557-2
GARFIELD COOKS UP TROUBLE	(#63)	978-0-425-28562-6
GARFIELD FEEDS HIS FACE	(#64)	978-0-425-28567-1
GARFIELD EATS AND RUNS	(#65)	978-0-425-28572-5
GARFIELD NUTTY AS A FRUITCAKE	(#66)	978-0-425-28576-3
GARFIELD SLURPS AND BURPS	(#67)	978-1-9848-1773-0
GARFIELD BELLY LAUGHS	(#68)	978-1-9848-1777-8
GARFIELD EASY AS PIE	(#69)	978-0-593-15640-7
GARFIELD GOES HOG WILD	(#70)	978-0-593-15642-1
GARFIELD WHAT LEFTOVERS?	(#71)	978-0-593-15644-5
GARFIELD LIVIN' THE SWEET LIFE	(#72)	978-0-593-15646-9

DVD TIE-INS

Title	ISBN
GARFIELD AS HIMSELF	978-0-345-47805-4
GARFIELD HOLIDAY CELEBRATIONS	978-0-345-47930-3
GARFIELD TRAVEL ADVENTURES	978-0-345-48087-3

AND DON'T MISS . . .

Title	ISBN
GARFIELD AT 25: IN DOG YEARS I'D BE DEAD	978-0-345-45204-7
GARFIELD'S JOKE ZONE/INSULTS	978-0-345-46263-3
GARFIELD FAT CAT 3-PACK/ VOL. 1	978-0-345-46455-2
GARFIELD FAT CAT 3-PACK/ VOL. 2	978-0-345-46465-1
GARFIELD FAT CAT 3-PACK/ VOL. 3	978-0-345-48088-0
GARFIELD FAT CAT 3-PACK/ VOL. 4	978-0-345-49171-8
GARFIELD FAT CAT 3-PACK/ VOL. 5	978-0-345-49180-8
GARFIELD FAT CAT 3-PACK/ VOL. 6	978-0-345-52420-1
GARFIELD FAT CAT 3-PACK/ VOL. 7	978-0-345-52588-8
GARFIELD FAT CAT 3-PACK/ VOL. 8	978-0-345-52599-4
GARFIELD FAT CAT 3-PACK/ VOL. 9	978-0-345-52607-6
GARFIELD FAT CAT 3-PACK/ VOL. 10	978-0-425-28558-9
GARFIELD FAT CAT 3-PACK/ VOL. 11	978-0-425-28566-4
GARFIELD FAT CAT 3-PACK/ VOL. 12	978-0-425-28578-7
GARFIELD FAT CAT 3-PACK/ VOL. 13	978-0-345-46460-6
GARFIELD FAT CAT 3-PACK/ VOL. 14	978-0-345-49175-6
GARFIELD FAT CAT 3-PACK/ VOL. 15	978-0-345-52585-7
GARFIELD FAT CAT 3-PACK/ VOL. 16	978-0-345-52592-5
GARFIELD FAT CAT 3-PACK/ VOL. 17	978-0-345-52603-8
GARFIELD FAT CAT 3-PACK/ VOL. 18	978-0-399-59440-3
GARFIELD FAT CAT 3-PACK/ VOL. 19	978-0-425-28561-9
GARFIELD FAT CAT 3-PACK/ VOL. 20	978-0-425-28571-8
GARFIELD FAT CAT 3-PACK/ VOL. 21	978-1-9848-1775-4
GARFIELD FAT CAT 3-PACK/ VOL. 22	978-0-593-15638-4
GARFIELD FAT CAT 3-PACK/ VOL. 23	978-0-593-15639-1
GARFIELD'S 20TH ANNIVERSARY COLLECTION	978-0-345-42126-5
SEASON'S EATINGS: A VERY MERRY GARFIELD CHRISTMAS	978-0-345-47560-2
GARFIELD'S GUIDE TO EVERYTHING	978-0-345-46461-3
ODIE UNLEASHED!	978-0-345-46464-4
GARFIELD'S BOOK OF CAT NAMES	978-0-345-48516-8
THE GARFIELD JOURNAL	978-0-345-46469-9
LIGHTS, CAMERA, HAIRBALLS!: GARFIELD AT THE MOVIES	978-0-345-49134-3
30 YEARS OF LAUGHS AND LASAGNA	978-0-345-50379-4
GARFIELD MINUS GARFIELD	978-0-345-51387-8
GARFIELD FROM THE TRASH BIN	978-0-345-51881-1
GARFIELD LEFT SPEECHLESS	978-0-345-53058-5
MY LAUGHABLE LIFE WITH GARFIELD	978-0-345-52591-8
GARFIELD'S SUNDAY FINEST	978-0-345-52597-0
AGE HAPPENS: GARFIELD HITS THE BIG 4-0	978-0-345-52609-0
GARFIELD COMPLETE WORKS: VOLUME ONE: 1978 & 1979	978-0-425-28712-5
GARFIELD COMPLETE WORKS: VOLUME TWO: 1980 & 1981	978-0-425-28713-2

✿ **New larger, full-color format!**